That Game of Life
The Transcendence of Opposites

Kin Lau

ISBN: 978-0-578-63252-0

<u>ACKNOWLEDGMENTS</u>

To my friends Jeaneen Sullivan and Dr. Stafford Cohen for their editorial feedbacks. To my high school English teacher David Lyons for providing me the skills and inspiration to write. To everyone who had to put up with me and provided me moral support during the time I was writing this book. I cannot thank everyone enough.

CONTENTS

FOREWORD

How did this book come to be? Perhaps I can attribute the inception of this book to the bewilderment and trepidation inside the head of a lost child. To his fortune and misfortune, he found himself in a strange land and strange places and having to traverse a series of dark mazes in his lifetime physically and mentally. Throughout the experience, part of him was seemingly always watching on a fence, questioning much that he experienced, feeling like never having a home to return to. Along the way, he was saved by guidance, encouragement, and knowledge from timely appearance of individuals and books. And it goes without saying, he got to where he is with a bit of luck. Obviously, that child was me.

In writing this book, I feel that I am not trying to teach others any specific skills, mental or procedural, at least not in the traditional sense. A friend recommended to position the book in the self-help genre, which it can do, but I fear that verges toward pleasing others and more about gaining readership. I hesitate that such a decision would steer the book with the improper spirit, so I resisted instinctively. Self-help and similar books typically teach by prescribing a set of skills or a defined mental framework for people to learn. That is not the case here. Rather, this is more like a dialogue, with a summarized report of my findings on my journey. My intention is to revitalize an innate sense or attitude of being a human being. Such attitude is something that we already possess but at the moment seems to be dormant.

If there must be a proposition, I would say it is a proposition that has been made in different contexts and explained in different ways by sages and philosophers in the past. So for you the readers, I can promise is that the content carries within it a pure intention to try to awake, to invoke an attitude that is innate in us all. Hopefully reading it helps some of you to regain a state of being that you can maintain to carry you through the lowest of the lows – mundane misfortune, betrayal, tragedy, catastrophic losses – and also during the highest of the highs in your life. Perhaps the new attitude can keep you balanced and grounded and thus you can avoid the crashing and the burning for yourself and for the people you care about.

Quoting Socrates, "An unexamined life is not worth living."

People inevitably have many problems in life. The larger society also has its myriads of problems. But what if the problem is not the problems? Also, the problem is not that there are problems? What if the true problem lies in the most elementary attitude from which we observe, approach, and solve problems? What about the fundamental axioms that govern our behaviors, arisen out of that attitude? What if there is an inherent flaw, fundamental weakness in the axioms that we are yet unaware of?

We can also construe that, the world is a simple place. It is because of the development of human consciousness that makes everything complicated. Human being and consciousness thus become the key complexity that needs inspection and contemplation. But in modern lifestyle, we have largely turned our attention toward the external, materialistic reality and away from seeking a solution from within.

I believe the truth is right in front of our eyes and in our surroundings. Few seem to notice nor pay attention. It is as if a veil had been pulled over our eyes. Perhaps it is the lack of time and space, both mental and physical in the hectic modern lifestyle.

What qualification do I have?

To answer that, let me share a quote from Maugham's novel *Of Human Bondage*. Maugham reflects on the average development of a person from childhood to young adulthood:

But he had grown very self-conscious. The new-born child does not realize that his body is more a part of himself than surrounding objects, and will play with his toes without any feeling that they belong to him more than the rattle by his side; and it is only by degrees, through pain, that he understands the fact of the body. And experiences of the same kind are necessary for the individual to become conscious of himself; but there is the difference that, although everyone becomes equally conscious of his body as a separate and complete organism, everyone does not become equally conscious of himself as a complete and separate personality. The feeling of apartness from others comes to most with puberty, but it is not always developed to such a degree as to make the difference between the individual and his fellows noticeable to the individual.

Maugham points to the bases for the drama of the novel that surrounds the protagonist Philips. The drama emerges out of his unique characteristics and the ensuing internal turmoil within Philips due to the many distinguishing factors that set him apart from his environment and his peers: orphaned as a teenager, adopted by his dogmatically religious and reserved uncle, having an impoverished background, and being born with a club foot. It is not hard to fathom just having one of the factors can wreak havoc and cause much duress during a child's ego development into adulthood. All the differences generate the intense magnification of his "apartness" from his peers. In contrast, his peers had a much smoother transition because they can blend in and share in their commonness.

That leads to some digging into my own history. As hinted at the very beginning, the stage for writing this book is set the day my family left Hong Kong to move to the United States. At that time, I was twelve.

I will always carry the memory of the day of departure of myself gazing lifelessly outward at the fading city of Hong Kong through the fogged and awfully small window of the airplane. For reasons unknown to myself, tears swelled and streamed down my face... though inevitably carrying the weight of sadness, perhaps it was also a premonition to the unknown difficulty that I had yet encountered. That was in the midst of December, it was as if I was "airdropped" from a place that I had complete familiarity, and tropical, to a place that is completely foreign, freezing cold with layers and layers of snow. The climate difference between Hong Kong and United

State's mid-west region certainly did not help the transition, but that was the least of the concerns. I suddenly found myself a stranger in a strange land. American culture was completely foreign, thus a little hostile but something that I must acclimate to. The Chinese culture and values that were already instilled within me took their time to recede into the background. While some of it provides me discipline and other advantages, it felt like more of it acted as handicaps while I was growing up as a teenager in the west. As such, a sense of disdain grew within me and questioning about my own position through and through, both regarding the new and the old. However, my survival instinct was helpful and seemed to have push me to adapt and learn to take what is useful. It is only later on that I regain the necessary respect and reverence for my own culture while also retaining the same attitudes for the newly acquired culture.

The fact that I am an easterner who came to United States in early teenage hood has become a source of my greatest advantage, despite also causing some of the greatest struggles. I retained adequate eastern values and Chinese language skill from the early twelve years to continue in self-study. At the same time, I was not too entrenched that I was inflexible in adopting western culture. I am somebody who is perfectly wedged between cultures, a chimera of sort, belonging to neither and unbeholden by either's ideals and traditions. During my journey to dive into the depth of both eastern and western, I discover the strength in religions, philosophy, and psychology from both. I feel less remorse in letting go certain aspects of one side for the other while retaining the advantages, like a tightrope walker who is all about striking the balance. I endeavor to assume the best of both worlds. It is not about judging which is better. After having to live on a fence for the longest time, such is my struggle, such is my advantage. I discover the strength of eastern culture in its holistic approach, encapsulating myth, philosophy, psychology, and metaphysics all together in an almost aggregated framework. On the contrary, the strength in western culture, since around Age of Enlightenment, lies in its understanding of myth, philosophy, psychology, and metaphysics categorically and in details. Renaissance man, philosophers, and scientists each contributed and developed specific approaches out of their individual strength. To generalize the weakness, the east can be vague, and the west can be fastidious. The right path is neither. Both are necessary. One way or the other is more applicable depending on the personality and propensity of an individual, timing, and circumstance.

Regardless, this leads me to make a request of you my readers.

I sincerely wish you will be able to read with the presupposition that you will set aside your ideology and rejecting thoughts and emotions. Be that as they are, as you read each topic, hopefully you will be able to draw out the meaning lying behind the text, map out meanings through reflecting on your own experience, and thus arrive at your own understanding.

Will you allow this invocation?

Nietzsche wrote in *Thus Spoke Zarathustra*:

> Of all that is written, I love only what a person had written with his blood ... It is no easy task to understand unfamiliar blood ... He that writeth in blood and proverbs doth not want to be read, but learnt by heart.

It is with the same intention that I write this text.

By shedding of the burden of nominal intellectual pursuit, by being able to distance from that, one regains something else. In Taoism, it is said:

> 為學日益 To obtain worldly knowledge, one accumulates/learns daily.
> 為道日損 To get to understand[align with] the Tao, one relinquishes/let go daily.

In a similar manner, ancient Greeks and Christianity both regard hubris as an act that violates natural order because if a man believes he already knows all, will he possess the sincerity and summon the necessary effort to know God?

At the outset, I began writing this book to clarify and orchestrate my own thinking, my own philosophy for myself. I wanted to bring my lower resolution understanding into high resolution. (But It quickly grew into a monster I never imagined.) That was my low expectation for this writing. A more nominal expectation is to interest and to guide a small number of readers to some level of inner peace. A fantastic outcome will be the result of inspiring a few individuals into their own deep investigation, introspection and therefore reaching their own understanding of life and truth. Because, it shall only be through these individuals that perhaps the unfolding chaos in the human world may be ameliorated.

Regardless, if this text serves you no other purpose, I sincerely hope it somehow offer some peace in your mind, thus in turn helps you to navigate through life events in a calm and collected manner.

The first part of this book is a macro level view, directly diving into the philosophical essence and universal principle in the game of life. The second part of this book is a more micro, psychological, detailed break-down. Because of that, if you are a more instinctual person, you may start with reading part one. But if you tend to take a more analytical approach in thinking, I suggest reading part two before part one.

Statement

The game of life as a human being is a game to be played in two modes. One mode is playing as a "human." The other mode is playing as a "being."

To be an integrated, individuated human being requires the ability to play in both modes simultaneously and seamlessly.

Mea Culpa

There is much that remains unknown to man. Worse yet, something that remains as mostly mystery even in modernity is man himself, his mind, and his consciousness.

That by itself is not a problem.

The great irony in modern age is that despite that fact, humans had begun to act on the assumption that all had been figured out. Outside of daily life tasks and their respective specialized career, people act as if there is little that requires their attention to take time to understand about themselves and the environment around them. Such assumption had pervaded even educational institutes with virtual unanimity and had transferred into the mind of students in recent decades. Students are to focus on more and more specialized subjects and explore little else.

The assumption is the problem. It leads to the loss of a sense of wonder, without which no one would seek inquiries into life's more substantial matter — values, purpose, philosophy, life and death. There is a huge loss of inquisitive minds in recent times.

Ex U.S. Secretary of Defense Donald Rumsfeld made a distinction on the categories of knowns and unknowns. *Known knowns* are what we know that we know. *Known unknowns* advise that there are some things we do not know. *Unknown knowns*, which was skipped in his anecdote, are available knowledge that someone is not yet aware of. Finally, *unknown unknowns* are things that we do not know that we do not know.

With said pervasive mindset, people had worsened in deficiency in both knowledge and wisdom on the individual level. That is, their eyes rest mostly on the known knowns and fail to adequately be accustomed to learning, to have a prepared mindset to handle the content, ideas, and experiences that are categorical in the other three unknowns. This inability leads to much dismay, surprises, and unintended consequences.

Therefore, even in the 21st century, or especially, it appears a case is required to be made on how we human beings yet understand little of ourselves, in order to recover a sense of wonder. A sense of wonder is required for anyone to really push hard to learn and think for himself. He can accept that he does not know. He dares himself to ponder about the past and the future. He lets himself be to feel his pain, sorrow, desire, happiness. Without that ability, he is non-participatory in life. He cannot discover more feasible ways forward. If he cannot do that for his own life, he cannot hope to viably stabilize the environment, the system that he lives in. He is liable to just be a pawn.

In 1999, cognitive psychologist Daniel Simons and Christopher Chabris performed a study that revealed how people can fixate their conscious attention so hard on a task that they become blind to something unexpected, even when it happened right in front of their eyes. The experiment asked the volunteers to watch a video where a group of people dressed in either black or white would pass a basketball around. The volunteers were tasked with counting how many times the ball has been passed around by those in white, ignoring the passes performed by those in black. The result is that about half of the volunteers completely overlooked that someone in a gorilla suit had slow-danced across the scene. Being too fixated on something leads us to easily miss unexpected details. This awareness test helps to also point out that we are far less aware of the world than we think we are.

In 1951, Polish psychologist Soloman Asch devised an experiment to test the influence of social pressure and how it affects individual's will to conform to the group. 50 participants were chosen to do a "vision test." Each participant is placed in a room with seven confederates of Asch, without his knowledge. The seven others will pre-picked either of the two noticeably wrong answers.

First an image with a line was shown and then another image with three labeled lines. One of the three lines will be of the same length as the one from the first image. 18 trials would be performed, and in 12 out of 18 trials (critical trials), all seven confederates will select the same wrong answer. Asch also conducted a control group where the participant was given the trials alone. On average, 32 percent of participants conformed while 75 percent of the participants conformed at least once during the 12 critical trials. In the control group, less than 1 percent of participants gave the wrong answer. This experiment provides some insight into how people may easily conform to social pressure.

In 1973, Stanford psychology researcher Philip Zimbardo conducted what was famously known as the Stanford prison experiment. The experiment aimed to gain insight into the effects of role-playing, labeling, and social expectation on an individual's identity and behaviors. 24 students evaluated to be physically and mentally healthy were selected out of 75 applicants. They were assigned randomly to be either prisoner or guard and were situated into a simulated prison. The prisoners were treated and processed as a criminal directly from their homes and booked into the prison. Instead of their names, they were to be called by an ID number. The prison guards were given the freedom as they deem fit to maintain peace and order as long as they do not physically harm the prisoners. The prisoners were required to follow the guards' orders. Both the guards and the prisoners were given mock uniforms.

The experiment was set to run for two weeks but had to be terminated after its sixth day. While the prisoners and guards had the freedom to interact however they wanted beyond the few ground rules, the guards' behavior quickly descended from basic derision into hostility, sadism, and dehumanization. The prisoners were no better and staged a rebellion on just the 2nd day. To maintain their authority, the guards became more and more aggressive and abusive despite the non-physical rule. They developed their own punishment-and-reward, prisoner-informant, and solitary confinement system in the mock prison. The prisoners, on the other hand, began to experience mental deterioration. They became passive, depressed, hopeless and had random crying, anxiety episodes. Several prisoners had to be released early as a result. Even

4

Zimbardo, who acted as the prison warden, lost sight of the fact of the experiment and ignored the radical behaviors and worsening conditions. The experiment was finally called to a halt at the protest from his graduate student Christina Maslach. Only a few of the guards were able to resist from being lost in the social identity assigned by the experiment. In his book The Lucifer Effect, Zimbardo lamented on how only a few can resist the contextual temptation and the lure of power based on social role while maintaining his own principle and morality.

Going back further in time to 1961, Yale University psychologist Stanley Milgrim, who was a classmate to Zimbardo and previous student under Soloman Asch, did a study to measure people's willingness to obey authority figure. The study's participants were purposely misled to believe the experiment to explore the relationship between negative stimuli, learning, and memorization. Through some trickery, they were always selected as the teacher while the "learner" was an actor from Milgrim's group.

The teacher and the learner were taken to a compartmented room. The learner was shown to the teacher to be strapped to a chair and had electrodes attached to his arms, connecting to a generator. The teacher was then led to the other compartment which allows them to communicate with each other via sound. They did not have visual contact through the compartment. One of Milgrim's colleagues would act as the "supervisor" in the teacher's compartment. The teacher was to teach the learner a predetermined list of word pairs so that he would memorize them. Each time a mistake was made, the teacher was told by the supervisor to administer an electric shock. The voltage was increased each time, going from 15-volt, labeled as "slight shock" all the way to 450-volt, labeled as "Danger: severe shock" even though no real shock would be delivered on the learner. The teacher was given a sample of the shock from the generator at the beginning of the session. During the session, the learner would purposely make mistakes. He would begin to scream in pain as the voltage reaches higher and eventually proclaim that he has a heart condition. Although the teacher sometimes hesitated to continue to give the electric shock, the supervisor would then urge the teacher to continue for up to four times using phrases beginning with "Please continue" to finally "You

5

have no other choice. You *must* go on." If the teacher expressed wishes to stop all four times, the experiment was stopped. Otherwise, the experiment continued until the learner was given the maximum 450-volt shock three times.

The result from the experiment was that 26 out of 40 participants (65%) administered the maximum 450-volt shock. All participants administered shocks up to 300-volt. Participants went on with the experiment as they were urged and ordered to obey, despite many exhibiting strong emotion and distress to continue administering the shock.

Prior to the experiment, Milgrim polled fourteen Yale University psychology seniors to predict the outcome of the experiment, and he also informally asked for his colleagues' opinions. The senior students predicted that if there were 100 teachers, almost none (average 1.2) would administer the maximum 450-volt electric shock and less than 4 would continue after 300-volt. Milgrim's colleagues provided similar opinions.

The result of the experiment was unnerving. Perhaps that is why the original experiment was critically questioned for its standards and methodologies. To that point, Milgrim and other scientists, such as Jerry Burger from Santa Clara University in 2007 and a group of Polish scientists from SWPS University of Social Sciences and Humanities, were able to replicate or perform variations of the same study with similar results. Some experiments demonstrated little variation between male and female. However, Milgrim's polling result was of equal significance, if not more, to the result of the experiment. It reveals that psychologists, who are the designated experts of human minds, can be as gravely inaccurate as a layman.

Following the end of World War II, the world sought justice against the Nazi officials at what is known as the "Nuremberg trials." It is there that the behaviors, anecdotes, evidence, and defense by the Nazi defendant both inspired many of the investigative studies and correlate their future result. Because most for the defendants, due to indisputable evidence of their crimes, were unable to argue for innocence and a high likelihood of death, the defense chosen by their lawyers was the Superior Orders. In essence, the defendants were making the plea that they were only following orders from superior officer. Even one of the most prominent Nazi Adolf Eichmann, a key organizer for the Holocaust, used that defense. Consequently, the Nuremberg Defense became synonymous with Superior Orders or the "I was just following order" excuse.

Whether the Nazi indeed acted by simply following orders or used the Nuremberg Defense just to absolve himself of responsibility, were moot. In either case, the people fell directly or indirectly slave to what Kant called the *self-induced tutelage*, "a man's inability to make use of his understanding because of a lack of resolution and courage to use it[reason] without the direction from other."

The lack of will and courage was an initial problem. Without them, a vicious cycle begins itself as fear and comfort keep the individual in place. The more he does not move, the less he knows, the stranger the world becomes, and the more reality shies away from him. The more he does not understand, the more frightening the world becomes, resulting in an almost irreconcilable wall of opaqueness between reality and what he thinks he knows.

The additional problem for the modern man now is that not only modern civilization provides too much comfort, too much safety, the assumption that "he knows" further keeps him in place from ever exploring what he yet does not know. All of that together enables him to hyper-focus on his own specific objective, and on his social identity.

So modern man has thus given up on his sense of wonder, for now. The old saying goes, "Be careful what you ask for, you may just get it." Without any extensive investigation, introspection, human beings are at risk of asking for something that we, at last, do not desire. Both Soren Kierkegaard and Fyodor Dostoyevsky attest to that.

> For when all combine in every way to make everything easier and easier, there remains only one possible danger, namely, that the easiness might become so great that it would be too great; then only one want is left, though not yet a felt want - that people will want difficulty.

- Soren Kierkegaard

Even if man really were nothing but a piano-key, even if this were proved to him by natural science and mathematics, even then he would not become reasonable, but would purposely do something perverse out of simple ingratitude, simply to gain his point. And if he does not find means he will contrive destruction and chaos, will contrive sufferings of all sorts, only to gain his point! He will launch a curse upon the world, and as only man can curse (it is his privilege, the primary distinction between him and other animals), may be by his curse alone he will attain his object—that is, convince himself that he is a man and not a piano-key! If you say that all this, too, can be calculated and tabulated—chaos and darkness and curses, so that the mere possibility of calculating it all beforehand would stop it all, and reason would reassert itself, then man would purposely go mad in order to be rid of reason and gain his point!

- Fyodor Dostoyevsky, Notes from the Underground

Kierkegaard's idea here can be applied to another aspect of life. Regarding the pursuit of happiness in the current social milieu, what if an individual finally satisfies all of his desires for happiness, only to come to the realization that he still suffers from the desire for the feeling of lacking and the feeling from the pursuit thereof? Is the pursuit of happiness the proper goal in life? That is to say that we need to thoroughly contemplate our assumption.

Do we know what we want? The answer yes is derived from the assumption that we know ourselves. That is far from the case for a majority of people. If people can accept that as a mistake, that is *mea culpa*. *Mea culpa* is the admittance of one's fault. It is the sincere bearing of the gravity of the mistake and also the bearing of the immense fear of the repercussion of accepting the mistake before one can move forward to repent. This is akin to the idea from clinical psychology that exposure to what one fears is only redemptive, transformative if it is done so voluntarily. In many cases, truth is also that which is most feared. The act of accepting that "there is something wrong with what I am doing" is paramount prior to repentance.

In the modern English translation of the Greek New Testament, the English word *repentance* takes the place of two Greek words *metanoia* and *metamelomai*. Repentance was used about ten times more for *metanoia* than *metamelomai*. *Metamelomai* carries the meaning of "remorseful regret" and that appears to be the meaning and general feeling that people embody when they think of repentance. They cling to the idea of sin and guilt, without ever knowing *metanoia*. *Metanoia* means a fundamental change in one's mind (heart). *Meta* means "beyond" and *noia* means "mind." The nuance is to go beyond the limitation of one's mind or to transcend what one already sees. Therefore, while *metamelomai* has a stronger sense of reflecting on past conduct, *metanoia* conveys a sense of seeing beyond what one already can and transcending one's current limitation.

We as human beings are so familiar yet at the same time strangers to ourselves. If we can allow ourselves again to contemplate the stranger part of ourselves, instead of willfully ignoring it, then perhaps we can reach a better understanding of ourselves and bring balance to our world. There is a good reason that there are many old warnings against pride, arrogance, hubris while promoting moderation, humbleness, and humility. If we are always sitting on a high horse, we look down on everything, when instead we need to take some time to look up and around.

In tarot, the Fool is the first card, numbered 0. It is a card indicating unlimited potentials and new beginnings, spurred by part optimism, part reckless courage. Adopting the role of a fool allows one to journey and discover new things, literally and metaphorically. Even if one decides to return to where one was, one would have gained new perspective and experience. That is why the fool is the antecedent of becoming a master.

Will you accept yourself to be a fool once again?

Part 1
Macrocosm / The Universal

Human Game

The game of human is playing as the individual social identity within society. Since its very inception, society is the game containing all human games. Within this game, there are games within games within games, overlapping and intermingling simultaneously. From the higher level of nation, to community, to family, all the way down to each individual, and then within the mind of every individual... we are playing elaborate games at every level.

The word game used here does not carry any pejorative connotation as a frivolous, useless pastime. Rather, the usage here infers a contest where certain rules are to be followed while success is measured based on certain conditions, or metrics if one is more mathematically inclined. Within each game, besides the direct rewards, each involved player would also strive to gain superiority over his peers. You can better observe the game once you identify the objective, the rewards for which you are aiming at.

If your reaction to the statement that life and civilization are games is one that deemed it offensive, maybe even blasphemous, "how dare you, life is not a game," "how could you say life is mere game," "life is so much more meaningful than just a game," then we shall explore what is hidden behind those thoughts.

It is as if the thoughts were shouting out a fervent hope that living as human in society is extremely important, meaningful, full of purposes and therefore should be taken very very *very* seriously. That spells the covert belief, "*This* social game is all there is to be and no one shall object."

Overarchingly and generically, these human games boil down to,

11

"I desire to go from point A to point B," with "point B" being the desired outcome that involves gaining of certain material possession, money, fame, or power. Frequently, it also involves having more of those elements in comparison to one's peers.

Excluding the topics of reason and motivation for the moment, within our gigantic civilization game and all its sublevels, we are all participating in this chasing toward point B sort of game, each with their own sets of rules and preferred winnings. Throughout our life, we play through an interminable amount of these one-upmanship games, each with their own set of rules that boil down to these aims:

"I have more money than you."
"I am more famous/popular than you."
"My status/title is higher than yours."
"I am prettier than you."
"I have a better partner/family than you."
"My religion is better than yours."
"I love you more than you love me."
"My god is more legit than yours."
"I am more spiritual than you are."

People live their life in a manner that regards the human game as the only reason to exist, to persist. The game and its sub-games are what motivate their on-going survival. For an internal sense of security and to sustain noninterrupted lifestyle improvement, we avoid the serious questioning of common social conventions and contemporary culture. Most people simply fall in line, supposing "If everyone is playing that way, I may as well. There must be reasonable grounds." To avoid hostility and perhaps ex-communication from our community, we dare not question the status quo. One simply goes along to get along.

So, the human game goes on like a merry-go-around.

The game must go on.

The consequence is that most of us do end up taking these games very seriously. Unfortunately, seriousness is a kind of weight. The phrase "life is a drag" is often heard and exposes such a fact of us living life entangled in some very undesirable solemnity.

We have been fooled. This is not an indictment. This is not a case against the human game of going from point A to point B. To live as if that is truth is to live an incomplete life. This is a case for life involving more than just going from point A to point B. Life is a game but playing the human game is not the only thing.

Every game has a *meta*-element. The catch of the human game is that to "win," you need to recognize these human games. They are perfectly fine games. It is just that there is more to life. One does not win by beating the human games.

To be seduced and be bamboozled by the human game is to lose the game of life. One becomes lost in the game when he thinks that he can beat the game and spends all his effort in doing so. Treating the human game as the entirety of reality, acting like the assortment of games as absolutely serious matter, one lives in deceit and conceit. That is to lose the game of life.

It is as if we are all hypnotized from birth.

The key to the game of life, is not to beat the human game. We must break the spell. Because if life is *only* human game and all we are is to strive to beat the game, is that not a self-defeating proposition?

How did we get so lost, or so hypnotized?

Limitation of Thinking

In modern days, the line is blurred when people speak of intelligence and wisdom. However, the distinction between intelligence and wisdom must be made. There is no correlation between intelligence and wisdom. Let us focus on intelligence first.

Specifically, the word intelligence in this context points to the capacity of our mind to perform analytical thinking. Current social milieu informs us that there are different dimensions of intelligence to be considered. For the discussion here, intelligence points to one's mental processing power during thinking, digestion of information. Thinking is also associated with what we may call rationality, reasoning, or logic. For the sake of simplicity, the word "logic" will be used in this chapter to refer to the embodiment of all of these ideas.

Logic is our prominent and esteemed method to interface with our reality as human beings in the 21st century. Logic is used in conjunction with human's conscious attention which is a laser-focused detection tool. By applying conscious attention and the processing ability of the logical part of our brain, we observe, analyze, dissect, hypothesize, prove, and finally devise a solution to a problem. That results in the collection of more and more knowledge.

However, logic is a problem solver that has a weakness. Its power is strictly linear. It is a problem solver that cannot solve itself. Math, language (hieroglyphics aside), and other byproducts such as computers and technology are almost too cumbersome in dealing with reality.

Of course, I can already hear the reverberation of people calling me crazy because of the processing power of computers today. I will simply point to the advent of Big Data and Cloud computing, artificial intelligence... had they been able to solve all our problems? The growth of data had been exponential, and it does not look like we had reduced the problems we are facing. Also imagine, if we continue to apply our incredible intelligence, develop computing power ad nauseum, will that result in the solutions of most of our problems?

We need to acknowledge a simple fact. Logic as a tool, including its byproducts, is not all-powerful.

It is a problem if we forget and it does seem frequently that we do. Too much emphasis and reliance on the application of logic had caused numerous problems. Our belief in its technological byproducts is almost zealous. Our propensity to confound the theoretical with reality is evident in the unintended consequences of our own doings. Even though not explicitly, our actions demonstrate the fact that we behave as if we believe in technological utopianism. "Technology will save us, bring us happiness, and end all sufferings." Meanwhile, much of the necessity and the ambition for scientific development is the consequence required to "cure" the unintended consequence of previous development. That is the result of ignoring the blind spots during the usage of logic and conscious attention. Like driving, accounting for blind spots is important.

Three notable points can be made regarding the blind spots, or weaknesses, in the manner human currently use logic.

One, the choice to apply logic is not logic itself at the root. Logic is not and will never be its own initiator. Put another way, the thinker behind the thoughts are not purely made of thoughts themselves. If one observes his own thinking, he will realize that he does not know where most of his thoughts come from. The human being is the entity behind thoughts that should not be overlooked.

Two, logic's power lies in its divide-and-conquer method for solving problems. It is and will always be divisive. Turning problem into digestible, solvable portion is its strength. Such is also its weakness. Its divisive nature will never be resolved by further applying itself. Unless it is someone with the capacity and audacity to proceed to an extreme level of applying his logical prowess to its very end, and through *reductio ad absurdum*, realizes the lapse of logic and what is beyond. In which case, he must accept and consider this "other element" that is beyond.

Three, logic is used in conjunction with conscious attention. Typically, they act as one unit. By focusing on more and more details, we acquire further details, but we also begin to discriminate, exclude, and ignore more of the surrounding data and information. Consequently, logic causes blind spots by rendering certain things irrelevant and ignoring the whole.

It is easy to find an example that demonstrates problems from the blind spots. United States 2008 financial crisis is such an example.

First, there can be little argument that the drivers behind the trading are traders, investors, analysts, and financial firms who were overwhelmingly motivated by greed. Second, the financial products that accelerated the downfall were risky derivatives (in some cases, derivatives on top of derivatives) originated from beautifully formulated, immense mathematical models (a byproduct of logic) that masqueraded the risk into oblivion to most eyes. Third and finally, due to the concern being mostly on the economics, citizens whose livelihood and wellbeing would be affected by the dire consequence were largely an afterthought in the aftermath.

If the basis of all our problems world-wide big and small begins from the basic flaws of logic, it becomes inherent that by further applying logic and its byproduct will only further worsen our crisis – focusing only on the details and losing out on seeing the whole.

The application of conscious attention and analysis of perceived details has become a stable of our modern lives. One is either thinking one's own thoughts or being distracted by the thoughts of others. In fact, it is not farfetched to say… thinking, thoughts are *the* component of modern life due to the advent of the internet and social media platforms. That in itself is not wrong. But what leads to devastating results is the mistaking of the thinking process in which we divide things into separate items and events as actuality.

Knowledge vs. Wisdom

Knowledge is a consequence of thinking. With numerous generations of prodigious thinkers, inventors, and philosophers as monumental forces behind us, the layers of analysis and conceptualization that we have come to rely on and accept had reached an unprecedented and overwhelming level.

Not every thought can be called knowledge, a tier below knowledge is information. Information is a combined set smaller pieces of data, such as names, labels, facts, and numbers. Information connect together to form knowledge. A wide array of knowledge may allow connections to happen between them. The connection, the reference of one thing to another provides positional information, values to inform decisions. On first thought, the occurrence of a large amount of these connections, and the observation of patterns that overlay the connections perhaps can be called wisdom.

As much knowledge as we have now, we have a more mind-numbing amount of data and information. It is multiplying at a rate worse than locusts during the plague. Unaware, modern man focuses and gorges on information. That leads to people lacking a wide range of knowledge. Constipated on the amount of information, lacking in knowledge and their connections to each other, we are living in a world seemingly devoid of wisdom. We have all encountered incredibly intelligent individual who had acted unwisely. It is also common to experience the reverse, encountering individual who we may not label as intelligent, but we nonetheless call wise. While wisdom does not preclude intelligence, intelligence does not guarantee wisdom.

How could that be?

I believe it may have to do with how wisdom has always lived a vague existence. Something which is vague is not easy to obtain and therefore out of reach, and in the end, few bothers to try. Alas, it can be said that we are not even doing a good job of teaching and absorbing knowledge, where many people simply concern themselves in information hoarding and subsequent regurgitation.

In the current 21st century, we are in dire need of wisdom. Perhaps it is time we place wisdom back as one of the highest virtues across the world.

Plenty of mythology and theological text stress the importance of wisdom. One interesting character that stands out among the stories is Odin the Norse God.

Odin is the head of gods living in Asgard among the Nine Worlds in Nordic myth. Odin possesses a relentless drive for wisdom, and he is willing to sacrifice anything and everything to obtain this mysterious understanding of life and reality. Briefly, the tales go like this…

Odin first overcame hurdles after hurdles for the Mead of Poetry that not only provides him the artistry and eloquence of poetry that will help spread wisdom. It is noteworthy that the Mead of Poetry's inspirational aspect that can invoke wisdom in others is of great value. Then there is the story of his discovery of the magic runes written on to the tree of life, Yggdrasil, by the three maidens of fate, the Norns, that dictate the fate and ordain the destiny of all that exists in the Nine Worlds. Magic runes are not mere old text but ones that convey wisdom, intention, and carries magic power. Such potent wisdom will only make itself understood to those who is deemed worthy. To demonstrate his deep intention and worthiness, Odin hanged himself on a branch of the Yggdrasil, pierced himself with a spear, urged his subordinates to grant no help nor sustenance. He dangled there between life and death for nine days. Only then, Odin, who is deemed "a god who sacrificed himself to himself," does the runes make themselves known to him. Finally, in the Well of Urd at the root of Yggdrasil, there lives the wisest being of all worlds named Mimir. Mimir received his cosmic understanding from drinking the water from the well. Odin made his way to Mimir and requested a drink of the water. As the guardian of the well who understood the potency of the water, Mimir asked for a sacrifice in exchange for one drink. Odin proceeded to offer one of his eyes for a drink that should grant him the deep wisdom he most desired.

The expression of the importance of wisdom is reflected in Odin's obsession. There are also the running themes of needing to sacrifice and being worthy of the acquisition of wisdom. Within the story, there is the fact of magic runes having an influence on the fate of the worlds. One who can understand the runes can catch a glimpse of the future. That speaks of the undeniable effect of wisdom on the outcome of future events - fate.

Comparing eon past to the 21st century, it appears our progenitors across the globe had more inclination to discern and apply wisdom in their value systems. Perhaps it is due to our ancestors having a slower pace of life. They also have not developed and allowed the dominating use of the rational mind. Conversely, it might have been easier to discover patterns, understand certain inconceivable things. Their perception is not preoccupied with details and is not flooded with an insurmountable amount of information. Perhaps that is why they had the better propensity for wisdom.

One may argue that there are plenty of horrible outcomes perpetrated by our ancestors. The counterargument is that the bloodsheds and atrocities that had happened in 20th century far outweigh the summation of those from before. Regardless, it is undeniable that the inclination to strive for wisdom and the conditions required to obtain it had eroded over the ages. A specific instance is the dearth of time and space for any idle introspection.

Wisdom can be the result of an integration process that happened by having awareness and introspection on experience. Experience includes past actions, feelings, thoughts, knowledge, intuition, and other kind of perceptions that an individual had. The result of that can be noticed in the optimal outcome as a result of a wise individual's action or reaction that can only be classified as "no-how" and "no-why."

(awareness + experience) → integration process into being → wisdom

The process from which we gain wisdom starts with awareness. By applying that non-discriminating non-judgmental introspection, one is not fastened to his egocentric view and can observe his experience thoroughly. He can detect and accept what truly happened.

Knowledge results from intellectual learning that is specialized, whereas wisdom results from the all-inclusive observation that is generalized. Our intellectual capacity excludes things and can get in the way of the integration process. The analytical mind tries to identify something as right or good, and something else as wrong or bad. It points out what is relevant and screens out other things that can be ignored. With predictive power, we became inclined to apply our intelligence to identify what is wrong and have geared ourselves toward the avoidance of problems. Another tendency is that we like to rationalize a bad outcome and paint it in a good light. With overapplication, we become more and more myopic from seeing the whole experience and failing to consider many other possibilities and perspectives. What if what is wrong is right and what is right is wrong? Conventional knowledge tells people to review their failures. What if what needs to be discovered resides in what the individual considered success?

If logical intelligence is a sword, wisdom is the wielder. It is the sword with which we divide things into like and dislike, right and wrong, good and evil. The greater the intelligence, the more dangerous it is if it is wielded by one without wisdom. It is the equivalent of giving a sharp katana to an apprentice who has just started learning about swordsmanship. He will very likely cut himself badly.

The degree of wisdom to which one would gain from any experience is proportional to the ability to detach from what was deemed right and wrong. In other words, one gains wisdom in life to the degree that one can transcend his belief of good and evil (and other various forms of polarized thinking).

The nature of this transcendence is not like the typical route of the learning of a skill. It is in nature more akin to taking off sunglasses to see light as it is. Logical thinking is like a veil that gets in the way. A new way cannot be paved by applying more logical thinking. That tends to dig deeper a hole that is already present. A new path needs to be discovered by detaching from that. It is about pulling back the veil so we can see things as they are. As opposed to a new skill, it is more about finding this state of mind, this perspective that we have always had within us but forgotten.

Why is it yet that so few possess wisdom?

Recall again the lore of Odin, the idea of sacrifice is paramount. How much discomfort is one willing to endure? What is one willing to give up? Odin's sacrifice of one eye to gain wisdom symbolizes the abnegation of previous worldly perception for a new kind of perspective. In other words, he symbolically gave up a large part of who he was, for something of which true nature he does not know exactly. It is a leap of faith that is painful and threatening to the mental structure of one's reality. To see deeper patterns, to understand the game of being requires just that - suspension of what one once believed and what one pedestalized as truth.

Duality

The game of being is the game of reality, the game of nature, and the game of existence. It is about understanding laws applicable universally, or natural laws. Of course, it is based on the assumption that there is certain eternal, objective, immutable truth in this universe.

Reality is of infinite possibilities. If one is to interact with nature with fluidity, one cannot be chained down by pre-existing thoughts. Holding on to a predetermined belief system absolutely is infeasible. But unavoidably, most people feel a need to have a grasp on nature, and they inevitably act with the intention to seize control of nature to control one's own destiny. It is an attitude of trying to beat nature into submission. That is the attitude being taught to new generations. Sometimes it is not done so explicitly but transferred osmotically by proximity. Monkeys see, monkeys do. That is especially true for children.

How can a person peer into nature of reality with such an overzealous attitude? How can one reach a profound understanding? For to understand is for one to "stand under something." This something is a law, the deepest pattern that naturally manifests in the game of being. This is something universal. Perhaps we can also call it *meta*-knowledge.

This is about the dualistic nature of existence. This nature is manifested in the male-female pairing of gods and beings that had existed across cultures, from the very beginning of human history. To name a few: Mesopotamian's Tiamat and Apsu, Egyptian's Osiris and Isis, Hindu's Shiva and Vishnu, Japan's Izanagi and Izanami, China's Fu-Xi and Nugua, Christian's Adam and Eve.

One message is without a doubt shared between the yin-yang symbol, the ouroboro, and the bird and serpent. Despite undeniable opposing forces within existence, underlying everything is a quiescent unity. Duality is the fundamental pattern for the game of being. Underneath the façade of reality, two sides are integral to each other. They are both separate and together simultaneously. One side annihilating the other results in the destruction of both. Such understanding has so far been out of reach of most people's understanding. Perhaps that is because such a realization is something that an intensely rational, shortsighted mindset cannot tolerate.

At this point, if we further allow ourselves to further defocus from this most basic dualistic pattern of yin and yang, good and evil, life and death, there is yet something amiss that may come into our awareness.

The white background enables us to see the yin-yang symbol. The whiteness also brings forth the imagery of ouroboros to our eyes. So what is that enable dualistic existence to be? Such a question leads us to investigate non-existence.

Void

Non-existence has also been labeled as the void, no-thingness, emptiness, non-being, vacuum, sunyata, or denoted by the Chinese character 無 (wu or mu). Note that it is not what is implied by the word "nothing" in vernacular usage.

Truth is, there are no words capable of conveying non-existence, for it is not something, nor is it nothing. Even if one may choose any and all words, it still cannot be talked about. One cannot assume the void to know of the void. Its ineffability is immutable but just that existence is its implication. None of that should prevent us from applying our mind, our senses, our whole being to contemplate about it. It is this exploration that is of great significance.

In Buddhism's Heart Sutra, it is written, "Form is not different from emptiness. Emptiness is not different from form. Form is emptiness. Emptiness is form." Here I will supply an approximated definition for the word "form." Form entails the infinite permutation of possibilities in existence. That includes all phenomena whether they are substantive, psychic, natural, etc. Thoughts is form. Feelings is form. Body is form. Ego is form. Social structures is form. On and on.

In Buddhistic context, form refers to things that are perceivable to our five main bodily senses. With modern scientific advancement, we can say that form extends to what can be detected, measured, and modeled by our technology. We can see "form" because of its contrast to space, or other forms, around it. It is also analogous to our ability to hear sound. We can hear the melody in music because of the silence between the notes. It is said that silence is the most powerful sound. If we want to be totally precise in words on what we hear, we hear sound-silence. If form and space, sound and silence are inseparable, categories such as object, sound, etc. do not inherently exist because they are dependent on the opposites that they arise from. Thus, the same goes for void and existence. In other words, void is a "real" phenomenon that tells us that existence and form are only parts of a whole equation. Instead of "Form is emptiness and emptiness is form", it could be that "Form implies emptiness and emptiness implies form."

In theology, there is the latin phrase *creatio ex nihilo*. It expresses the same notion – creation out of void (though literal translation points to nothing). From the reality of existence, lives and things we know reach death which is another nature of the void and from the void, existence may once again happen. In other words, all categorization and differentiation by the intellect are a fundamentally false dichotomy.

The concept of void is related to awareness that was discussed previously. If the void is the background that enables the illumination of dualistic existence that which we experience, to be aware is to be able to detach from identification with existence only and to accept void. To see only form is to miss the void. Regaining understanding of both form and void and their relationship is the path to regain perception of our personal dualistic thoughts and then ultimately understanding of our own being. Therefore, to fear the void, to be afraid of not existing, to shy away from death is essentially the avoidance of one of the deepest understanding to life one may gain.

It is not without coincidence that Odin sacrificed an eye to gain the highest form of wisdom. The contemplation of the void requires a voluntary detachment from physical reality which includes how we ordinarily think. So symbolically, he gave up an eye that was used to perceive the physical world or the world of forms. There was an established model, a belief structure on what reality supposed to be, but one must let go of it. Rationality and logic which belong to the world of forms will only prevent the acceptance of formlessness. This is in opposition to how everyone lives every day, where they desperately hold on to anything and everything, physically, mentally, emotionally and even spiritually. One *must* hold on. But any kind of attachment becomes the very barricade from the true vision of reality.

A more transcendental type of wisdom involves the understanding of this ineffable, formless void that is always with us. The void which is always contributing to the intractable impermanence and cyclical nature of all matter.

Inevitably, writing or talking about void and non-existence results in some almost incomprehensible paradoxical utterance. And I shall leave mine...

Understanding the void, thus also wholeness, is the grasping of the non-grasping without grasping.

If ye realize the Emptiness of All Things,
Compassion will arise within your hearts;
If ye lose all differentiation between yourselves and others,
fit to serve others ye will be;
And when in serving others ye shall win success,
then shall ye meet with me;
And finding me, ye shall attain to Buddhahood.
 - Milarepa, Songs of Milarepa

Beyond Language and Symbols

Shall one take any direction of inquiry to its extreme end, as we had done, we will ultimately reach a realm where rational thoughts, linear languages no longer suffice. You may feel at this point that everything is yet so vague, but I want to point out that is a feeling common in being in touch with any object or subject which is new. And in this case, something that is seldom explored. It can be attributed to our dedicated reliance on the intellect, while this exploration is within the realm that exists beyond the intellect. It is wisdom and formlessness that can only be partially conveyed through art and symbolism. We can also say that at the extreme end of the exploration of symbols and art lies the presence of divinity. Human languages in their current state are cumbersome and inadequate in this sense.

One can do nothing else but to apply one's whole being and be sincerely receptive of this realm. By forcing ourselves to attempt to understand "this" through means of logic will cause "blocking." How can we hope to define "all" with any language or symbol? Putting constraints on understanding strictly at the levels of language and symbols would be akin to staring at the finger that is pointing at the moon when what one really wants is to perceive and understand the moon.

In mathematics, there is the concept of the superset. The superset contains the elements of all its subsets, which includes the null set, and all of the elements' permutation (thus again, void and forms). There is no way to define the superset by subsets of itself. Putting all of the elements together also does not suffice to explain the idea of the superset.

Well, the superset of existence is the notion of oneness.

Tao – Oneness

Using the term Tao foremost is my way to pay respect to my eastern root. Tao is oneness. Oneness is the totality of being that includes both dualistic existence and its background the void (non-duality).

The oneness of reality, or of this universe is the ultimate law. The whole of nature simply is. The inter-connectedness of all that exists also is. It is the complete emptiness, and it is also the complete fullness. The wholeness of it includes both the void and the forms. Whether we decide it to be so or not decide it to be so have no influence.

To truly see the world is to know oneness. It is to be aware of all the interconnected relationships within and without.

You can call it the many names given across eons and across cultures and religions. Some of them are wholeness, oneness, Tao, Dharma, God, Brahman, YHWH or IHVH (The Tetragrammaton), Jehovah, the infinite, cosmic energy, suchness, ultimate reality, Self, Ahura Mazda, ein sof, or simply nature or universe.

In the end, it does not matter its name. Being beholden to names is to sin, which in ancient Greek is *hermatia*, meaning to miss the point. Naming and then forcing a concept, a definition on it to grasp and unable to let go would be further blasphemy. It is the mistaking of a smaller part as the sum. So do not strive to divide the totality of being and the energy behind it in order to lock it down and grasp it with the analytical mind. Such mistake is called avidyā in Sanskrit, where vidyā means to see, to know, to understand, or to perceive. The a- prefix means "not." Avidyā means not knowing, not understanding, or blindness. In Buddhism and Hinduism, avidyā is the root of suffering, that is, misconception of the nature of reality causes suffering.

Various ancient passages and tales give clues to initiate a mindset in people under studies to ward off sin and avidyā.

The beginning of *Tao Te Ching* by Lao Tzu states:

道可道，非常道。名可名，非常名。

That translates to "The Tao that is called Tao is not the changeless Tao. The name that can be named is not the changeless name."

In *Upanishad*, "He among us who knows the meaning of 'Neither do I not know, nor do I know'—knows Brahman." Similarly in *Vedanta*, it is stated that "Truth is one; sages call it by various names."

With a striking resemblance to the Upanishad, a Zen poem reads, "You cannot catch hold of it, nor can you get rid of it. In not being able to get it you get it. When you speak it's silent, when you are silent it speaks."

In ancient Hebrew, the tetragrammaton IHVH is a symbol of existence and devout Hebrews prohibit themselves from pronouncing it. Thus, its true pronunciation remains a secret and it is said, "He who can rightly pronounce it, causeth heaven and earth to tremble, for it is the name which rusheth through the universe." Because the pronunciation was lost, it leads to the future development of the name Jehovah by translators, which means "He who will be, is, and has been."

Once again, the implication of oneness is everywhere around us. In human's paradigm whose life is based on the concept of time, it is something that was, is, and always will be. And that, could be saying too much. No words, no language, no thought, no concept, no book can perfectly capture what oneness truly means.

That is why, in Buddhism and for many masters, the only way to teach, is to use negation and continuous rejection of man-made notions until a student realizes what is. When the students are utterly and completely frustrated, when all his answers that arise out of typical intelligence and his ego, are not the answers, and when everything is futile… only then, he has a chance for a breakthrough.

Oneness sits at the basis of the game of being. From there, void and duality, and from duality more subsets arise and complexity multiply. Yet fundamentally, they remain connected, still one.

Oneness back to Duality

From the chapter *Awareness* up to this point, the investigative journey from the thought-driven mind-divided reality that is founded upon duality to oneness has been made. To complete the full circle of life, we must follow the "rediscovered" perception of the world of oneness back into existence – duality.

In the Christian myth, God first created heaven and earth. Then from the soil of the earth, he created Adam. Then out of a piece of Adam's body, he created Eve. These are all analogous to the "from one comes two opposites and two opposites made one whole" idea in the physical realm. Furthermore, when Adam and Eve ate the fruit from the Tree of Knowledge of Good and Evil, self-consciousness develops and the dualistic division in man's perception of the world is made real. That is knowledge and what it does. "And the eyes of them both were opened" in Genesis. The world that was simply whole is split apart. "Self and other" becomes real, thus embarrassment arises as they realize they are naked in front of each other. Before that, they did not detect and perceive one and the other as "something else." And because conscious attention allows them to differentiate., what follows is the ability to categorize things in the world. They can now decide and choose what they like and dislike. "Good and evil" had come to be, resulting in them being "kicked out" of the holy (wholly) Garden of Eden, and utopia is no more.

In the Buddhist context, Gautama, before he came to be known as the Buddha, was born a prince. A renowned seer from far away land prophesized at Gautama's birth ceremony that Gautama will either become a great king or an epoch-making religious figure. His father being king predictably desired Gautama to inherit his kingdom than becoming a clergy. To achieve that, he chose to completely shelter Gautama physically inside a well-guarded palace and mentally under an abundance of material pleasure. Such a shelter draws a strong parallel to the Garden of Eden. Upon adulthood, irresistible to the innate human desire to adventure, Gautama decided to venture outside of his confined realm despite objections. The first time he ventured outside, he met an old man and realized his youth in contrast with old age. The second time, he met a sick man and realized his health in contrast with sickness. The third time, he encountered a corpse and discovered life versus death. Finally, he crossed paths with a monk and realized abundance in contrast with lack. His reality is utterly shattered at this point, where order used to be, chaos has taken root. His mind previously was of one, but the new perceptions had introduced division. It is at this point that Gautama departed from his kingdom and began his journey in search of liberation from the duality of being. His journey culminated in the *Middle Way*, a freedom that is possible by the transcendental understanding of opposites such as limitless indulgence and extreme asceticism.

The world is composed of myriads of dualistic opposites founded upon oneness. This is the undeniable undercurrent of reality and world events. From the perspective of human, we have come to neglect such reality due to our ability to differentiate and subsequently picking sides. We are mesmerized by such power. Triumph and liberation are not found in having one side dominate or annihilate the other. Such an attitude is life oppressing and destroying. Triumph and liberation are to be discovered in the knowing and reconciliation of the opposites. If we can transcend them and see from afar, duality is founded in implicit unity, in oneness. Knowing, in this case, does not mean in the sense of the learning of knowledge but knowing as in knowing how to breathe, knowing how to move our hands - somehow we know it but we do not know how we do it, while we can also voluntarily have some control over it. This is true understanding. If one comes to this level of understanding, one shall see opposites and their oneness everywhere and in everything. One would have come to know the ground of being, in the game of being. This is the re-discovery that can lead to balance that invigorates life. With that serving as the foundation, one may cease to be confounded by the superficially chaotic patterns in the human games.

All world's grandest guiding principles must arise out of such understanding. Love, harmony, compassion, kindness, peace, enlightenment. If the understanding is missing, these intentions tend to become misguided in action. Although this is not something meant to be fully "grasp" in the intellectual sense, nor can it be fully grasped, the ceaseless spirit in approaching the full understanding is a key element to a fruitful, integrated life and the continuation of human beings. Perhaps such spirit should be the highest ideal as a human being. Such spirit may carry us to the utmost approximation to embody the paradoxical yet symbiotic duality of being, the examination beyond that, without the desire and intention of grasping and ownership, is perhaps as close as we humans can get to... Truth.

Why is this important? Furthermore, why has everything written in part 1 been important? You ask yet you remain because something inside you wants to know. In Joseph Campbell's word, you have answered your calling and are in search of the highest treasure. Let us continue the search from a more personal viewpoint, with more in-depth details in part 2.

If all is connected, then there is no isolated event.
If all is connected, then there is no isolated individual.
If all is connected, then there is no isolated thought process.
If all simply is, we are no different than the source.

Part 2
Microcosm / The Individual

Discovery of Blindness

I quit my software engineering career and took up the mantle of freelance photography in 2016. For an extended period of time afterward, I remained brim with hesitance when the occasion arises for me to tell others that I am a professional photographer. Perhaps hesitating at first is understandable, but it is not as if I had not accumulated the skills, expertise, and experience after the many jobs and ventures I partook in. Why the hesitancy?

I began taking photos in high school with the now-forgotten disposable cameras. That was almost two decades ago. They had very limited functions – one telephoto length, single automatic flash, and 30-some frames of films. Over the coming years, I gradually moved up the equipment chain, from a brick-sized digital point and shoot camera in college to a full-frame digital SLR camera.

Along the way, I learned about the various technical capabilities of digital cameras and lenses that seemed most important at the initial stage of being an enthusiast. But as I carried on, there came a need to study and master the technical skills involved in how, when, where to use settings such as aperture, shutter speed, ISO, mode of autofocusing, etc. It took more than a decade to progress from shooting in Auto-mode, then Program-mode, then Av-mode, and then the final necessary switch to Manual-mode. Like any other discipline, the rabbit hole of improvement continues to go deeper. After taking many seemingly purposeless photos and creating many sorry excuses at art, I began to observe and apply composition techniques like using leading lines, patterns, colors, dramatic contrast, etc. And not long after I began shooting professionally, I found myself adopting the use of more peripherals such as reflectors, basic flash, off-camera flash(es), and other light modifiers. Now in the age of computer, there is an entirely additional set of skills one may learn in post-production software.

Beyond those more technical skills mentioned, there are various abilities required to do different types of photoshoots. In interactive settings, the ability to anticipate moments and subjects' reactions are as critical as quick reaction time – if one desires to capture all the precious candid moments. That is an aspect of photography that I personally enjoy and strive to excel in. In portrait photography settings, I had to learn various ways to pose models and provide proper, understandable instructions on posture, movement, and facial expressions. That is subject to adjustment depending on how the people being photographed react and also their unique features. In a tightly scheduled event that requires photography coverage, it is vital to communicate and coordinate with the event planner and perhaps other vendors. In handling the photographing of large groups, I had to give direction with authority along with some patience, in order to properly set up a good photo; however, a sense of urgency is also required because of how quickly sometimes people lose their patience. Finally, as clients and venues always vary, I learned to anticipate different personality's expectations and adapt fluidly to sudden and unforeseen changes.

Even after having gained all the experience and learned all those skills, there is one competency I received from my mentor Todd Rafalovich in the last few years – though he never explicitly made a point of it – which makes me hesitate to call myself professional. And that is the ability to see light.

You may think that sounds silly. *"If you can see, you can certainly see light."*

The fact is that after learning from observing how Todd works and my own experience, it is as though I did not know how to see light before the endeavor of the last few years. In other words, despite living with eyesight for more than three decades, I realize that this was akin to being blind!

What used to be brightness and darkness, and a few shades in between previously had multiplied into a large spectrum with infinite possibilities. There is now direct light, diffused light, bounced light, ambient light, etc. Shadows can present themselves in so many manners. The color temperature of light becomes an on-going factor. All those factors together would cause different presentations of the subject. There is also the combination of light bouncing off surfaces and skins and if absence, the shadows produced. In any given photography setting, a photographer will need to observe, account for, and decide how to make use of said factors and elements of light, sometimes with very little time, in order to capture aesthetically pleasing photographs while accounting also for the time and other contextual demands. It is like learning how to perform different dances with light in each unique scenario. Similarly, with regard to shadow, this is also an awakening into seeing darkness and so, this is not just a dance with light but also a dance with darkness.

Despite having eyesight, like everyone else, one key aspect for a skillful photographer is the never-ending pursuit in the mastery to see light and the gradients created in all its glory. It is this unending pursuit to learn to dance with light, in any given setting, and with swiftness, that contributes to my hesitance to fully claim the title of photographer. Perhaps we can also call this feeling the ultimate reverence of art that lives inside all kinds of artists, where one can never truly "possess it all" and be a master. Instead, as Bruce Lee put it, one is always a student-master who is skillful to teach but never quits in furthering his mastery.

The more experience I gathered working with digital cameras, the stronger my appreciation grows for the gift of eyesight because, despite the advent of sensor technology, a camera sensor's capability still pales in comparison to human eyes in many ways. One specific attribute to consider is the dynamic range coverage. There is a rising category of photography in the past decade categorically known as high dynamic range (HDR). In order to capture an HDR, multiple frames of varying exposure need to be taken. The higher the contrasting luminosity within a scene, the higher the number of frames that need to be taken with varying exposure. Afterward, these multiple frames are composited in post-processing to generate the final HDR photograph. Even with the latest generation of camera sensors which have greatly improved dynamic range, without the process to generate an HDR photo, post-processing edit is still required to even out the bright and dark sections in a photo. Such an amount of effort is required to generate an image that our eyes can naturally perform.

Having said everything previously, it was a long-winded story to surmise the following critical notion. Although we all possess the gift of eyesight, it does not mean everyone realizes the potential and utilizes their vision to the same degree. The extent, manner, and awareness in everyone's application of vision vary widely. Though we may not be physically blind, we live like we are blind because of our lack of attention and investigation. Truth is, how many of us ever come to such degree of realization to appreciate such a gift, along with many other similar gifts of our biology, and of nature.

How much appreciation and sensitivity do we truly exhibit over our senses of taste, touch, smell, and sound? More importantly, what about the gift of life, the awareness behind the senses, the consciousness that is bestowed upon each of us? Although everyone possesses it, how many truly seek to understand and utilize it to its fullest? Although everyone possesses, how many have willingly and bravely dived into the depth of the psyche to learn to "see" and understand oneself? Furthermore, it is straightforward and savory to observe and deal with light, but how many are willing to acquaint and grapple with darkness?

The Ignorance of Being

The following is a fable that I stumbled upon on the internet once. It has stuck in my mind, though I cannot find the originating author upon much searching.

An American businessman was standing at the pier of a small coastal Mexican village when a small boat with just one fisherman docked. Inside the small boat were several large yellowfin tuna. The American complimented the Mexican on the quality of his fish.

"How long it took you to catch them?" The American asked.

"Only a little while." The Mexican replied.

"Why don't you stay out longer and catch more fish?" The American then asked.

"I have enough to support my family's immediate needs." The Mexican said.

"But," The American then asked, "What do you do with the rest of your time?"

The Mexican fisherman said, "I sleep late, fish a little, play with my children, take a siesta with my wife, Maria, stroll into the village each evening where I sip wine and play guitar with my amigos, I have a full and busy life, senor."

The American scoffed, "I am a Harvard MBA and could help you. You should spend more time fishing and with the proceeds you buy a bigger boat, and with the proceeds from the bigger boat you could buy several boats, eventually you would have a fleet of fishing boats."

"Instead of selling your catch to a middleman you would sell directly to the consumers, eventually opening your own can factory. You would control the product, processing and distribution. You would need to leave this small coastal fishing village and move to Mexico City, then LA and eventually NYC where you will run your expanding enterprise."

The Mexican fisherman asked, "But senor, how long will this all take?"

To which the American replied, "15-20 years."

"But what then, senor?"

The American laughed and said, "That's the best part. When the time is right you would announce an IPO (Initial Public Offering) and sell your company stock to the public and become very rich, you would make millions."

"Millions huh? Then what?"

The American said slowly, "Then you would retire. Move to a small coastal fishing village where you would sleep late, fish a little, play with your kids, take a siesta with your wife, stroll to the village in the evenings where you could sip wine and play your guitar with your amigos…"

-   Author Unknown

The moral of the story for me points to the truth that despite how we genuinely desire to be "here" deeply, we have developed a mentality that ignores that desire and provokes us to scramble and go on many journeys to other places. Hopefully, in the end, we bring ourselves back "here" in very roundabout ways. Put in this way, it is a silly way to live, but perhaps this is how the circle of life works.

We can describe life as an analogy of a trip from the maternity ward to the burial ground. In between, society and culture have prearranged and preconditioned that we make certain stops. From a toddler, one must learn to talk, crawl, and walk, better sooner than later because the race has begun. When physically allowed, off to preschool an infant goes to learn how to socialize. Things are starting to heat up here. Next, we have kindergarten, middle school, and high school. Throughout this time, kids must make those precious grades. But in the 21st century, that is not enough. One must have accomplishments in all kinds of extracurricular activities to boot. Then we have universities. There better be some prestigious internships in the summers in between. Upon graduation, hopefully this ends with some high honors. Finishing university grants you a certificate and a celebratory event called commencement. That means the beginning of searching for employment. But perhaps a bachelor's degree is still inadequate in the 21st century for gainful employment, or perhaps you grew tired of your monotonous and sterile office environment after a few years, you feel angsty and in need of a change. That causes you to return to the comfort blanket known as academia for a master's degree, PhD, or MBA, which then hopefully land you a better, or a dream job afterward.

As you continue your career path, you are required to fulfill certain quota or performance metrics. Achieving these will get you those delightful promotions, along with materialistic rewards; however, it also comes with exponentially multiplying duty and higher quotas to be met, disproportionate to the new title. Meanwhile, you are also supposed to find a mate in life, get married, purchase a property, and have children. Hopefully the ludicrous job enables the attracting of a prospective partner. You need to be able to meet the demands of each other. Then if you are able to stay together long enough, you can have a baby together. Later on, hopefully your children can get into the schools and careers that you yourself deem prestigious.

And so we push and push and push. We push toward our goals steadily, obediently, and with gusto, with nil a critical thought. Every step of the way, one is supposed to act with excitement. Each milestone is necessarily celebrated. "The pursuit of happiness," we exclaim. That is how the story goes. The script has been written and so we follow. Yes yes, we must follow it… That is until a point of deep dissatisfaction is reached. That is all too common. The mistakes, disappointment, resentment, and suffering that were carefully swept under the rug would pile up. Upon accumulating past a threshold, they come gushing out and transform into crisis, a catastrophe, a tragic life event that occurs suddenly and plunges life into irredeemable chaos. Only with a sufficiently gargantuan chaotic mess in view, we may then stop ignoring life, as human, and as being, all together.

At such juncture, the human game has stalled. Then what?

Like a mule being led by a carrot on the stick, that is how we followed the script through a good part of life. But after disappointment after disappointment, we come face to face with a lack of fulfillment that made it worse than the mule's life, who at least gets to enjoy the satisfaction of eating the carrot at the end of his day. We think, "we are supposed to get there," but upon landing in the crisis, we realize we are not getting there at all. Sometimes it is called a mid-life crisis; however, nowadays there is also the quarter-life crisis.

"I have played my part in all these things. I have followed what is socially accepted. I did as I was told. I tried to be a good person. I did my best to contribute to society!"

Again and again and again throughout life, we somehow did not realize how unconsciously we have been living. And in unconsciousness, we humans live life running around in circles continuously and hastily. We even have a name for it, the rat race. Money, power, and vanity have become the gods of the modern age. Arguments can be made whether this circle is spiraling upward or downward. The more important question is whether we will destabilize and spin out of control before long. What may determine society and civilization to spin out of control is hinged on how consciously people live their individual lives. The less conscious the people become, the more the society they build will be a house of cards.

In an age where we are ever more technologically advanced, we are becoming less and less aware of ourselves. By focusing only on the human game, we ignore the mechanisms that have to do with reality and our own being, which include everything outside of conscious attention and what cannot be qualified by the intellect.

Adding to the dilemma, contemporary societies across the globe function on analytical models and technology that are only exacerbating this unconsciousness, amplifying our hectic lifestyle, amplifying the incessant yearning for carnal desire, and increasing demand for material and superficial convenience. Systems had been developed and are being developed to rely and thrive on this unconsciousness. We are fed with a myriad of distractions that prevent us from introspection and asking important questions in life.

"What do I really want?"
"Do I really want what I think I want?"
"What are my values?"
"What gives meaning to my life?"
"What kind of guiding principle should I live by?"

Anyone who observes the happenings in their own country and around the globe with their eyes wide open must on some level realizes that something is off. As Marcellus famously said in *Hamlet...*

Something is rotten in the state of Denmark.

After that, the question that each of us must first answer for ourselves is whether we accept that notion fully or not. Without such acceptance, one cannot begin to confront and resolve any problem.

Remember *mea culpa*.

Fixation on Human Game

Abstraction is defined as the process of generalization of a phenomenon by retaining only information which is relevant for a specific purpose and rendering all other information irrelevant.

One can say contemporary society is a massive apparatus constituted of abstractions piled on top of each other that encapsulates us physically, emotionally, mentally, and spiritually to enable us to live among ourselves and in nature. Because nature is inherently of infinitude, it is a necessity to limit the scope of reality that we encounter daily. The rules and systems that arise out of abstraction are confining the realm of infinite possibility to prevent us from continuously living in fight-or-flight mode so we can function within a "normal" spectrum. They provide us with a realm of "known" so we do not have to continuously engage in the terror of the "unknown," and that allows us to be productive citizens. That is the great benefit of human society. It is a supporting "structure" that enables a civilized life with reduced stress and danger. For the sake of simplification, I lump all facets and mechanisms of human society together and call it the human game.

Despite the human game's benefit, it is also a curse. The curse is that we are liable to forget what it is and its origination. If the game is an illusion, the longer the game has gone on, the more we are ensnared in the illusion. It is the move toward complete ignorance from what lies outside of the illusory game that is the great danger. Instead of the society functioning for the people, the people are to function to uphold the social system at all cost.

Human's ancestors from eons past did not develop societal rules arbitrarily. They arise out of deep, instinctive understanding into reality and being. There is wisdom that lies at the bedrock of the initial abstractions. Old abstraction – old social rituals and traditions – may seem primitive but they are informed by a certain insight into the intangible, distilled content, patterns of nature.

As civilization matured over the ages and after abstractions layered upon abstractions layered upon abstractions, the originating wisdom had become ambiguous and gradually faded into the background. More and more complex abstraction continued to pile on, completely burying that wisdom. That coincides with the expansion and overreliance of our intellect. Without the proper effort to excavate and rediscover, humans begin to make rules and systems that are more and more disassociated from reality and adversarial to our being. The ultimate symptom is a worsening condition where humans will fight senselessly over more and more convoluted rules and concepts. At the final stage of these unfolding conditions, the downfall of various civilizations or dynasties become inevitable.

The fortunate part is, many rules and abstractions in the realm of knowledge in the human game still contain traces of the original wisdom. Much still have their effects in governing human behaviors and social rituals. The unfortunate part of the 21st century is, we are recklessly doing away, ignoring, or destroying such abstractions without the understanding of wisdom. Like the lack of an appreciation for eyesight, we can say society and civilization are blindly surviving on the fumes of our ancestral wisdom. Ironically, we believe that we are very clever and therefore can create our own destiny, while undermining the foundation that which we still walk on.

The majority of modern man no longer holds much respect for older myths, customs, and traditions. They carry the attitude that such things are outdated, and therefore stupid and senseless. This leads to the closure of a door that may allow us to understand our culture, and ultimately ourselves.

The situation is exacerbating due to a hyper-focus on the human game which is based on over- or pseudo-(under) intellectualism that bestows a false sense of security, due to our belief that our intellectual by-products – abstractions, words, mathematics, science, and technology – allow us to wrangle and bend the fabric of reality. There is an illusion that humans now possess the power to control everything. People will readily deny that if asked, but nonetheless their behaviors demonstrate such an assumption which they apply in daily life. We are overestimating ourselves. Such arrogance leads to the ignorance of the individual psyche, which enables people to be handily subliminally manipulated. Consequently, we now witness a society that functions on using sensationalism to appeal to people's raw emotions. Such atmosphere reeks of the mass hysteria that consumed the people during the Salem witch trials. Over-intellectualism and sensationalism congregate into a deadly combination. In such a scenario, there arises a deafening silence on a call for the pursuit of wisdom and the pursuit of Truth.

Meanwhile, a voice that speaks that there is no such thing as foundational truth slowly envelops the globe in the 21st century. When such a claim increasingly takes root in the minds of the masses, supplanting Truth in society, ideologies that are pretentious half-truth, thus more digestible and appetizing for the analytical mind and common egos, become the motivating force of groups. Demagogues, cult of personality, and false prophets shall spring into power and reign supreme. Individuals will cede self-exploration and invite themselves into cults of personality. Society absorbs the influence from the more fanatical, imbalanced personalities that are shaped by half-truth. People are no longer individuals but have become mere herds with everyone merely selecting and following the same few sets of written scripts. They would talk the same, feel the same, think the same, and even look about the same. People will feel like plastics and robots to each other. Consequently, everyone would finally become bored with each other. That is the state of affair we are fast approaching if not already arrived at...

Everyone is alone.
Everyone is empty.
People no longer have need of others.
You can always find a spare for any talent.
Any relationship can be replaced.
A world that is bored with itself...
- Shogo Makishima, Psycho-Pass (anime)

The word "psyche" originates from Greek, which is the name of the goddess of the soul *Psykhe*. Appropriately, the manners in which the mass of humans live demonstrates a complete disregard of the psyche and its natural flow. As human beings, we have come to ignore our psyche at our own peril. The disregard of the psyche, and the soul, necessarily leads to a lack of understanding in ourselves. This loss of understanding is not necessary. Meanwhile as we willfully ignore it, problems that lie in the recess of our psyche turn into neurosis, then gradually become psychosis that translates into the reality in individual life, communities, and the greater society.

If the universe is the macrocosm, then we are each a microcosm of the universe through which the universe reflects itself. If our view and understanding of our self becomes tainted, distorted, corrupted, or marred by egotism, the reality around us shall reflect such perversion. If who we think we are is out of sync with who we actually are and conversely, if what and how we think and perceive the world is out of sync with what and how the world actually is, such misalignment and disassociation will actualize in reality. Individually, we may think and believe in things we do not act out, and our actions more and more cannot be correlated to what we think because what we think and feel consciously versus what we think and feel unconsciously are dangerously fragmented. In such a manner, people are living with a modality that is sufficiently inadequate in relation to reality. As such modality sweeps across society, the populace and state will uphold grandiose ideals that ring hollow and are implicitly betrayed, truth and facts will be denied their rightful place, malevolence will be acted out in the name of kindness, means become the ends, and all other manners of events that equivocate "putting the cart before the horse" will occur.

Therefore, it is not the belief in the power of reason that will save us. Neither its rejection. Quite the contrary. For it is the fervent hope that we can be entities of pure rationality that has led us into the intellectual cul-de-sac in the modern age. We can no longer afford to mistake intelligence and knowledge for wisdom. In other words, it is inadequate and savage to forcefully filter thoughts and perceptions through the intellectual lens. It has come time to accept and include the being that is beyond the faculty of reasoning. It is time to let go of our "fetishized analytic logical rigor," just as

Schopenhauer argued against the notion of people treating philosophy as a mean to earn one's living and therefore inevitably betraying the philosophical essence of truth-seeking. More rationality is not the antidote. Sadly, the academic field of philosophy has fallen prey to the deconstructing nature of intelligence... rigorously.

We think we are seeing the result of a loss of rationality demonstrated by a populace that is increasingly blindly ideological. That is not accurate. We are seeing the result of the extreme adoption of trying to fit reality into pure rational constructs, hyper-rationalization, and a blind trust in intellect... In such a case, *enantiodromian* effect occurs, where the behaviors of people are becoming increasingly senseless and out of touch with reality. While we think we are gaining the upper hand and control over reality, we are losing control faster than ever. We believe we are free, but freedom has been, and is gradually being eroded. We believe we are creating peace, trust, and security but are unconsciously introducing more danger, mistrust, and instability among ourselves and into our systems. And how can any man hope to steer reality toward balance unless he has discovered balance within himself?

Or, must mankind reach the point driven home by Ivan Ilyich's realization:

> It is as if I had been going downhill while I imagined I was going up. And that is really what it was. I was going in public opinion, but to the same extent life was ebbing away from me. And now it is all done and there is only death.

Detaching from Rules

Although my major was in computer science when I was attending graduate school at Stanford, my curiosity led me to enroll in a few additional courses in the management science and engineering department, on the subjects of decision and risk analysis. Among those courses, nothing else stuck with me better than one phrase quoted in one of the texts. And here I will be paraphrasing because I cannot locate the original text, "All statistical/mathematical models are flawed. They are all wrong. They are useful in so far they provide you certain insight, knowledge, and prediction that can inform your decision." That is a warning against mistaking the mathematical models for reality, lab results for guaranteed outcome.

Backtracking a few years from my graduate school days... I was an undergraduate student at Michigan State University and fenced competitively as part of the school team in the Midwest Fencing conference. My main weapon was the foil. A concept in foil fencing is known as the "right of way". It is a key factor for the referee to determine which fencer gets a point. In the most basic scenario, the fencer who initiates the attack on the opponent, aka begins the threat of a target area, gains the right of way. If the opponent simply counters, and the fencers hit each other simultaneously, or even if the counterattack lands first, the point is given to the fencer with the right of way. Thus, the threatened fencer's proper reaction should be to parry the opponent's blade, therefore seizing the right of way, before attempting a riposte to take the point. It gets more complex and nuanced, but for the purpose of the writing here, this explanation should suffice to continue.

A beginning fencer will practice fundamentals such as basic posture, footwork, point control. Due to the concept of the right of way, the motion of a basic parry and riposte will be taught early on. The motion is to be repeated endless times, drilled into muscle memory, and beaten into the bones from the very beginning.

During the learning of the various forms of parry and riposte, frequently the motion of parry and the motion of riposte are practiced separately. It is always parry first, then riposte... parry first, then riposte, parry, riposte.

In my third year of fencing at MSU, I had finally improved to a level that warranted a few lessons with our retired head coach, Fred Freiheit. Despite being in his 70s, there was no doubt that I would be annihilated if he fenced me with the slightest intention of seriousness. I received two key points from him which resulted in a key improvement in my fencing skill from that point on but more importantly, continued to benefit me to this day inside and outside of sports.

The first point is that, though I had tremendous speed with my hand, there was much excessive movement that can be trimmed. I needed to eliminate the unnecessary actions. Secondly, my movement of parry and riposte are performed separately, but why? That was because they were concepts that are taught separately to beginners. It was a necessity to isolate them during the learning process but that had resulted in physical and psychological compartmentalization of movement and a key minuscule yet clear distinction in execution. Fred taught me to blend the motion together in one fluid and swift movement without repercussion. However, it was also necessary for me to eradicate the notion of them being separate within. From then on, the consistent practice was required to also remove the unnecessary separation of the two movements to make one. If a sliver of separate concepts yet lives in me, they will manifest in my actions. Put differently, I had to disavow completely what I once believed to be true if I was to improve.

Carrying the idea of the second lesson a bit further, is the idea of being formless in Bruce Lee's famous Jeet Kune Do – the boiling down of many forms of martial arts and movement into a teaching of seemingly basic, fluid, but expedient motion – a form based on formlessness. It has a strong focus on the fluidity of motion and only the essentials.

We all live by some simplified model of the world by interacting with it guided by some frameworks which were infused in us without much of our own input. So let me ask you, how many "parry," and how many "riposte" do you carry within the framework of beliefs and ideas through which you perceive and make decisions in your life? How many of those you hold and apply as absolute? What if those systems and beliefs you hold dearly appear false in the face of a given situation? What if rules need to be broken? What if rules need to be unlearned? What if you have to give up all your ideals, your hopes and dreams, all your psychic and physical possession to obtain what you truly want, to be who you are? What then?

Are you willing to make the sacrifice?

To Go, or Not to Go

What if you must abandon your entire existing internal model and framework with which you interact and define your purpose within society? What if all the meanings and values you hold in the highest esteem are found to be delusive?

No, nobody wants to fathom that. Most people cannot alter their thought process easily, however trivial, and consequently, we have phenomena such as groupthink, confirmation bias, and cognitive dissonance. Thoughts are so precious to people that they congregate into homogenous groups and huddle only with people who think like them. To venture beyond that seems certain death. That being the case, how is it ever possible to steer anybody to confront the unknown of all unknowns that is the inner world, the psyche.

But that is something to be accepted. Such behavior is perfectly normal. People's reprehension is perfectly understandable. One can only greet that with compassion. (and if you ever desire to be a "teacher" figure, you must possess this deep understanding, refer to Part 3. Learning, Teaching, and Being a teacher)

In the game of life, it is far easier to live only being conscious of the human game. For these games exist largely within the confine of logical intelligence and its derived cleverness, skills, and methods. Pre-existing, tangible, well-defined sets of skills and methods are readily available in abundance for one to choose.

By remaining unaware of the game of life on the level of being, one takes on much less responsibilities for himself and his surroundings. The game of being involves the exploration of the more intangible aspects of life. One will come to contend with revaluating one's own axioms. One will discover new connections to his environment. Everything internal and external previously unknown will begin to surface. Such realization renders the unavoidable necessity to face the blunt force of nature. To be on the path to explore the game on the level of being is to chase ideals while incessantly redefining them. For most people, the choice is far better and easier to not ever define a goal. It may be too crushing to set a lofty goal only to face failures.

It is far easier to rule a nation than to rule one's self.

By merely following scripts that are readily laid out, one follows a safe path, physically but especially psychologically. By never questioning yourself, one can simply obey the plan laid out by others and never be wrong. By acting in the ideals supplied by others, one is never responsible. By acting the same as others who also follow the safe path, one seemingly gains immunity from loneliness, though it lurks in tow like a shadow. By not specifying one's condition of success, one never fails. By not finding and presenting the world one's authentic self, one is never vulnerable.

Emerson warns against such a tempted path of conformity:

> What I must do is all that concerns me, not what the people think. This rule, equally arduous in actual and in intellectual life, may serve the whole distinction between greatness and meanness. It is the harder, because you will always find those who think they know what is your duty better than you know it. It is easy in the world to live after the world's opinion; it is easy in solitude to live after our own; but the great man is he who in the midst of the crowd keeps with perfect sweetness the independence of solitude.

This kind of one-sided existence may suffice for many but not all.

For those who like to ask questions… for those who all the worldly materials do not find fulfilling… for those who cannot seem to find joy from consuming the prepackaged… for those who feel something is missing perpetually… for those striving to be "normal" but can no longer feel normal… for those who, like Odin, have intrinsic hunger for wisdom…

And, if those feelings and questions are embraced, accepted… for those who listen to the calling of their being…

They may not realize it or know it while in the moment, but they will each go on a personal journey, unique but the same. But unlike other kinds of journey in life where one may find companions, this one is achieved alone. One may discover tools, guides, friends, teachers, and gurus that may inspire along the way, but this journey is traveled inwardly accompanied by solitude. How far one goes on this journey is entirely up to one's own will. Yet, the same destiny awaits those that may emerge from each of their unique quests.

A quest for self-discovery, where you will contend with all the elements within yourself.

And may each follow his own path.

Resolve

Huike (Shinko Eka in Japanese), known as the Second Patriarch of Zen, has an extensive background in Taoism and Confucianism because of his Chinese family background. After the death of his parents, Huike began his study in Buddhism. After eight years of study in Buddhism, he found himself yet full of questions and doubts. He was also criticized for not having a master, so Huike decided to seek out Bodhidharma. Bodhidharma was known as the First Patriarch who originally cross the Himalayas from India to spread his message in China. His identity remains shrouded in mysteries.

Huike finally encountered Bodhidharma in a cave near Shaolin Temple while he was amidst the famed nine-year wall gazing meditation. Huike waited outside as days and nights passed. He kept waiting even when snow began to fall and piled up to his knees. Bodhidharma yet refused to accept Huike as a disciple. Finally, to show his resolve, he cut off one of his arms, presented it to Bodhidharma, and said, "This is the beginning. Either you turn, or my head will be falling before you. I am going to cut my head too."

With such a sign of sincerity and determination to undergo any kind of sacrifice to obtain wisdom, Bodhidharma accepted Huike as his first pupil. And, they held their first conversation that gave Huike his first glimpse into certain realization... more on this in the chapter Zen.

On the flipped side of the world at a much later time, Patrick Henry, the famed American orator impressed upon his fellows at a Virginia assembly in a key moment during the Independence War, "Is life so dear, or peace so sweet, as to be purchased at the price of chains and slavery? Forbid it, Almighty God! I know not what course others may take; but as for me, *give me liberty or give me death!*"

At the time of the speech, the general attitude of the public to oppose British rule remained weak and irresolute within the American colonies. However, Henry realized a fateful moment to argue against complacency and the necessity to arouse the will of his people. He did so despite knowing full well that such rhetoric was not the popular opinion among his fellow colonists. Speaking out any way he did. For he knew he had to speak out. Despite the weight of the decision for everyone involved – inevitable mayhem and a considerable certainty of death in war – despite knowing the weight, he spoke out because he knew the stake was something larger than life. That is something worthy of risking one's life, not just his own but also everyone in the colonies. And that very important thing is freedom.

Such is the will necessary for one to go on an inward journey to understand one's self fully. That is also how he will understand the nature around him. Both kinds of understandings lead to the possibility of the development of one's own individuality. One must possess the will that allows one to contend and remain stern and determined even in the face of death; otherwise one shall only cower in fear. One must be open and accept what is to come, be it self-empowerment or self-immolation; otherwise, one shall be shrouded in denial. One must remember the courage that pushed one toward the first leap on to the path that leads to new possibilities toward truth; otherwise, one can easily be corrupted and be pulled off or stopped in his path. One must learn to listen to the calling of one's own being; otherwise, one shall ultimately betray himself… leaving him no ground to stand on, no foundation to grow, no beginning, no end, but a mere shell that blends in with the common.

Perhaps such will, such resolve can be called the Will to Truth, or Will to Being, or Will to Wisdom? It can be given so many names, yet the essence is the same. This… indomitable Will is essential for the journey ahead. For the sake of this writing, let's settle on calling it the Will to Understanding.

Such resolve allows one to persevere when necessary changes are challenging and at times appear impossible. Such resolve allows one to persevere when everywhere one looks things appear foggy and seems to be trapped in an endless space like in Waiting for Godot. Such resolve allows one to persevere when wit tempts and ostensible shortcuts shimmer. Such resolve allows one to persevere when hindrance and obstacles of all manners begin to thwart. Such resolve allows one to persevere when clobbered by uneasiness, ridicule, animosity, contempt, and reproach from others. Such resolve allows one to persevere when friends become enemies and family become strangers. Such resolve allows one's own defense when the tyranny of the crowds seeks to subjugate. Such resolve allows one to persevere when loneliness stirs, and the alluring siren song of normality and conformity ring aloud. Such resolve allows one to sacrifice all if such is what it takes when the moment arises.

Half-heartedness has no place in the game of being.

These forceful messages are not to be mistaken as heed to rebel against one's external world. The Will to Understanding is not a force for dominance and control. Behind an action lies a thought. Behind a thought lies an intention. The resolve is to always maintain the Will to Understanding as a source of the intention. The prerequisite and indispensability of such resolve for one to reach true self-understanding and inner transformation cannot be more emphasized.

All the described repercussions become possibilities when one's inner world begins to transform in large and small ways. Typically, people either choose to ignore arising issues or exert tyranny to ensure such unknown and ignored issues remain tightly sealed away. There is a high chance that others can neither comprehend nor entertain such a personal venture. Although one may be circumspect and keep to one's own council, and even with the utmost tactfulness one exhibit in calibrating one's own behaviors among the presence of others, repercussion cannot be avoided. Because, mere existence can signify threat.

Additionally, as one expands one's knowledge and understanding, with wider perspective every step of the way, comes the inevitability to encounter and overcome scenarios and choices that one neither fathomed nor considered before. This occurrence will iterate itself numerously. Eventually and perhaps to one's utter surprise, he comes to the startling realization that the crowd is far in distance behind, scenery and perspective completely different, and he is standing dreadfully alone…

Such risks and dangers are inevitable in such an undertaking. This is why both Friedrich Nietzsche and Carl Jung had both written to convey certain warnings.

> It is the business of the very few to be independent; it is a privilege of the strong. And whoever attempts it, even with the best right, but without being OBLIGED to do so, proves that he is probably not only strong, but also daring beyond measure. He enters into a labyrinth, he multiplies a thousandfold the dangers which life in itself already brings with it; not the least of which is that no one can see how and where he loses his way, becomes isolated, and is torn piecemeal by some minotaur of conscience. Supposing such a one comes to grief, it is so far from the comprehension of men that they neither feel it, nor sympathize with it. And he cannot any longer go back! He cannot even go back again to the sympathy of men!
> - Friedrich Nietzsche, Beyond Good and Evil

Similarly, Jung referred to an old saying in *The Development of Personality* regarding the treacherous nature of the undertaking, "For many are called, but few are chosen." He followed up that saying by pointing out how "the development of personality is a favor that must be paid for dearly" and no members outside of himself can save himself in the endeavor.

It sounds risky and grim but accompanied by the Will to Understanding, although far removed from his fellow men, such a person in such a seemingly perilous state, who dared to assume such dire risk, will finally feel he is exactly where he needs to be, despite any and all turmoil. That will be his greatest discovery – Solitary solidarity will be the company that grants peace, creativity, and fulfillment. It is within solitude that one undergoes the trials afforded by the full assault of one's entirety of being, the only path to transformation. For a while one may be in a maze, for a while one may be in the desert, for a while one may experience hell, but all these will become the source of his strength. One may agonize and writhe in the suffocating aloneness as the sole awakened being who trudges within a sea of sleepwalkers. But so long as he captures a glimpse of his highest ideal, even if he shall perish in the most pathetic state, he will know in his heart that this is a better outcome than living like a caged beast.

In Taoism, it was written that "朝聞道，夕死可矣". That translates to, "If one acquires understanding of the Tao in the morning, one can die with content in the evening" with Tao representing the ultimate universal truth.

Most modern people would readily choose the blanket of security and safety in the most trodden paths. Only they forget…

Life itself is inherently a risk. There is a necessary risk to continuously confront incessant waves of unknowns, because of the infinitude of possibility. Despite the impossibility to know everything, it does not excuse one to abdicate his responsibility to try his best to understand nature.

If one is instead willing to risk it, let that conviction be the guide to life. This is the emphasis to this calling in the Sermon on the Mount:

> Therefore I say unto you, Take no thought for your life, what ye shall eat, or what ye shall drink; nor yet for your body, what ye shall put on. Is not the life more than meat, and the body than raiment? Behold the fowls of the air: for they sow not, neither do they reap, nor gather into barns; yet your heavenly Father feedeth them. Are ye not much better than they? And why take ye thought for raiment? Consider the lilies of the field, how they grow; they toil not, neither do they spin: And yet I say unto you, That even Solomon in all his glory was not arrayed like one of these. Which of you by taking thought can add one cubit unto his stature? Wherefore, if God so clothe the grass of the field, which to day is, and to morrow is cast into the oven, shall he not much more clothe you, O ye of little faith? Therefore take no thought, saying, What shall we eat? or, What shall we drink? or, Wherewithal shall we be clothed? (For after all these things do the Gentiles seek:) for your heavenly Father knoweth that ye have need of all these things. But seek ye first the kingdom of God, and his righteousness; and all these things shall be added unto you. Take therefore no thought for the morrow: for the morrow shall take thought for the things of itself. Sufficient unto the day is the evil thereof.

- Matthew 6:25 – 6:34, King James

It is easy to be suckered into the struggles of daily life and forget all lofty aims beyond the superficial and the materials. Due to their struggles, people desire even more materials and pleasure. Power(money) and vanity(fame) are means through which people obtain those pleasures, so naturally they follow the old tales of becoming completely mesmerized in their pursuit. Eventually, power and vanity would even supplant materials and pleasure and become the all-dominating goal in one's life. That is why one should "take no thought in what we shall eat, drink, and be clothed with," even though we must participate in the motion of society daily. This sermon resonates with the teaching in Buddhism that warns people against the *five hindrances* - *kāmacchanda* (desire for sensory stimuli, or greed-related), *vyāpāda* (ill-will, or anger-related), *thīna-middha* (laziness, or sloth-related), *uddhacca-kukkucca* (restlessness, or attachment-related), and *vicikicchā* (doubt, or distrust-related). Each may serve as a fatal trapping that impedes the development of deeper understanding. We can observe people in modern lifestyle who are becoming increasingly ensnared in the pursuit and rumination indicated by these hindrances. They are mentally trapped and cannot look beyond. It is without wonder that the minimization and detachment from the hindrances (by seeing through, not suppression) is a key step on the path of enlightenment in Buddhism.

One is to pay attention to the highest conceivable apotheosis in the moment. One is to iteratively aim at that and not detract in an inner path of self-understanding. One must continuously make this difficult choice, for such aim is not achieved in a short time but rather akin to the construction of a new kingdom. One cannot stop as distractions are abundant. Otherwise, having no aim or worse yet, aiming low or aiming downward, will have the eventual consequence of coming to a stand-still in one's life. As still water grows stale, a stagnant soul will fester and become diseased.

Such is the conclusion with the natural ratiocination later in Matthew:

For whosoever hath, to him shall be given, and he shall have more abundance: but whosoever hath not, from him shall be taken away even that he hath.
- Matthew 13:12, King James

This seemingly cruel, cold-blooded utterance directly reckons the precept that the pursuit of an individual's highest aim, which is ever-evolving, is to be ignored at one's own peril.

Did you allow life's everyday issues to dominate its entirety? Did you allow yourself to wallow in self-pity or self-loathing, anger or jealousy? Did you allow yourself to be enamored by the drama and gossips of the day? Did you give in yourself to the indulgence of incessant entertainment and distraction? Did you honestly not have even five minutes to spare for silence, solitude, contemplation, and self-reflection?

Modern man often quickly claims that life is simply too busy for any such "loafing" endeavors; however, as the inadequate understanding of oneself persists, as such uncaring attitude continues to influence, complexities in life as well as the errors caused by such deliberate ineptitude will multiply. These ineptitudes and errors will reach their influential hands outward and becoming an indomitable, repercussive force against the individual. Instead of a gradual iterative, transformation process, one will encounter the instant accumulated destructive force of reality of his own creation… and an attempt to recover has to be made, with much graver danger.

The decision is yours. First, to aim or not to aim. Second, where will you aim at?

If in the heart of hearts, you are able to find your inner resolve, and you have come to terms with your own sincere desire to seek Truth, and thus striving for inner understanding despite all the perils that lay ahead, and retain sincerity all the way… you will at some point come across the true meaning behind:

Ask, and it shall be given to you; seek, and ye shall find; knock, and it shall be opened unto you: For every one that asketh receiveth; and he that seeketh findeth; and to him that knocketh

it shall be opened.
-    Matthew 7:7 – 7:8, King James

The quote carries the same nuance as the old saying:

When the pupil is ready, the Master appears.

Just don't forget to hold on to your resolve, your Will to Understanding. With purity. With sincerity.

Hero's Journey

The idea of heroism and myths of heroic characters are timeless and universal. They transcend cultures, time, and geography. Even in modern times, the sheer fact of the popularity of film watching exposes such a fact, especially with the multitude of superhero movies. As audience watch, they knowingly and unknowingly place themselves into the roles of the characters. The concept of the transcendental hero contains qualities and patterns that exude from the characters in books and movies. The concept apprises us in how we can fundamentally and necessarily interact with reality. There is a reason why so many of us are enticed to go to theaters repeatedly, or otherwise read fictional stories.

The hero archetype has a special allure for us. Archetypes can be loosely defined as patterns of patterns or meta-patterns. It could be said their summation exist even beyond the realm of meta-patterns. Because of their peculiarity, they can help us to catch a glimpse into the true nature of things. One may say they live inside the many universal symbols and imagery of the human world. As such, they are recognizable and understandable to the human psyche. They are mysteriously appealing. They exert influence subliminally. However, it is not a case of archetypes being controllers in man-made phenomena. More accurately, they are an objective element of reality that manifest themselves spontaneously and are not to be mistaken as governing forces. These archetypes are like latent guides in the cognitive structures in our psyche. They may be thought of as a set or a conglomerate of characteristics that are personified as spirits, deities or other mystical entities in stories. As a result, archetypes reveal themselves within the concretization into mythological characters: gods, demons, angels, other supernatural entities... Each character corresponds to a manifestation of key aspects of one archetype though sometimes several. Moreover, these characters are often not rigidly defined and had variations of tales and origin stories. For example, the stories of Greek and Roman mythology have differing details and maybe even conflicting stories for the same god. Fittingly, archetypes remain vague as such. Though each archetype contains certain key qualities, it remains a nebulous entity that is intellectually malleable. Archetypes require new investigation and insight by individuals from an era to bring forth the uniqueness and the meanings, which make the archetypes' power accessible for their people. That is why, archetypes are like living beings that exist in the hidden part of our minds, and arts. They, if properly nurtured, become allies, if dreadfully neglected, become atrophied, or perhaps dangerous enemies.

The hero is one such archetype. Examples of other archetypes are mother, father, maiden, mentor (wise old man), fool, child, joker, etc.

Why are we so attracted to heroes and heroism? We are enamored when the simplest act of heroism is displayed on the news. We feel compelled to tune in and hear the stories. We love to hurl praise at those heroes. Even more so, people love to be labeled as a hero. With more lengthy stories, we become slowly absorbed into the role of the hero. It is as if we are experiencing the character's struggles. Through witnessing the process of struggles, our heartstrings are pulled, and our own body becomes writhed with emotions. We feel as the character does in the midst of the failures, the tragedies, and finally the overcoming of all odds that finally grants a transcendental sense of relief and joy.

Why is that?

Joseph Campbell performed a most in-depth analysis of mythological stories across space and time and provided us with a commensurate break down of the transgression of the monomyth, a hero's journey in the book *The Hero with a Thousand Faces*. And upon comparison, the hero's path can guide us on playing the role of a human being.

As one gains familiarity with the patterns of the hero's journey and the ideas of archetypes, the ascribed steps become easier and easier to be identified within all kinds of stories, despite varying in degree, in sequence, and in details.

As indicated, the hero's journey always begins with a "call to adventure." This call often manifests after the hero's encounter with an entity, whether as a magical creature, enigmatic person, or mystical symbol that ignites an instinctual desire within the hero to seek a new experience. The new experience juxtaposes the status quo, which creates a special kind of yearning.

The hero often hesitates and leaves the calling unanswered; however, while he may have ignored the call, a significant failure or disastrous scenario typically occurs which acts as a grave warning and jolts him out of his sloth. "*You better get on this or watch out… it will not be pretty for you, and all those around you.*" Because of fear, frustration, but also with a hint of exhilaration, the hero is nudged toward making the decision. Together with the appearance and urging of some natural force that may be personified as a mentor, the hero eventually readies himself for a journey into an unknown realm, be it physical or imaginary. In some cases, the hero may get forcefully removed from his status quo which could turn the character into an *antihero*, a reversed role model who demonstrates traits that we should not aspire to possess.

To cross over into the new strange territory, the hero encounters a guardian figure at the boundary who will test him, partly for his qualification for imminent tasks, partly for the hero's own safety because of the danger ahead. If he proves his abilities and passes, he enters and explores the new realm. During this exploratory period, he endures and overcomes additional trials and obstacles that will be bruising yet enhancing. He may be enticed by the opposing evil, his inner darkness, or an alluring temptress. These temptations will remain an on-going presence in the background.

When the hero hits his most dire strait, a guardian spirit, a fair maiden, or a mother figure appears. She will calm the hero's nerves, heal a critical injury or past-wound, and re-energize his inner strength to continue to battle with the unknown, the evil. Despite being in a different realm than where he came from, the hero must also reconcile with a father figure, or make amend with his own culture. The hero is doomed to fail if he begrudges his own origin and denies his own roots because that is which can provide him the values, rules, tools, skills, and knowledge useful in future conflicts. And while the hero needs to accept the values, the trickiness lies in not being encumbered and knowing when to break those rules.

Armed with the newly gained experience from various trials, a maiden's blessing, and acceptance of his own origin, only now is the hero equipped to make a final descent to confront his "ultimate ordeal."

To emphasize the universal nature of how one cannot mature without both knowing his root, the father figure, and accepting his hidden nurturing potential, the mother figure, I would like to mention the lyrics from *Kimi wo Nosete (Carrying you)*. The song comes from the Japanese animated film *Laputa* and beautifully captures what a hero must necessarily inherit to carry out his journey:

> Tousan ga nokoshita, atsui omoi (the burning passion**, left over from father*)
> Kaasan ga kureta, ano manazashi (the vision/gaze**, given by mother*)
> * father/mother interpreted as symbols that inhabit all the qualities of father/mother
> ** passion/gaze are the icons that harbor all the essential values and power from father/mother

Without the inheritance from the father, the hero will lack the supportive strength to persevere. Without the inheritance from the mother, the hero will also lack the invigorating, creative force to mature.

The "ultimate ordeal" stands in the way as a final trial for the hero to obtain the "ultimate boon." During this final struggle, the hero must use everything he has at his disposal, including some untapped potential that he may not realize before. Something new must come forth from within. He must also apply rules and knowledge that are inherited from his origin, yet he must consciously violate some in this entirely new scenario. In order to do that, he is propelled forward by certain strength from the maiden's blessing. Upon the success in this act, a boon or a treasure is obtained.

Often time, this treasure is represented physically as a physical object, in the forms of a weapon, relic, or elixir. More relevantly, this object either finds its origination from or has a strong relationship with the anti-thesis of the hero. Even if the ultimate ordeal does not produce a physical treasure, the treasure can be signified by a monumental transformation in the hero. After all the trials and the ordeal, the hero's old self is disintegrated, merged with new potentials and the claimed treasure, and reintegrated to form a more capable, nobler character. Therefore, often the script for this part of the journey is symbolized in entering a dark cave or forest or venturing to the most dangerous part of the labyrinth. Here the hero must sacrifice part of himself, or experience a kind of death, to re-emerge and rebirth.

Despite the hurdles of the trials and the ordeal, more awaits the hero. With his newfound power or attributes, the hero has effectively become a disparate character from the beginning of the journey. This often coincides with a new look, a new expression on his face in films. His transformed self may feel alienated from others back in his own world, so he struggles to assimilate back into his own culture. Or his newly unearthed potential may not be noticed and recognized by others, causing frustration. Or he may become delusional with the new power and loses himself in vanity and grandiosity, forgetting his original sense of purpose. He can also experience difficulties in how to utilize the power in a final confrontation against his archenemy.

If at last the hero succeeds in overcoming these predicaments, he has succeeded in mastering the two worlds. Not only he retains knowledge of the old status quo, he also possesses the new experience and perspective from his journey. Within him, he has synthesized all those content into his being. As a result, he can find fulfillment, resolve the central dilemma of the story, benefit his society, and discover a new position for himself in the rejuvenated society.

Campbell's works are of tremendous value in that... Rather than treating stories as mere fantasy and entertainment, it is highly useful to learn to recognize their deep patterns. They can provide us the knowledge to better understand and realize what to do with ourselves. We humans can adapt and exhibit these patterns into our own behaviors throughout our lives, both physically and psychologically. They can greatly inform our actions and decisions if we can interpret them properly. In other words, the hero archetype provides an idealistic suggestion for our behaviors to improve our life. Concretely, it is when people try to model their actions after heroic characters such as Achilles or the Iron Man. The inspirational aspect of the heroic story inherently resonates with people and generates a timeless appeal.

An essential characteristic of the hero archetype is the hero's voluntary confrontation with the unknow, despite all fears and all odds. Such characteristic is what allows self-transformation to take place. Without which, nothing can happen.

From infancy, humans as babies are born into the world surrounded by unknowns. As babies touch various things, they become familiar with them. One can only suppose the reason behind the fact that babies always put objects in their mouths is to learn about foreign objects. It may be because the mouths or lips being the most sensitive body parts. Moving on to the stage of the toddler, kids move around with a kind of reckless enthusiasm, as if possessed by an instinct to explore. When they move on to the stage of a preschooler and other new environments, children who are less exploratory are nudged and encouraged by parents to join the other children. Sometimes they are forcefully pushed to venture beyond their comfort zone. Because how else would one adapt to a new environment and become familiar with new people? From the perspective of a child, the entire world as a giant unknown can make it difficult.

The consistent and repeated facing of new challenges and situations that require one to push beyond known abilities is that which fosters growth. Children into their teenage years are like sponges. Every step they learn and grow rapidly physiologically and mentally, learning new motor skills, growing muscles, new languages, new thinking. Their limit is only set by the protectiveness of parents, family resources, and their own natural tendency and willingness to be put in new situations.

As humans mature into adulthood, namely from late teens to early 20s, a decent-sized pool of conventional thoughts, cultural ethos, knowledge, and other miscellaneous concepts had been gathered. They are joined and hardened together to form a psychological entity, typically called the ego. It consists of all the knowns and reactionary guidelines for the individual to operate appropriately within society. After this period, most stagnate in this realm of knowns and rarely venture far from it.

As a home is a shelter for the physical being, these knowns are a kind of shelter for our psychological being. Framing reality into intellectual boxes is akin to building fences and walls around your home, garden, village, city, state, nation... and within the security of the walls, the environment is perceived with a reduced number of possibilities which enables the easier definition for identifiable course of action.

It can be said that the current modality of human behavior is one where we live largely based on the knowns. That is, we operate on the presupposition that we act and make decisions based on pre-existing knowledge and facts that are grasped by our conscious attention. But inevitably, nature throws us curve balls in the forms of unexpected events and failures which in turn leads to physical and emotional reactions such as anxiety and depression. In these scenarios, we experience the calling to cross over from known to unknown, order to chaos. The subsequent conquests of the unknown and chaos resembles the hero's journey from his world into the netherworld.

Correlating our own life to the hero's refusal to call to action, refusal is often the answer we give. That is in contrast with our courageous selves in childhood, as if we embodied the archetype of the child/fool, with a bit of recklessness. Having misplaced that as adult... We fear. We hesitate. We agonize. We drown in sorrows. We choose to ignore the real problem. We betray our potentials. We repeat these things over and over again. However, quoting Campbell, "not all who hesitate are lost." In many ways, nature has structured life benevolently in that for most, it is set up in a manner that allows an uncanny amount of wrong decisions. Mistakes can be made upon mistakes, piles on top of piles before an "event horizon" that spells a person's ruin. At every turn in life, there is the possibility of changing the course of direction, down to the smallest action, until it is too late to do so.

But for many, the choice is to continuously ignore the calling as one clamor to the comfort and safety of the known, of the "home." This is where the story ends for them, not with an adventure but endless ennui, or maybe endless, spiraling drudgery and misery. If they persist in such life, they then teach their progeny to behave accordingly also.

For the others who instead choose to answer the "call to action," they have chosen to embody the archetype of a hero. They have chosen to voluntarily confront the unknown and chaos in their life, despite hesitation and fear. Although risky and scary, this is the sensible attitude to face transitions in life that allows for excavation of potentials and growth. New materials need to be discovered for self-transformation. But answering the call is just the beginning, the beginning of the uncovering and forging of potentiality. This is what coincides with Campbell's idea of "follow your bliss." It is a key step. But at the same time, it is but a preliminary step to a long journey ahead.

A creature that cannot transform will inevitably grow stale, wither, and die. Worse yet, a creature that is unwilling to transform shall inflame his surroundings such that they die along with him. If enough individuals follow this course in their society, they will surely bring about the deterioration of it.

In conclusion, it is this endless and repeated embodiment of the hero archetype that is the revivifying mechanism within the individual. By doing so, the individual can also renew his society and culture. The hero is a transcendental force dormant in humans. Its traits are what enable each human being to expand his horizon. If that force is not cultivated, the human world will undoubtedly enter a degenerating spiral that culminates in disintegration.

Do you hear your own calling? Will you do your best to answer it?

Religious Spirit

Religious spirit is the emanation of the innate aspiration to connect and to understand that which is greater and beyond oneself.

Religions are eminent staples across world culture, and many are the results of late sages' answered religious spirit. What religious archetype people believe en masse can be called the spirit of their age.

Religious spirits and religions are related but they exist on different planes.

Let's imagine a simpler world that has sparse and scattered groups of humans. This world has a colossal mountain in the center and vast fertile grounds around it. As time goes by, humans begin to assemble at the roots of the mountain. Each group is isolated from each other. These groups gradually prosper into tribes, and tribes turned into larger society so they can protect themselves from the elements of nature. Their cultures and civilizations continue to mature without knowing the existence of other societies.

Despite the peaceful and structured life within the confinement of their societies, a small set of individuals would begin to wonder what lies beyond the confinement.

What is this place? What are the things I see in the distance? Who am I? Why am I here? What do "I" even mean? Is there something greater than I?

A yet smaller subset of these individuals would muster up enough courage (call to adventure), risk everything from their common orderly lives (embracing the resolve), pack up some luggage (inheriting their own culture), face the perils to journey up the mountain (confronting unknowns), contend with their fear and other emotional inadequacy (facing their own shadow and unconscious), be willing to sacrifice some burdening useless luggage (sacrifice or detachment from existing ideals and the ego), adapt to random events (excavating unconscious potentials), and finally reaches the top of the mountain.

Not all who venture will make it to the top. Some would give up and return home. Some would fail to pass the obstacles. Some would get lost mid-way. Some would mistake vista points as the top and languish. Some would perish.

What does it mean to reach the top?

At the top of the mountain, they finally witness the world as it is. They see the glory of the world in its vastness, view unblocked, everything connected. The limiting, narrow personal perspective that we each exist alone cannot help but pales in comparison in front of the spectacle. Such a nearsighted personal view can no longer be accepted. The isolating bubble of their society is also vaporized. They have obtained a new kind of vision, another way to see the world.

It is not just this new vision. On their way up the mountain, they would have had the space and time for introspection. Alone, they had experienced themselves and the world in a way not achievable while in the comfort of society and the company of others. Additionally, the many difficult challenges along the way would have further driven them into the confrontation with their fear, weaknesses, and many other parts of themselves that were hidden before. They had encountered and overcome their inner demons to reach the apex.

As they bask in the new spectacle in conjunction with the experience of overcoming trials and tribulations, they gain a much deeper understanding of the world and themselves. Moreover, one can say an all-encompassing perspective of reality is discovered. A new understanding is formed from the integration of self-knowledge from the journey and the perspective of the old life in society. This is beyond an intellectual experience. It will take time to immerse in the new perspective where they infuse what they witness into their being, thus developing a whole new sense of the self, the world, and their relationship.

What relationship? Ordinarily, people act on the axiom that they are each an isolated entity, who searches and gathers from the external world to define themselves. And there is also the presupposition that to survive, we need to spend tremendous effort to guard ourselves against others. *I will only act out of my own best interest.* This is akin to someone who first looks at a forest, sees all the trees and makes a quick, shallow conclusion that there are many separate trees. *I am surrounded. I am a tree by myself and I must defend myself from other trees and other things in the forests.* Though appearing separate, the trees are not so separate after all. As one allows oneself to expand his perception and observe more details, one will discover the intertwining roots, the interaction between the many organisms and different types of trees, the sharing of soil nutrients, and the forest's effect on climate which affects the forest in return, etc.

The people who made it to the peak see past all that. They are the sages of the past who peer directly at the nature of being. They had gone through physical pilgrimage and tracked the depth of psychological maze to reach "the peak" to obtain such a vision. Each of them had achieved it by following their own paths, with the force of their own culture and their own unique individual traits serving as both support and hindrance.

No longer do people appear as individuals who need to triumph over the collective or society as a collective that smothers the individuals. It is simultaneously both and neither. It is a false dichotomy from the very beginning. The sages are the ones who realized the potential for such a drastically different perspective, a state of being that is available in everyone.

Such a magnificent gift is that they would love to share with everyone in their respective society. Consequently, after spending ample time at "the peak" to deepen their understanding, they return to their society. They know that people will only fully reach understanding by journeying up the mountain themselves. Thus, they set up *stations* around the lower tier of the mountain intending to guide the people up. And at these stations, they spread their message in the language and symbolism that are available in their own culture. So, they teach. They motivate. They guide. But they cannot do the journeys for their disciples.

These *stations* at the waist of the mountain expand and become larger organizations as their popularity grows. They attract people with both strong and mild interest in exploring the mountain. Their duty is to support and inspire people to obtain their own vision by traveling the distance themselves. At least, that is the wishes of the founders who possessed the religious spirits. However, over time, as leadership changes through the generations, leaders with the religious spirits and had reached "the peak" are no more. Future leadership eventually falls into the hands of individuals who lack religious spirits. Some feint genuine vision but never traveled to the peak. Some, who out of the gravity of sheer kindness and ignorant compassion, falls prey to the over-protective spirit of the oedipal mother, and they suffocate any future possibility with love by preventing people from their personal struggles. And then there are always those, brimming with personal ambition, decide to focus solely on the maintenance of the institution for his personal benefits and popularity. For these individuals, upon the discovery of other similar stations existing around the waist of the mountain, they grow jealous and ambitious. Because these other stations speak different languages and because they may compete for power and popularity, a war will be declared to assert the title of being the "right" passage.

These *stations* analogize the state of affairs of modern religions.

Over long periods, these stations would have misplaced all the original meanings and intentions of the guiding principles. Worse yet, people who aspire, people who possess the religious spirit to seek, to understand can become ensnared by readily prepared "answers" provided by the stations. Their innocence and inexperience deprive them of knowing to walk their own path being the only way to reach understanding. The *stations* are mistaken as destinations. The fortunate part, though, is that somehow there are still a select few individuals who possessed the religious spirit, managed to keep pushing in their journey, and came back to tell the tales from the peak. It is by these individuals that culture and society are being revivified.

In short... if enlightenment is to arrive at the peak, the stations are guiding posts that point one towards the peak. If enlightenment is the moon, religions are the fingers pointing at the moon. Humans first mistake seeking the finger for the seeking of the moon. They make their second grave mistake on being completely pre-occupied in arguing which finger is the best.

Only, they neglect the fact that the fingers only differ because the sages can only base their teachings on the context of their contemporary culture and language. Moreover, there are and had existed many false sages. Thus, there is also the tricky business in how one can tell whether a sage is the "genuine good" or a phony if one is not already a sage, which makes following one's religious spirit the more essential. As such, it is warned that one cannot idolize anything or anyone but seeks only to understand the messages.

If you meet the Buddha on the road, kill him.

However, everyone is simply too busy competing about "which fingers are better," and trying to enforce the dogmas that were formulated out of a central transcendental understanding while completely ignoring and overlooking the essential message.

Religions are the guides, and the guide must not be confused with the destination. Also, each religion spreads into many sects, and their doctrines and methods multiply like mitosis. Inadvertently, the original meaning becomes even more diluted, and students get hung up on the many choices and words.

Religions lacking in religious spirit are nothing but soulless, meaningless endeavors that cannot liberate. Such practicing further leads people into the quicksand of foolishness and ignorance. Simply reversing that and reject religion is also missing the point. Setting them on fire outright will not help. Religions including the institutes, the rules, the dogma are the visible shell. They are the concrete, intellectual formulations under the context of different eras, but lying deep underneath is a profound understanding reached by following the religious spirit. Therefore, religions differ and are useful in the context they are developed but should not be mistaken as the goal.

God is Dead

In the movie *The Dark Knight (2008),* Harvey Dent said, "You either die a hero, or you live long enough to see yourself become the villain."

This leads back to the topic of the hero. Within every heroic story, the hero must take a firm stance in opposition against evil, typically embodied by a villain. This is the archetypical struggle between good and evil, one of the most classic representations of dualistic forces in nature.

Though a hero stands on the side of good, he as a human consists not of pure goodness. Rarely can we find a story that has the hero as purely good and the villain as purely evil. Unless it is a story for kids, it will be boring and certainly fail to captivate the audience. Its characters will be uni-dimensional. Rather, the most fascinating stories are those that manage to paint an ever-flourishing ever-changing landscape within the inner workings of the characters, littered with intermingling and contravening aspects of both good and evil.

As touched upon in the chapter *Hero's Journey,* a key milestone in a hero's journey requires him to encounter, overcome, and integrate his own dark side. Achieving this required feat, the hero possesses the strength to defeat the villain. Otherwise, he will lack the capacity, such as the cunning or otherwise the perspective, to anticipate his enemy. At the story's conclusion, we react with excitement that good had triumphed over evil.

However, the story does not end there if we allow our imagination to extend the story. Even as the hero overcame the villain at the end, evil is never truly eradicated. The nature of reality is that so long as goodness exists, evil follows closely in its tow in the shadow, however anemic it may be. If the villain and all the evil associated with him are annihilated, the seed of evil will fester within his disciples, someone related to him, or even the very hero that defeated him.

> Gradually it was disclosed to me that the line separating good and evil passes not through states, nor between classes, nor between political parties either -- but right through every human heart -- and through all human hearts. This line shifts. Inside us, it oscillates with the years. And even within hearts overwhelmed by evil, one small bridgehead of good is retained. And even in the best of all hearts, there remains ... an unuprooted small corner of evil.
> -   Aleksandr Solzhenitsyn

A hero who refuses to let go of the identity of hero and without an existing countering opposition is destined to succumb to his own villainy. This will occur through his unquenched desire to act out his role, forcing him to manufacture and project evil in his mind to justify his heroic existence. That is the seed of corruption. The hero may assume the most righteous high ground. With blindness both inwardly toward himself and outwardly against his surroundings, he shall proceed to commit the most heinous act in the name of peace, justice, morality, and banishment of evil. That is how "You either die a hero, or you live long enough to see yourself become the villain." This does not solely apply to the individual but also people in a group. It is common for an organization to identify with an objective or ideology zealously. When there comes a time that the resulting action no longer serves the group's best interest or the well-being of the majority, the organization often fail to recognize the need to change course but doubles down instead. We can certainly observe such tendency in the current decade, where people are frequently possessed by ideology.

A similar phenomenon is one where an individual developed a grandiose desire for the identity and fame of being a hero. Upon hitting a mental threshold, he would venture to commit fraud in order to deceive and rouse the mass to win himself the glory and heralds of a hero. If ever a society and its masses begin to overemphasize a specific set of heroic righteous qualities and even pedestalized those qualities above all else, such fraudulent phenomenon will surge as people clamor over each other to be a hero, a winner to gain the benefits.

Such an occurrence would highlight the potential danger of morality that is shallow, too well defined, and blind. Moral behaviors that are not based on individual sovereign choice, founded upon deeper guiding principles, is a slow poison that will diminish the life of a culture, leading to dilapidated city, state, and eventually nation.

Lao Tzu expressed the perils of morality in the second prose in *Tao Te Ching*:

天下皆知美之為美，斯惡已，皆知善之為善，斯不善已。

That means "As the world comes to identify what is preferable as preferable, the undesired thus born. As the mass learns what is virtuous and knows only what is virtuous as virtuous, immorality thus arises."

Friedrich Nietzsche had the foresight to detect the inconspicuous underlying trajectory of western culture and was keenly aware of the incoming onslaught of such great malice by morality. He understood the festering, the inner rot within the populace. Nietzsche saw it within the people of his time… not just as a current event but as a historical trajectory from the compounding effects from events from previous centuries. That is a reason for him to venture as far as to famously extol "God is dead" in his books. The phrase first appears in Gay Science (1882) and later Thus spoke Zarathustra (1883 and 1885). With regards to Thus Spoke Zarathustra, Nietzsche has said:

> People have never asked me, as they should have done, what the name Zarathustra precisely means in my mouth, in the mouth of the first Immoralist; for what distinguishes that philosopher from all others in the past is the very fact that he was exactly the reverse of an immoralist. Zarathustra was the first to see in the struggle between good and evil the essential wheel in the working of things. The translation of morality into the metaphysical, as force, cause, end in itself, was HIS work. But the very question suggests its own answer. Zarathustra CREATED the most portentous

error, MORALITY, consequently he should also be the first to PERCEIVE that error, not only because he has had longer and greater experience of the subject than any other thinker - all history is the experimental refutation of the theory of the so-called moral order of things: the more important point is that Zarathustra was more truthful than any other thinker. In his teaching alone do we meet with truthfulness upheld as the highest virtue i.e.: the reverse of the COWARDICE of the 'idealist' who flees from reality. Zarathustra had more courage in his body than any other thinker before or after him. To tell the truth and TO AIM STRAIGHT: that is the first Persian virtue. Am I understood?...The overcoming of morality through itself through truthfulness, the overcoming of the moralist through his opposite THROUGH ME--: that is what the name Zarathustra means in my mouth.

- Friedrich Nietzsche, Thus Spoke Zarathustra, Introduction

Religions provide morality within the cultures across the world. Zoroastrianism exists as one of the oldest religions that remains to this day. Thus, Zarathustra as the avant-garde prophet plays a significant role in the modernistic adoption of morality in society. On one hand, Nietzsche foresees and seeks to warn against the danger of crowd's tendency for thoughtless acceptance of morality, and on the other hand, the detrimental effect of the enforced morality through religious groups, peer pressure, and tribalism, which can further reinforce the crowd's docility and individual sloth. The result is a positive feedback loop that will undoubtedly undermine the sovereignty of the individual.

The exceedingly dangerous act is the worsening *hang-up* with what is "good," and increasingly obvious is also such blind faith in morality is bringing western culture toward a cliff.

The dominance of our conscious intellect leads to our tendency to myopically focus on words such as "good" and "righteous" which are littered through the verses in the Gathas. However, the essence behind such historic "good" and the present-day "good" are worlds apart. The chasm could not be bigger between what is "good" in reference to social morals nowadays and what is "good" in reference to the act of approximating Truth in the past (recall religious spirit). Conversely, that which deny and hide Truth is what is "evil."

There is significance in the Gathas being written as hymns and in verses format. It likens to a song. A note does not a piece of music make. Notes are put together into chords. Chords serve as the basis that accompanies the melody. Melody is made across measures. Measures are put together to form a section, and sections together with dynamics to form the mood and climax in the music. A song is the integration of all these components, each with their significance joined to make something more valuable. The Gathas, like many other religious texts, is a culmination of many hymns together to deliver a more complete message. Though read and deciphered separately, there requires an eventual point that they are understood together, like a delicately painted art. Can one pierce through the art and see the meaning behind it? This must be kept in mind of all who seek to contemplate and understand these texts. If one fails to do so, one will inevitably grasp on to a few notes and decree their superficial meanings to be the whole song. Instead of the proper attitude to understand a song, modern man has turned to the hyper-focus and extraction of morality into well-defined superficial definitions. Few people care for the less conspicuous values.

Rather than an utterance serves simply to debase religions, Nietzsche's implication of "God is dead" can be made relevant in three fragments. This is reflected in the timing and interval between the moments when he wrote the phrase in *Gay Science* and later *Thus Spoke Zarathustra*, within which time his vision in the future was becoming clearer and better formulated and is further developed during the process of him writing *Thus Spoke Zarathustra*.

The practice of religions evolved gradually over the centuries to become mostly about the translation of doctrine into applicable moral values across society. Consequently, God is pedestalized and relegated to be an enforcing figure for the morality of the good. Whoever strays from the written rules based on the doctrine, and thus also against the group's morality, is to be justifiably punished in His name. In other words, societal rules and practice of religion have morphed into a mode where the dogmatic sustenance of shallow morality and rules takes precedence to the aspiration to divinity. This is the first implication of "God is dead."

What follows in trend is a situation where the group's morality that was according to the doctrine is subtly and gradually substituted by the group's will despite punishment remains issued in His name. At this stage, the people had not only strayed from the essence of divinity, the seeking of the real message has also been cast aside. Moreover, the people's behaviors had largely detracted even from the superficial meaning of the doctrine while morality is widely preached. In name, God may yet exist, but the image had been replaced by man's shallow understanding, egotistic will, and unconscious projection. Man had usurped God's will as his own, so in fact, "God is *demonstrably* dead" through the behaviors, manners, and attitude in the practicing of religions. This is the second implication of "God is dead."

The described state of affair is a truly dire situation. We are living through its procession in the 21st century currently. It is fathomable for anyone to perceive the real underlying situation to at once face a unique brand of despair, but Nietzsche dug himself out the turmoil and provided his best vision for a path forward. This is where he channeled Zarathustra, and I sincerely believe that it is more than what Nietzsche indicated in the quote, where it is a case of the person who created the problem would best know the solution to it. He understands the necessity of the rediscovery of divinity within the individual. A rediscovery that is self-chosen and paved not by the veneer of morality, traditions, nor conventional religious thoughts and practice. Neither is it done with praise from others but in private. This is the path to overcome the darkness that had arisen and will exacerbate due to the denial of the individual by group mentality, in conjunction with the abandonment of religions and traditions resulting from nihilism. Religions may yet stand publicly but in spirit, they are mere walking corpses.

This leads to the addendum to Nietzsche's condemnation of morality. Even though Nietzsche demonstrates abhorrence and fervent protestation against the moralistic standard of religions where he labels himself an Immoralist, it is as if Nietzsche instinctively realizes the essentiality of the religious spirit in his choice of the original Zoroastrian prophet Zarathustra to be his mouthpiece. This entire backdrop and the demonstrated reality of "God is dead" in society lead to the requirement that people need to accept the previous descriptions of "God is dead." Only then, they can usher in the renewal and rediscovery of the religious spirit for a brighter future. This is the third implication of "God is dead."

The gate behind us is now closed. For the sake of God, it shall be recognized that "God is dead." We must now discover a new way forward.

Therefore, in the modern 21st century and in the same spirit, shall we also not make a proclamation that "Heroes are dead"?

Beyond Good and Evil

What Nietzsche hinted at is not a lone occurrence within the western culture with Christianity. A similar trend has gradually encroached the world such as also in the east within their treatment and practices of Confucianism and other eastern religions. That is to state that, we are talking about a universal concern that applies to every individual across the human world.

As for the viable path forward, it is not about simply taking a contrarian stance to common morality and raging against contemporary social values. That is not the point nor a complete solution. Simply following a set of existing values require little personal effort. It is the push for "Morality (contemporary values) is good!" Simply going against the same set of values also requires little personal dedicated investigation. It is just flipping side calling "Morality is bad!" Both paths remove the necessity of a sovereign individual from the equation. Either path if strictly adhered prevents the creation of anything new.

But if not standing in opposition to morality, what then?

Another way to interpret the fact is that it is neither about being for nor against morality. Within either case, one would still be trying to find a solution within the realm of knowns. But like the hero who descends into the underworld to finally triumph, the solution for us to seek now exists in the realm of unknown. Even though antagonism toward morality and religion appears as a theme in *Thus Spoke Zarathustra*, what Nietzsche envisioned was implicit but is disclosed in the name of his ensuing book – *Beyond Good and Evil*.

How does one transcend good and evil? What does that even

mean? Regardless of the answer at this point, to even begin to consider such a question requires substantially more involvement and effort on the individual part, which again explains why this is a path seldom chosen.

Perhaps a starting point is to consider, can we accept the premises put forth regarding "God is dead"? Or is it only embraced shallowly, without grasping the nuance? Or shall we outright reject such notions?

The key lies in the observation of our own reaction when confronted with such notions. It is not about either forthrightly accepting or rejecting the notions; however, if one reacts so, the reaction conveys that one possesses an immutable mindset. And if such a mindset remains, it will render the perpetual fruitless course of action and reactions in such an individual's life.

But even if our immediate reaction takes the form of sudden outburst, there is still value to be gathered from it, if one can observe it later. Can we afterward allow ourselves to have free space and moments to contemplate what lies behind the curtain of blind acceptance or eager belligerence? This is an important opportunity to begin inner-reflection.

His reasons may be good, and no one may have been able to refute them. But if he is equally unable to refute the reasons on the opposite side; if he does not so much as know what they are, he has no ground for preferring either opinion. The rational position for him would be suspension of judgment, and unless he contents himself with that, he is either led by authority, or adopts, like the generality of the world, the side to which he feels most inclination. Nor is it enough that he should hear the arguments of adversaries from his own teachers, presented as they state them, and accompanied by what they offer as refutations. That is not the way to do justice to the arguments, or bring them into real contact with his own mind. He must be able to hear them from persons who actually believe them; who defend them in earnest, and do their very utmost for them. He must know them in their most plausible and persuasive form; he must feel the whole force of the difficulty which the true view of the subject has to encounter and dispose of; else he will never really possess himself of the portion of truth which meets and removes that difficulty.

- John Stuart Mill, On Liberty

Mill indicates that to achieve true critical thinking, to arrive at a real understanding, each of us individually must journey down a path to learn to stand alone and understand opposing sides equally well. To learn that is the first step to obtain the ability to see beyond good and evil. From there on, one can proceed to understand his own opposing thoughts, his own opposing feelings, and other opposing elements in his personality. It is a requirement to thoroughly understand oneself. That is the only possibility to allow one to observe one's axiom, one's philosophy, one's ego, one's shadow, and ultimately one's total being whom he is operating from. Leave no rocks unturned within. This is the process of revaluation of all values. This is the only way that may lead to a needed transformation of the image of God and understanding of divinity within the personal realm, which then may manifest to bring renewal for the individual and conversely society.

In the current 21st century's state of affairs, single-mindedly putting on the cloak of old rituals and traditions no longer suffice to mitigate the chaos that had permeated all facets of life, in all levels individual or national. The fragmentation is too deep for we had recklessly lay torches to our traditions, cultures, and religions. Their mangled forms are beyond repair, pathetically decomposed in the gutter of our rampant ignorance; however, we can rebuild by finding the will to understanding and regaining our religious spirit. We need to relearn ourselves.

In current time, it is imperative for each individual to relearn independent introspection more than ever. Unlike the cacophonic chant of "You can change the world" that is relentlessly repeated in a bombastic, force-feeding manner into the youth's brain in modern society, the opposite is true. That is because the "I-need-to-go-change-the-world" mentality, especially if adopted by the youth, creates herds and they eventually turn into adults who become useful idiots. They are natural preys, easily exploited by individuals who are capable of exerting powerful will on others, whether through unequivocal charisma or psychological manipulative techniques. "You can change the world", then, easily becomes the reason for the world being destroyed. Moreover, it is heinously criminal to indoctrinate youth with such sensational rhetoric for they have yet the mental development to defend against it. Take the following quote:

> The world is yours, as well as ours, but in the last analysis, it is yours. You young people, full of vigor and vitality, are in the bloom of life, like the sun at eight or nine in the morning. Our hope is placed on you ... The world belongs to you... [blank].

On a quick look, the quote draws strong similarity with how speech in modern society energizes their youth. It can be construed as something that is written in brochures for a youth program. The part that is purposely blanked out reads, "China's future belongs to you" which makes it a lot easier to guess the origin of the quote. The quote is written in *The Little Red Book of Chairman Mao* in Chapter 30 by Mao Ze Dong, who reigned over the infamously atrocious, murderous periods in China, the Great Leap Forward and the Cultural Revolution.

During the Cultural Revolution, Mao created the Red Guards that consisted of masses of young students by fanning their enthusiasm over the tipping point. He did so through the promise and dream of a certain utopian future shaped by his communist party, that is an escape from the tumultuous, devastated society that is also shaped by him and his party, insidiously. Mao was able to possess them by his will and had them committed to his ideology to do his bidding. Mao mobilized them to wage his desired war against the established Chinese culture, and all other cultures or ideology that are threatening to a communist regime. To protect and enforce an ideology, no chink in the armor is allowed. So, there can be no wrong thinking. The Red Guards helped him to fulfill that requirement. They destroyed incalculable pre-communist artifacts, sites, books, and values. Moreover, the Red Guards also did his bidding of speech and thought censorship where they betrayed and turned violently against their own parents, siblings, grandparents, teachers, friends, neighbors... It is, therefore, no wonder that Mao's communist predecessor Lenin said:

> Give me just one generation of youth, and I'll transform the whole world.
> -   Vladimir Lenin

Lenin underlines the devastatingly effective propaganda strategy of targeting the youth. This strategy bears almost no weakness in the expansion of communism or for that matter, any dictatorial attempt with an ounce of intelligence. It is a brilliant strategy to undermine any existing culture, but one that takes time and patience. We can only surmise two possible defenses. One is raising youth that is backed by a strong and grounded culture. The other is the fostering of sovereign individuals, who are self-motivated in the pursuit of knowledge and wisdom. As such, a wise society needs to be mindful of its own culture. Additionally, it should be a duty for the adults, parents, society, and culture to safeguard their youth for their mental, psychological, and spiritual development. That is as opposed to the heinous act of usurping the youth's minds to exploit them as tools, that carry out ideologically, politically motivated biddings. This is yet another strong reason why we individually each is responsible to come to an adequate level of understanding of ourselves so that we do not do so inadvertently.

The result of Mao's two ruling periods, Hitler's Nazism and concentration camps, and Lenin/Stalin's soviet and gulags culminated in a combined total of hundreds of millions of deaths. Even without exact figures, even without accounting for other wars and man-made catastrophes, the 20th century is handily the bloodiest in documented human history.

Unfortunately, humans are slow to learn from lessons in their own life individually, much fewer learns from national history as citizens, and worse, much less learns from world history as members of a species. We have yet recognized that each of the murderous episodes occurs not because of a few individuals, and definitely not by accidents. It is convenient to put the blame solely on the likes of Hitler, Stalin, and other top leaders of the groups. After all, it is profusely easier a practice to designate someone else as evil and say, "Not me!" However, the bible provides a strong dictum against that. When a crowd brought an adulterous woman in front of Jesus for judgment, Jesus responded:

> He that is without sin among you, let him first cast a stone at her.
> -   John 8 (King James)

97

Upon Jesus' utterance and moments of contemplation, the crowds slowly departed one by one as they realized the error of their ways upon introspection. This story provides a warning against anyone to hastily judge and condemn, without an ounce of self-reflection. Without that, we are liable to be blind not only to our own flaws, but we will also be unable to detect the involvement of our own crimes. As such, there is no possibility to take responsibility for an ounce of our contribution to the various malicious forces in play. Famous Russian author of the Gulag Archipelago recognizes that and he says:

> If only it were all so simple! If only there were evil people somewhere insidiously committing evil deeds, and it were necessary only to separate them from the rest of us and destroy them. But the line dividing good and evil cuts through the heart of every human being. And who is willing to destroy a piece of his own heart?
> - Aleksandr Solzhenitsyn

This echoes the old saying of "The way to hell is paved with good intentions." We cannot change the world by trying to conquer it with force and shape it to our will. A person can naively believe that he can force changes in the world without first achieving an adequate level of self-examination and without a certain level of understanding of the implicated mechanisms in existing systems. But it will equate to building a structure while ignoring the necessary foundation. Because he has no solid ground to stand on, to avert fear and maintain a sense of security, it will result in him consorting a crowd where he can find safety in numbers. Consequently, he will be crusading in a movement that exhibits all the quality and values of someone else's intention, thought, ideology, and hidden agenda. He is mesmerized and preoccupied with the superficial rhetoric that soothes his inner suffering and insecurity. And when the movement comes to pass, he will just as easily abdicate his involvement and squares himself by joining the choir that lays all blame, accusation, and responsibility on the mastermind. In other words, this person was used in another person's game, but precisely because of that, he can absolve himself from any crime committed during the involvement. This is the seduction behind mob mentality, with the scariest part being that the individual is allowed to relegate himself into a position where he can gain benefits during the occurrence but free from responsibility, accountability, and consequence afterward… because he is serving "The Greater Good," "The Utopian Dream," or "The Will of the People."

If we do not understand ourselves thoroughly, then it is inevitable that as we alter the world, the transformed reality will be filled with the trauma, distortion, psychosis, pathology, and other demons that had festered out of sight in our psyche. And when we cannot get away from the habit of reacting to reality by differentiating everything into likes and dislikes, accepting one and rejecting the other, and conjoining ourselves with what is good and condemning what is evil, we will never address the fundamental factor, consciousness, that had plagued humanity because we are operating from a position of blindness (sin, avidyā). When one calls one side good, one makes the other side evil and becomes blind to their evil within. Vice versa. It is exponentially more dangerous if this tendency moves toward absolutism. How does one transcend by identification with either side? Put differently, if one identifies wholly with either side, one is bounded and becomes its slave. How does one become a master of good and evil when one is a slave to either? If we cannot detach, we will not find the transcendental awareness that helps us absolve ourselves. Without which, again, we are blind. We will continue to enact solutions that solve one problem while spawning numerous side effects, unintended consequences. Or in other words, the benefits of any solution that we choose in our current state of mind, be it technological, cultural, social, political, etc., will always be outweighed by the downsides and unintended consequences finally. Sometimes the downsides are intangible until much further down the road, and sometimes we would claim them as non-scientifically substantiated. In other words, we will ignore them. Surely, we change the world this way, and we had, but it would come at the cost of ever-increasing chaos.

While it is far easier and tempting to play heroics and charge forward with glorious chant and promises of utopian visions, we must resist it. Rather, it is incumbent on each individual to investigate, understand, and reconcile the depth of his individuality, that which includes the most magnificent benevolence and the most horrific malevolence. While each person must function mundanely in society, a consistent focus on a self-reflective path is the only possibility to bring about balance. By changing oneself, one may affect the world through the manifestation of new understanding. At the basest of it, one will have formulated a principle, philosophy regarding one's own relation to past, present, and future, and to all of his surroundings, to nature.

For modern man, his psyche is the most unexplored universe that needs the light of awareness. And only this light may shine a viable path. Marcus Aurelius said, "He who lives in harmony with himself lives in harmony with the universe." The reverse also stands true, "He who lives in disharmony with himself lives in disharmony with the universe." His reality shall reflect that.

Thus, I find the human species must first break out of a shell that it had forced itself into. *If only there is justice for all, if there is happiness for all, if there is equality for all, if we apply more rationality to reinforce our morals, if only we collect more external data... the world would be a utopia.* That is an assumption that is missing pieces of reality, hence the fruitlessness of all the labor across millennia as the fear of annihilation encroaches more than ever. That is our foolish wishful thinking.

By making the pursuit of happiness a central theme of modern life, where sometimes that is substituted by the positivity movement, we had inadvertently magnified the sadness, suffering, and negativity in our life. It is true that some degree of optimism can help render better outcomes sometimes. But as we increasingly and forcefully polish all experience in the glamor of positivity, the real negative force that gets ignored and allowed to incubate grows and grows. We desperately hide them from the public's eyes. The fear of these unavoidable, unfavored, and now commonly unobserved and unacceptable elements in life further multiply their force manifolds. Because of that, they will inevitably return to bite us with forces magnified many folds when exposed unexpectedly, like the hazardous phenomenon of backdraft.

By emphasizing a smaller and smaller subset of goodness, positives, morals, and kind acts, we make extinct other virtues and behaviors that may be advantageous in different scenarios. Additionally, we will inadvertently treat more and more things as if they are incarnate of evils.

If mere advocacy of benevolence over malevolence, identification with decency and morality against all that is immoral shall bring resolution for human problems and peace to the world, we would be flooded by hordes of gurus, army of saints and legions of sages by now. Yet here we are as a species.

An old saying goes, "When the wrong man uses the right means, the right means work in the wrong way."

Here I dare to summon the influence and voices of people in the past who braved a less coveted path on their own. In their own words, they tried to point out such an essential path, the ultimate becoming of man...

> I am only an experimenter. Do not set the least value on what I do, or the least discredit on what I do not, as if I pretended to settle any thing as true or false. I unsettle all things. No facts are to me sacred; none are profane; I simply experiment, an endless seeker.
> -   Ralph Waldo Emerson, Circles

According to Emerson, the task of all tasks, path of all paths is for the individual to live as an "endless seeker" who must unsettle all things, which include all manners of information, knowledge, and idealism, to achieve self-reliance.

According to Abraham Maslow, he regards self-actualization as the highest need, that should not be forgotten, despite an individual also needs to satisfy his other needs. Here it is important to indicate that a pyramid is somewhat a mis-conceptualization because, it leads people to think self-actualization should only occur after other needs are satisfied. So it is worth repeating, self-actualization is the highest need that must not be forgotten as an individual.

According to Fredrich Nietzsche, he urges man to embody the free spirit within, to go beyond good and evil, and to become an *Übermensch*. *Übermensch* is often translated to Overman or Superman but this is perhaps to the original author's chagrin. That is because of how easily the term Superman, within our contemporary context, can be and has been mistaken to emphasize merely the physical, or genetic aspects of perfection. That assumption cannot be further from Nietzsche's vision. As a result, the term *free spirit* appears to be a more appropriate choice.

> Need I say expressly after all this that they will be free, VERY free spirits, these philosophers of the future—as certainly also they will not be merely free spirits, but something more, higher, greater, and fundamentally different, which does not wish to be misunderstood and mistaken? But while I say this, I feel under OBLIGATION almost as much to them as to ourselves (we free spirits who are their heralds and forerunners), to sweep away from ourselves altogether a stupid old prejudice and misunderstanding, which, like a fog, has too long made the conception of 'free spirit' obscure.
>
> - Friedrich Nietzsche, Beyond Good and Evil, 44

According to alchemists, whose proposed alchemical transformation is fitting in describing man's psychic transformation process, together with artists, they call it the Magnum Opus, the great work. Man is to discover the *prima materia* in order to create the philosopher stone that is the symbol for rejuvenation, enlightenment. Philosopher stone is the source that enables the creation and manifestation of all other materials through transmutation. Man needs to discover his metaphysical philosopher stone. Without which, man is unable to manifest himself.

In the later stage in his life, Carl Jung arrived at calling man's psychological process of transformation, individuation. "The realization was that the [S]elf is the goal of individuation and that the process of individuation was not linear, but consisted in a circumambulation of the [S]elf." (Jung, Liber Novus, 217) I made the change from "self" to "Self." Its deeper meaning and reason for the change will be further discussed in chapter *Depth Psychology – Map of Psyche*.

Hinduism and Buddhism regard Prajna, *prajna paramita*, as the highest of the paths that lead to moksha, nirvana, or liberation. Even though Prajna means "wisdom," it is distinguished from conventional, worldly wisdom. It is only with transcendental wisdom, Prajna, that man may discover Self. Man can arrive at a level of awareness that enables his connection to the Self, without which, a man yet has the power of free will.

The Self is like a compass imbued in us by nature, grander than that of our conscious perception, our intellect... without a compass, without a direction, man is stuck in being led by something unknown to himself. Whoever it is, be it a person, an organization. Or whatever it is, be it his own burrowed thought or someone else's ideology. It is in this manner that man is led to create horror and catastrophe despite the best intention.

We can describe this problem of problems in all kinds of words. Without a connection with the Self, man is missing his connection to nature. Such a man is isolated on his own island. He feels alienated from his world because he believes he is disconnected. Such a man can only react to the world with mistrust. He is surviving in a free-for-all, dog-eat-dog world. Thus, he holds on tightly to his belief because to him, that is all he has. He cannot genuinely connect with other people. He is a man without his roots. He is a lost child. He is disconnected from nature. He is insecure. And he will find the world hostile. He will act out of accordance with reality and show contempt to any universal law.

Sages and the greatest minds of the past were trying to address a few central themes of humanity's problems. They were able to arrive and converge principally into addressing the problem of all problems... the development of consciousness, which is the ultimate subject, the final frontier of religion, psychology, philosophy, and science. It is a matter of the soul. And the irrevocable fact that... it needs to be accompanied by a sincere religious spirit, Will to Understanding, and a leap of faith to dare to explore the Truth beyond what we call "truths" (illusory forms).

To see beyond good and evil is to understand universal laws, such as duality. (refer to part 1. Chapter *Duality*). To see and understand the basis of such law manifesting in existence is to step into a complete view of the world as opposed to the differentiated reality of separate "things"... from there, one may gain the perspective and the capability to embody both differentiation and non-differentiation. This is to be done without a combating attitude, for as long as one retains a combative mindset, such individuals will always try to discriminate "this" is better than "the other." This is also not to be done with an attitude to overpower nature but through sincere resolve and clear understanding. The apogee of such a path, the aggregate of all experience from it, is the direct knowing of the Self.

> From one thing, know ten thousand things. When you attain the Way of strategy there will not be one thing you cannot see.
> -   Miyamoto Musashi, Book of Five Rings

> The philosopher has a highly inquiring mind and thus feels at home in remarkably many areas of study; he is not only an exact analytical thinker but also likes to study the "book of the world".
> -   Immanuel Kant

> See one promontory, one mountain, one sea, one river and see all.
> — Socrates

> Ever-newer waters flow on those who step into the same rivers.
> — Heraclitus

At this point, it must be iterated that Self is not something that can be pin down by conventional mental processes and definition to the likes of knowledge. But despite the inapprehensible and incorporeal nature, Musashi, Kant, Socrates, Heraclitus, and others have undoubtedly come to recognize it and connect with it, understand its timeless, omnipresent, indispensable, luminescent, yet self-concealing nature. They all hinted in their writings how such a connection will surely serve as a shining beacon for the individual on what needs to be known in a world overshadowed by ignorance.

Different yet Same Path

Generally speaking, we can surmise that there are two types of path (though uniquely infinite in individual perspective by the power of intellectual categorization) in searching for transcendental wisdom and reconnection with the Self.

One is a step-by-step approach where one advances through levels. The other is with direct or sudden understanding. This is not an either-or scenario, nor one is better than the other.

However, due to the modern dominating mode of thinking, the gradual step-by-step approach appears as the most viable approach. Additionally, that is also the umbrella under which exist most well-known approaches, be it Jung's Depth Psychology or the practices of Hinduism, Buddhism, and Christianity. The important point is, despite the gradual nature, for those on this path a "direct experience" or "direct understanding" is eventually required. It is an understanding that is beyond and without the interference of conscious intellect. Whether it happens through planning or unintentionally is of no significance. The one discipline that immediately emphasizes in direct and sudden understanding is Zen, despite it also having incalculable techniques, rules under Zen's many sects which could be categorized under the "step-by-step" path. The drive for sudden understanding can be observed in the obsession of certain new joiners for what is called the Satori.

To dive deeper into the "step-by-step" path, it is helpful to review what is called the "vehicles" in Buddhism. Note that "vehicle," translated from Yāna can also mean mode or method. It can be helpful to keep in mind that these paths, though vary in styles, are aimed at achieving very similar tasks.

The Theravada branch consists of doctrine from the earlier development of Buddhism. It later received the name Hinayana, the Little/Lesser Vehicle, in contrast to the later formed Mahayana branch, the Large/Greater Vehicle. Another name that applies is Śrāvakayāna. The focus of Theravada is the desires and their accompanying complications that arise out of Sadindriya. Sadindriya includes the six generic senses through which we interact with the world – sight, hearing, smell, taste, physical feeling, and conscious attention/analytical mind. It is easy to become overly attached to the six senses due to positive stimuli and become enthralled with the endless cycles of ups and downs. To avoid that, an individual would choose an ascetic or monastic lifestyle to minimize disturbance and attachment emerging from the experience through the six senses. An individual who succeeds in "cutting the cords" from the senses can achieve a state of liberation for himself, ending his personal suffering.

Although there is nothing officially named the Middle Vehicle, it can be represented by Pratyeka Buddhāna. This path centers on the samsara concept that depicts the endless cycle of life, death, and rebirth. In literal translation, samsara means "flowing around." Applying that definition to a more temporal level, this path is about shifting the mindset from the conventional way of observing the world in terms of separate things and events into seeing life and all occurrence in it as one process. Suffering is ultimately due to blindness of not seeing the process. Such blindness leads to ill intention. Ill intention leads to action. Action leads to possession. Possession leads to attachment. Attachment leads to suffering. Suffering leads to further blindness. If one remains blind, the cycle repeats. This echoes the idea of cause and effect. Until one completely understands one's own involvement in the cause, one cannot be free from the effect. If one cannot see the process, one cannot break the cycle. Because one's continuous involvement in worldly affairs will endlessly generate more effects, which can counteract the effort in seeking to understand, one on this path is also instructed to live a subdued, monastic lifestyle, similar to Hinayana. If an individual can end his blindness and maintains a clear understanding of samsara, he can eliminate the ill intention, and he can find liberation in this path for himself.

Finally, there is the later developed Mahayana Buddhism, also the Large/Greater Vehicle or the Bodhisattva Vehicle. Mahayana focuses on six paramita (perfection, completeness): dana (generosity), sila (virtuous conduct), ksanti (tolerance), virya (diligence), dhyana (concentration), and prajna (wisdom). Prajna, though listed last, is the most important. Prajna is the complete wisdom, or otherwise also known as the Perfection of Wisdom, that which through it the other paramita and all practices, discipline, and rituals can be born, can be understood, as natural insight. One with Prajna can see and gain insight like one knows how to breathe, without ever being taught. Without it, all practices remain compulsory dogma, and the practitioner is liable to misstep due to incomplete understanding. If one achieves Prajna, a feat that can also be called "Understand thy Heart, see thy Self" (Ming Xin Jian Xing, 明心見性), an individual has become an awakened one, which is the meaning of the word buddha. Thus, it can be said that Prajna is an inherent aspect of a buddha. Not only is he liberated, but he can also extend true compassion and assist others on their paths with his wisdom, meanwhile as he continues to further his practice and deepen his own understanding. This concept of sharing of teachings, assisting others is a key differentiation of Mahayana to the other two vehicles, which focus on the liberation of one's own suffering.

Here we have discussed three paths of Buddhism very briefly (perhaps criminally so) that fall under the general "step-by-step" path. Scholars and theologians may argue there are more styles and denominations to Buddhism. Whether there is a Middle Vehicle may also be up for debate. Regardless, that is beside the point in this discussion. The point to be noted here is that there can be as many pointers, methods, techniques, paths as we wish to intellectually or academically categorize, but if we examine them, they are not mutually exclusive and share much in common, beyond the veil of terminology. More importantly, they endeavor the same aim — to become awakened to the Self, a return to Self.

Buddhism provides a progression of studies and practices that attempt to lead a student to Prajna and the Self as the key achievement. Over the ages, various venerated Buddhas and sages contributed new understanding, alternative guidance, and additional paths for students to arrive at their own insight. Those insights are founded on their own illumination into human nature. For this reason, as illumination is universal, it is not surprising that comparison and correlation of Buddhist doctrine to modern psychological concepts had been made.

Such a comparison may seem strange and crazy to some. Not only are their origination years and years apart, one comes from the East while the other comes from the West. There is also the issue that in current time, there are a million and one problems that everyone experiences every day (and growing!) that are exceedingly more complicated. But the truth is, a person's basic needs had not changed.

We like to have things. We hate to be hungry. We need companionship. We want to feel like we belong. We freak out when there is an earthquake. We freeze up when we are shocked. We like to believe in some sort of a something somewhere, hopefully, that will ultimately "save" us. We all get anxious. We dread meaninglessness in life. If we pick a million people from across the world, likely all can agree to these statements. We have only forgotten such commonness in the current moments due to the amount of new technological advances, with the evermore promises to address some vaguely new "needs" that are more specialized forms of convenience, instant gratification, thrills, and self-validation. Those are not our natural needs, but they have become the unnecessary must-have distraction that captures our attention. Meanwhile, our basic nature had not changed for centuries, nor has our *modus operandi*. That is why Buddhism is as timeless and relevant as modern psychoanalytical theory.

Psychology's official definition is the study of the mind. But if we break up the word, the result is "psych-" and "-ology." Again, the word psyche has its origin in the goddess of the soul, *Psykhe*. Psychology thus translates to the study of the soul. And psychoanalysis is the analysis of one's soul.

Buddhism's path is paved for us with a deep insight into human nature, the product of our psyche. If one can maintain an open mind in the study of Buddhism and not pigeon-hole it as mere religion, it is easy to observe that it contains a mixture of psychology, philosophy, and other practical disciplines that arise out of deep understanding. In more recent times, Carl Jung first began to pave a path, of which the foundation was laid by his many predecessors. His path was seemingly parallel to Buddhism. But with his in-depth pursuit into western mythology, alchemical texts, and religious symbolism in relation to mankind's psychological development, his path met up with Buddhism as he realized that the goal of individuation is the Self. Jung at the end of his journey arrived at a tier akin to Buddhism, and historical sages, that seeks to exposit a process to resolve human suffering and guide the rediscovery of the Self.

Mahayana Buddhism describes the progression of the enlightenment process:

戒 (Discipline), 定 (Stillness/Samadhi), 慧 (Prajna)

That translates into, "Through discipline, one arrives at stillness. Upon achieving stillness, Prajna arises from within." The elimination of sensory desire, sacrifice of worldly views and habits, relinquishment of illusory karmic involvement, and practice of all other disciplinary action and good deeds, though could be beneficial by their own merit, are engagement to establish the condition for the blossoming of Prajna within oneself. This is akin to seeds requiring fertile soil and proper environment in order to germinate. That is the reason about concentrating, going deep, through and through, with one path (or pick a sutra to study) to "get to" stillness, and thus finally obtainment of Prajna. After this feat, it is said that "Know one sutra, know all sutras" or "One method understood, all methods understood." As one peers directly into the nature of being, one may derive teaching methods and skills suitable for new context and people, such as Siddhartha Gautama's Four Noble Truths. Prajna is the source of the development of the vehicles and thus it is also upon such illumination where one may yet differentiate between vehicles but may act as if to regard vehicles as not real. They are different tools useful on different occasions. Without stillness, true dedication, and a stern aim, such a feat is nigh impossible. But if one possesses them all, it may happen quickly. We can ask adversely, how can one possibly discover, recognize, and receive the gift of Prajna when one always busies himself with external pleasures, mired in attachments, avoiding discomfort at all costs, living erratically, and not being able to concentrate on anything at all? How can a seed germinate and grow into size with corrupted soil, dirtied water, and lack of sunshine? More concretely, would one even be able to maintain a somewhat peaceful state if the mind is preoccupied with scheming for money, thirsting for vengeance, or lusting after sensuous experience?

In the past century, psychoanalytical methods had been developed that seek to resolve mental conflicts that are remnants of traumatic life experience. The goal of the currently evolved therapeutic practice is the alleviation of such conflict that allows the individual to become respectable again within his social context. In short, it is about the mending of the ego to once again fit into the normality. That is the driving force behind modern psychotherapy. The devil in the detail is… normality is dependent upon the contemporary social context. Therein lies an important question, "What if what normality is construed to be is detrimental to the natural human psyche?" Or put differently, "What if what normality constitutes is against an individual's mental well-being?"

Even if we avoid addressing those questions, when it comes to addressing the deeper question about futility in the face of nature, existential angst, and generally life's suffering, modern psychotherapeutic methods and treatments are sorely inadequate and unable to provide any lasting "cure." Worse yet, a pervasive engineering, reductionistic approach in problem-solving that has permeated all fields including psychology had led to deteriorating consequences. That leads to the one-pill/one-method solving one-symptom/ one-deficiency mentality that dominates doctor-patient interaction. That leads to worsening quality of doctor-patient relationship. Instead of treating the patient as unique individual, who has unique lifestyle, unique personality, unique past, unique physiological disposition… the emphasis is put on the diagnostic of a particular "disease" while who he is, is made irrelevant. This is a generalization because there are yet effective and sincere doctors and therapists out there. However, it is notable such attitude is commonly found regarding modern therapeutic practices, where even patients are glad to be diagnosed with a specific disease because then he feels a "cure" can be prescribed and that he can be "fixed."

The reality is that in the face of a unique individual's psyche, there is no hope such myopic, simplistic approach can provide any reparative and curative long-term effect. So alleviation of "symptoms" are all but short-lived, as people live on intermittent episodes of temporary relief from chemical dosage. While behind the scene, the actual illness worsens.

With Jung's psychology, he had further matured the original intention in psychoanalysis by quite a few steps. Essentially, he has reoriented it toward a new goal. That is in contrast to the previously described approach of modern psychotherapy.

Per his insight, it is only through a prolonged process that consists of a series of inner overcoming that one may achieve what he calls Personality. Regarding Personality, it is an adequate level of integration of one's ego and shadow. With that being a semi-prerequisite, individuation may then be possible and attempted. Here the parallelism to Buddhism can be observed. The culmination of Jung's experience and conception meets up with Buddhism in principle. Both paths serve as means to ease and untangle one's inner turmoil, which encompasses one's conflict with the external world. If successful, that will impart a state of balance and stillness. It is within such a state that one has the possibility to connect with the Self, and that is also a state where the Self has the room to emanate through the individual. That is the task of all tasks. Only modern man seems to have lost track of such discipline, nor do they possess such aim. They know of no such aim. Their minds are always distracted and spirit scattered. In an age where money, power, vanity reign supreme, that is no surprise. Aren't we such sinners?

Both Depth Psychology and Buddhism's *vehicle*s that are briefly discussed fall under the umbrella of the "step-by-step" path. Diametrically, there is the "sudden" path that emphasizes more on directly cutting through the illusion of the ego. This notion is a strong driving force within Zen Buddhism. That is, despite its many denominations that had adopted methodology from the "gradual" path.

Whether one chooses one method on either path over the other is a matter dependent upon one's personality, upbringing, culture, and timing. Maybe one needs to try various methods before deciding on one… but ultimately, each individual must choose and progress on one path deeply, thoroughly, and sincerely. There are also factors such as timing and luck that will play a role, as happenstance and random life experience always play a role. Despite different choices and paths, all who heed their callings are striving for what is the same in essence. For it is through this path of discovery, his overcoming of himself, reconnecting with the Self, that man finds wisdom. Only then he is truly creative in discovering and using knowledge of all kinds in ways that enliven. Therein lies the possibility to bring balance into the human world that is experiencing a self-destructive pattern.

Mindset: Jung vs Modern Psychotherapy

Jung slowly came to a deep perception of the progression of human consciousness and sensed the dangerous trend that mankind is following. As a result, he dedicated himself on a path to find ways for man to heal and regain familiarity with the soul. Despite his effort during his lifetime, and even in the modern field of psychology, the content that he provided is yet largely sidelined or misunderstood.

Jung's work and conception are the consequence of him in the role of a psychologist and a clinician. His desire is to help his patients to grow into a more integrated personality. Through his writings, he seeks to do the same. Moreover, as he aged, beyond his academic writings, he elaborated on his vision and theories with hopes to turn the tide against the fragmentation of mankind's psyche. His intention and sincerity to assist people in developing psychic well beings cannot be doubted and should be clear for anyone who had amply surveyed his works.

As mentioned in the last chapter, there is a distinction that I observed within the intention standing behind contemporary psychotherapy and Jung's conception.

The focus of treatment in modern psychotherapy is drawn around the identification of a diagnostic conclusion about a patient. Namely, a doctor is to label each patient with disorders based on a set of specific symptoms. From there, a treatment path is chosen by the doctor. Additionally, the intent behind modern psychotherapy is the seeking to restore one's mental shapeliness, or to repair one's ego into a respectable state that enables the patient to again fit in with the social status quo. This is about curing the individual in so far that he would be functional and useful again within contemporary normality. This diagnostic and treatment approach to solving mental issues draws a strong similarity with the modern medicine approach to our physiological body. That is no surprise because they originate from the same supposition of reality. That supposition is an implicit, absolute belief in a mechanical view of the universe and an engineering view in solving all problems that exist in this fundamentally mechanical universe.

The overzealous application of such an attitude forces us to treat ourselves, human beings, likened to cars or robots. Applying that to resolve a problem, it means to separate larger parts into smaller problems to tackle with concentrated effort, and then locate and replace the broken individual parts. This is the engineering mindset of divide and conquer. We must recognize this as a central driving force behind the medical methodology. It has enabled wondrous technological advances and worked effectively enough in dealing with our physiological bodies. The word "enough" is used here to point out that despite the usefulness of modern medicine, there exist plentiful of cases where doctors are unable to diagnose an illness or even if diagnosed, the reasons why someone gets sick remain unknown.

The methodology dictates the prerequisite of determination of scientifically tangible symptoms which are chosen among a predetermined and scientifically approved set of symptoms. The symptoms are then combined to help the doctor to deduce a disease, which also must be scientifically approved. Based on the specific disease, pre-existing treatments will be chosen and applied.

There are several problems with that. First, there are cross matches between the symptoms among the diseases. Second, the deeper we dive into our physiological bodies in detecting problems, the harder it is to clearly distinguish if something is physical, neurological, or psychological/emotional. Third, the necessity to hammer down precise, tangible symptoms in a system (labeling of the illness) sometimes excludes the possibility of discovering the real, originating problem that may be influential yet subtle, or even frivolous, beyond the scope of detection outside the selected system. In other words, there is a hyper-focus on elements on just one end of the spectrum and negligence on others. And what if such a factor originates from a separate system or factors outside of all the observed systems? Such a mindset is not conducive to taking further steps to discover those issues. Forth, what about symptoms and diseases that do not exist yet, or that exist permeably among the many predetermined ones. Last but not least, the advent of sophisticated methods and apparatus that allow scientists and doctors to delve into an immense amount of measurements, had led to a tacit ignoring of the person behind the numbers.

Despite the described issues, modern medicine has brought about improvement and had been doing a very respectable job in the healing of our physical bodies. However, with the described issues, adding on the increasing concentration in generating short-term profits in more recent times has led the focus of modern medicine to shift even further away from the care and restoration of patients' physical well-being. Instead, the focus is more placed on sustaining persistent income from treatment and prescription so long as the patients remain alive, disregarding long-term side effects that can be devastating to quality of life.

The perversion that happens in treatment for the physiological body is mirrored in psychotherapy. This implicates the assumption that we can treat and cure the mind, the same ways we are doing with our bodies. The issue then is that the problematic scenarios described earlier are much worse when applied in the matters of the mind, the treatment of the psyche. The focus is so strong in treatment that the theory of chemical imbalance in the brain leading to mental illness is treated as fact while it was never proven and remains inconclusive from studies.

In short, a terrifyingly myopic view has been established in both the professionals and laymen, which does not include the bringing about of well-being and integration of the individual. Curing someone's mental illness has more to do with making compliance of an individual's mental state and behaviors into what is known as "normal," or arguably, "morally correct." That could be productive in terms of the individual's well-being and wholeness dependent upon what constitutes within the range of "normal" in the contemporary culture. As things currently stand in 2019, the crevice between "normal" versus the needs for the psychic health of the individual is very broad. This is a natural consequence of the giant gap between our attitude and model of reality versus how reality truly works. And despite the incessant push to address mental illness, we are rather primitive in handling our own psyche.

Diving deeper into the modern therapeutic approach, there exists a strong reliance on one-size-fits-all methods and in more recent times, pharmaceutical prescriptions such as anti-anxiety drugs, antidepressants, and antipsychotics. It demonstrates our sense of self-mistrust. We have moved away from the notion that there could be an innate curative force of our own psyche. Akin to our bio-physical body that has an immune system, it is only reasonable that our psyche contains a force that strives for a healthy outcome, like a psychic immune system. Instead, we have trended toward a position of mistrust. But even rationally speaking, how can we feasibly operate from a position that begins with mistrust? One cannot trust the mistrust that is founded on mistrust. Such attitude contrasts with the method of Carl Roger's proposed *non-directive therapy* which places a trust in the patient's own expertise in his own experience and his will to follow a necessary course to conceive his own cure. Such mistrust is also in opposition to Jung's adherence to follow patients' own paths without prejudice, even if apparently mistaken, for an eventual best outcome. That is, instead of thinking the psychic symptoms as deeply flawed and abnormal, a trust is to be placed in the patient's own nature that reveals the direction the patient is supposed to take. Thus, the symptoms or illness are not to be suppressed but to be understood. The symptom can inform a new way. Is it so hard to fathom that if one has veered off-path for a lengthy period, one must retrace past steps before finding the right direction again? Does it not make sense that if the problem is a buried side of our personality screaming out for help through psychic phenomenon, the path to freedom is to be discovered by understanding the phenomenon, just as our physical body signals issues through the sensation of pain and other symptoms?

A reductionistic system and a rigid mentality cannot hope to correspond to the human psyche in complexity. By serving the patients with labels of disorders, such as antisocial, general anxiety, bipolar, depressive, schizophrenic, borderline, narcissistic, a preconceived notion is almost dead-set upfront regarding what the problem is… and just as bad are the "easy" solutions to suppress psychic phenomenon. Procedurally working with labels and names may be helpful for initial approach, but it is no longer helpful if both the doctor and patients become close-minded and fixated on the label. That fixation disregards individuality and is a mistreatment of the psyche. Being close-minded with a preconceived notion can lead astray the patient from where he may naturally need to go. If we can safely assume that the problem originates from somewhere unknown and that our conscious self no longer suffices to resolve the issue, then applying pre-conceived notions, inflexible frameworks that are founded upon the conscious part of the psyche will fail to heal the person. The root of the problems will not be addressed.

In current times, quite often between people's conversation, be it between friends, acquaintances, or family members, when one person begins to divulge some more profound experience, he can quickly be met with push-back by the other party's suggestion to go speak with a therapist. It is especially likely if the experience is deemed "negative." Although not everyone is equipped, suitable, or has the time and energy to listen to others' dark secrets or traumatic experiences, but such a reaction is a direct rejection in the face of someone ready to be vulnerable. "*I think you should go see a therapist about this.*" It is as if nothing considered even slightly depressing, negative is permitted to be discussed nowadays. Jung once wrote, "condemnation does not liberate." You are the condemner of the person you turn away. Indeed, I am generalizing here… but what happens when the attitude of condemnation is pervasive in the everyday interactions among everybody? What happens when condemnation is embedded in the approach that is taught throughout the psychotherapy fields? And what if our methods to solve mental "illness" are inherently hostile against our psychic need? It is no surprise that it is so rare, so difficult, and so scary for people to open up to each other now.

The ever-encroaching modern approach in solving problems, applied in psychotherapy, ignores the individual. The experience of the individual is not being addressed at the source of issues. Worse, the result from such ignorance often feeds further suppression of a patient's psychic issue. It is as if we have forgotten that every single person is unique through both nature and nurture. There are differences in temperament, personality, parents, siblings, friends, culture, and fortuity. But we act as if those no longer matter. The focus is narrowly on the symptoms and diagnosis... Once a diagnosis is made, if it's the same diagnosis, the individual human beings behind it make little difference. Treatment will be prescribed as "If A, then Y. If B, then Z." That is it.

One may ask if there are such problems among the psychoanalytical or therapeutic arena, how is it that some people's condition genuinely improves after sessions with clinicians? Regarding this, I will attribute that to a handful of factors. The doctor may have performed self-analysis and overcame his own past and personal trauma. He has reached a level of self-mastery. He also likely has a sincere desire to help the patient and willing to take time to understand him. As a prerequisite, the patient must also possess his own will to improve. Only together in such a resonating relationship between the doctor and the patient will there be any true long-term improvement in the patient.

Putting all that had been written in this chapter together, it can be said that modern man has put himself in a warring state with himself. It is reflected in our behaviors. It is reflected in our reality in many people's deteriorating mental health. The approach and methods that modern man is to rely on for the restoration of mental health and resolution of trauma have become instruments that sow yet more conflicts. The relationship between doctor and patient and our treatment between each other are now in a state that is insensitive to the psychic forces behind the individual's skin-level character. Our ignoring of the individual's true nature is a desecration of our psyche. The "fitting" of an individual's mental state into what is known as "normal" is proving more detrimental than beneficial.

Another perspective is that it is no accident that modern man's growing distrust and estrangement from traditional religions coincide with the birth of psychology fields in the 20th century. The belief systems and rituals of days past provided an outlet for man's intangible psychic needs. Modern man is unwittingly trying to satisfy those same needs through channels developed through the rational mind and scientific means. As modern men thumb their noses toward old practices, traditions, and religion, they simultaneously defer themselves toward the haven of secular groups and ideologies that bear fundamental resemblance with the zealous, dogmatic groups in the past.

The failure of such a path is bearing fruit right in front of our eyes. There is a loneliness epidemic across modern nations, where the number of people who say they have no one to confide personal matters more than double from 1985 to 2006. In 2006, that amount is 25% of the American population. During the same period, the number of people Americans would include as their closest confidants had decreased from three to two. Anxiety disorder had increased dramatically in the last 50 years. In current year 2019, it affects 18.1 percent of adults in the United States (approximately 40 million adults between the ages of 18 to 54), according to National Institute of Mental Health (NIMH), while estimates put the number much higher at approximately 30 percent due to people being unaware of issues with anxiety.

Asides from statistics showing lack of connection, depression, alcohol abuse, drug use, and suicides had also been on the rise in the last few decades. Between 1999 and 2017, alcohol-related deaths doubled from 36,000 to 73,000 according to National Center for Health Statistics. The suicide rate for young Americans, aged between 10 and 24, jumped 56 percent between 2007 and 2017. Also, the suicide rates increase across all the U.S. states between 1999 and 2016, averaged at 33%. This is according to Centers for Disease Control and Prevention. The data all points in the same direction. Our mental(psychic) regression does not only affect what we do to ourselves. It also manifests itself through the chaos, fragmentation, escalating tension, neurosis, and psychosis in all layers of society across the world, in person-to-person, in family, in friends, in business, in local community, in politics and in between nations. These "superficial" symptoms are expressions of a deeper problem. Because of that, our techniques and attitude in handling ourselves and dealing with our psychic nature need to be reviewed.

Jung was famously known to have collaborated with Sigmund Freud. The relationship came to a dead-end when Jung realized that

Freud's conception, from which Freud appeared intractable, is confining for what he came to realize and sought to convey. Despite being the main force in popularizing the notion of the unconscious, Freud chose to focus on the influence of human sexuality, namely libido. He focused on libido-related abuse, trauma, aggression, perversion, and repression, and their influence on the unconscious. Such a view is too narrow and cannot embody the psychic whole that Jung slowly came to observe. Thinking libido is all that is influencing the psyche is akin to seeing only the tail of the elephant and then proceeds to describe the tail as the entire elephant.

Jung as a psychologist, in the development of his visionary, metaphysical, pictorial representation of the psyche, insists on the importance and necessary adherence to deal with facts and whole human experience (leaving nothing out), this includes values and elements of reality that lie beyond what is scientifically provable. In a scientifically dogmatic world, Jung becomes the odd-ball as his vision, theories, and images stand outside the "testable" realm of the scientific world. How could it not be this way? As Jung attempts to "speak in images" to describe the universal, modern science, its tools, and scientific methods continue to further specialize in testifying for the *unique*. Now because of that trend, even Freudian theories are being pushed to the wayside in psychology. It is no wonder that much of what Jung conceptualized and had written are considered non-fashionable, too pseudo, too mystical, and so excluded from the academia. Perhaps we can go as far as to say that the climate in the current field of science simply has no room nor tolerance for the field of psychoanalysis or any of its theories created by Jung, Freud and others like them.

Jung is interested in the whole picture of the psychic life that lives inside all of us. That is why beyond the materials and publications where Jung adhered to scientific standards, he dared to allow himself to explore beyond. The journey of his own inner exploration, revelation, and transformation was painstakingly documented in manuscripts between 1915-1930s that are composed into the book *Liber Novus*, also known as the *Red Book*, which was published recently in 2010.

There are some issues for any individual wanting to delve into

Jung's work to properly read through and digest them. Some of Jung's individual works alone are difficult enough to read and digest by themselves, but put together, they may be cryptic for someone to string together a coherent understanding. One can easily get hung up on one of the many sub-topics and aspects of psychoanalysis (such as transference, projection, etc.), or too focused on specific archetypes, or lost in the many symbolisms from legends, myths, and alchemy, or stuck trying to memorize all the information. One can spend his entire life and analyze the specifics to death and give a sorry attempt to remember them by heart. Regarding reading Jung's materials, I will give my opinions on an approach.

All of Jung's work is but an amalgamated vision from his inner journey through different parts of his life. While some of his works are strictly scientific, a lot of his works bear the essence of his inner experience and originates from a place where he called the depths (or the collective unconscious). He hopes for others to see it and arrive at their own understanding and thus inner transformation. Imagine a running stream that springs forth all of Jung's works, the undercurrent of that stream is his personal journey. That experience is partly expressed through *Liber Novus*. His other works are like the surface level waves and ripples from the undercurrent, seemingly separate but sustained and connected by it. So perhaps the way to go is to read some of his other works prior to reading *Liber Novus* which establishes some foundational understanding. One can read with speed and without worrying too much that one must understand everything. Afterward, reading *Liber Novus* will provide the essence. It will redefine and reorient your understanding and how those foundational pieces fit together. Then once again after reading *Liber Novus,* one can revisit the other works or those that were previously studied. New light will be shined on these contents.

If *Liber Novus* is Jung's schema to the individuation process, perhaps we can also view his other works as the branches, tools, and techniques that he provides for us to help ourselves. They are supposed to be optional and suitable for the occasion and not to be taken as gospels individually because in the end is not any single method that will help… but the choices and efforts of the individual. An important message to remember is, as stated in the previous chapter, that the goal of individuation is the Self.

The intuitive understanding of the whole is the epochal matter versus the grasping of individual abstraction and theories.

Depth Psychology – Map of Psyche

Depth psychology is the name given to the therapeutic approaches that explore the unconscious operation in the human psyche in addition to and with reference to the conscious portion. As such, the study of dreams, images, psychological complexes, archetypes, myths, and their symbolism are included. Because all these experiences are included in consideration, there is a strong transpersonal aspect in the exploration of depth psychology and the psyche. So, the scope vastly expands to knowledge in history, theology, philosophy, linguistics, biology, genetics, etc. In the end, depth psychology has to do with facts and real human experience. In other academic studies, the students will always seek to learn more specialized abstract concepts in one field. For depth psychology, it helps to learn as much specialized knowledge as possible, but in the end, one needs to generalize all of them into a coherent image.

Perhaps it is with good reasons that depth psychology is not so pervasive in academia. The inherent problem in academia is that each subject has been becoming narrower in coverage and requiring students to specialize in niche fields which is a trend, an attitude counter-productive to learning more about depth psychology.

However far and wide one may or may not have gone in the study of depth psychology. The key remains that it is meant to provide a way to interpret real experience, and real experience entails the happenings in every level and every facet that relates to the human mind – physical, neurological, psychological, conscious, subconscious, and the most subliminal. It is no longer merely a study into the psychological but more existential. Perhaps this is the inherent mismatch with academic studies where one strives to make grades and to get a diploma finally. More concretely, depth psychology acts more like a bridge between the real, material, scientific world which we are accustomed to and the more mystical, spiritual, religious side of life. This correlates with how humans deal with reality. Because we human beings do not interact directly with reality but with many mental layers in between, exploring depth psychology provides a more comprehensive mapping to understanding ourselves and those layers.

As far as we know, we still know very little about our brain (versus what is there to know), and even less so about consciousness. Therefore, inevitably we are discussing matters of the intangibles here. It means that one must first be open to such a premise and accepting to envisioning the more nebulous aspects of life. In other words, one needs to allow considerations of the strange, gooey side of life that is often objectionable to the rational mind of the modern century.

Below is a pictorial representation of key factors and terminology within depth psychology and some explanation. It is my proposition of what a map of psyche looks like. For that, I want to stress that nothing is to be taken too strictly and too literally, and the lines drawn between the different factors are more vague than definite. It is a provisional layout and how the different pieces relate and interact within our psychic being. If life is like a journey, then treat this as a map. A map can be useful in so far that it provides your current position and can guide you in a direction. On a physical map, you may know something about the various locations, but sometimes the importance lies not in knowing all their details. This is that case here. It is in understanding the different locations in reference to each other which is information that a map provides so that one can choose the direction to head to next. In the physical world, there are global satellites that can assist in triangulating position and provides us with GPS navigation system. But in the arena of our own life in its flow, we must, each person with his own brain, awareness, and consciousness act as his own GPS.

The factors that will be discussed are the forces in play in our psyche, and their quality and interplays affect each of us as a human being.

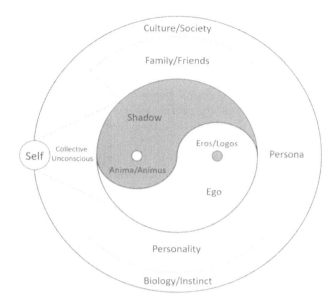

First of all, the factors Culture/Society, Family/Friends, Personality, and Biology/Instinct are more or less self-evident and will not be subjects of extensive discussion. Culture/Society is the values held by the culture and social milieu. Family/Friends are strongly related and similar to Culture/Society but have more direct impact and influence. Personality is the inborn, unlearned predisposition of the individual that has a strong correlation to Biology/Instinct. Biology/Instinct are the effects of our physiological body, autonomous nervous system, neurological programming, and other primordial circuitry. They are all essential factors that are part and parcel an individual's psyche. It is just as the study of an animal cannot exclude the environment and built-in biological traits. They are all connected.

From the Freudian perspective, Culture/Society together with Family/Friends is analogous to the Super-ego, and Biology/Instinct together with Personality is analogous to the Id. The Super-ego exerts pressure and control on the ego as a moralizing role while the Id influences and may usurp an individual's control on himself in the forms of primordial and instinctual impulses.

Ego is typically what the oft-spoken "I" or "myself" points at. It is the assumed psychic center of a person's everyday conscious state. This is what is deemed as the individual's identity. Furthermore, when the word "self" is used, frequently in other texts, it is referring to this identity, the ego. That includes the self that is oft spoken of in translated Buddhist scripture. In this chapter and the following, the self (with a lowercase "s") refers to the ego, as opposed to the "Self" (with an uppercase "S") described later in this chapter.

Surrounded by the other factors, the ego is comprised of and influenced by qualities and elements from those factors. That explains the ego's complexity. The factors' all-together interplays affect the artifacts within these factors that will be infused and remain as part of the ego during a person's development.

Artifacts from these factors may include social rules, historical heritage, academic knowledge, family precept, cultural traditions, moral structures, other belief systems, hackneyed mottos from elders, principles from books, advice from close friends, a subset of personality traits that one accepts as part of himself. Typically, family, parents, friends, and personality will have a more direct and apparent role in contributing to one's ego. Additionally, as the years go by, there is also other content such as life experience, memories, feeling-impression that lingers in cognizance in the individual's mind.

These rules, belief systems, and other content intertwine and congregate into the framework that is our ego. The ego would filter and provide a person his perception of reality, helping him to distill the infinite reality into finite possibilities. Unless one gains the ability to understand, see-through, and detach from his ego, his perception is reality. The perceived reality that gets retained as experience and memory modifies those rules and systems that lead us in everyday life.

As years progress, people accumulate more artifacts and experience that pool into the framework of ego based on the feedback of successful adaptation. What proves to be "successful" either get integrated as addition or reaffirms what was incorporated. The success that is spoken here does not necessarily infer success that is determined by the values in the contemporary social values, or family values. Rather, success is qualified by how valuable it is in the sustenance of one's identity, or the preservation of the ego. It may mean content that is acceptable to someone's identity. What is acceptable may be strongly influenced by what constitutes as "sane" or "normal" in the individual's contemporary environment or dictated by thoughts and ideologies pervasive in social settings. For example, if someone's ego is strongly influenced by his personality and he takes pride in his straightforwardness and presenting himself as he is, then speaking out his thoughts will be of great value to his ego. The straight forwardness becomes prominent in the preservation of his ego even though it is not the "sane" choice. That may lead to a detrimental effect on his social standing if reservedness and tactfulness are considered worthy instead.

During this accumulation process of a person's ego development, thoughts, emotions, values, memories, and other contents are incorporated into the ego. At the same time, what is not accepted either involuntarily resigns or is relegated to the *shadow*. So, what lies within the shadow can be things that we are no longer aware of (from the other factors), or what are considered not useful or "bad" from the perspective of the ego. As such, depends on which factor is the strongest in someone's life, either the society, or someone in the family, or a strong part his personality, that is that which imposes its will most on the molding of the ego and through the ego, its will puts its imprints on his life. To a different degree, such kind of "weeding out", conflicts, and tug-of-war happen between values from the different factors will shape an individual's ego and what lies in his shadow. It can be between the values of the society vs. his personality, natural impulses vs. what his family or friends advise him, personal values vs. cultural values, etc.

The shadow personifies everything that an individual had consciously rebuked as part of himself that he sincerely believes to be "not of himself." That includes content that he had repressed and thus are forgotten, but these aspects of that individual always assert their influence somehow and are manifested inadvertently in his life experience, despite his greatest endeavor. Because despite what he thinks of as himself, the shadow remains part of his psyche. Perhaps for a time, an individual may keep these content - such as unfashionable thoughts and feelings, antagonizing personalities, personal failures in the eyes of community standards, or inferior traits of character – hidden for a while. But inevitably, if dully repressed, they poke their heads out like groundhogs in spring in unforeseen ways.

Though shadow regularly bears a negative connotation, it should not be assumed that everything that lies in the shadow is bad. It is more appropriate to visualize the ego as the anterior of the body and the shadow as the posterior. It is difficult physically to get a clear look at our own back. Translating that to the context of self-exploration, it is harder to pay attention and learn about aspects of ourselves that lie in the shadow. Regardless, both front and back are parts of the body.

Although an individual may think of himself and identify himself with certain values, he does not necessarily present himself externally to others as such. This results in the formation of the *persona*. Translated from Latin, persona originally refers to the mask worn by an actor in theatres. Appropriately, the persona for a civilized man is the image that he presents to the world and wishes for himself to be realized as in others' eyes. The social culture also exerts a strong influence on the persona through designating what values constitute "right" and "moral." Therefore, the persona's qualities can resemble exactly what comprised the ego, but it may differ from the ego drastically as dictated by social values.

In modern psychological research, there had been research studies covering the subject of basic distinctions between male and female psychology. One example is that there is a difference where the average male is more attracted to tools and abstract ideas while the average female is attracted to people and understanding relationships. Within depth psychology, the ego is oriented by different archetypes, the Logos for the male ego and the Eros for the female.

In the chapter Duality, yin and yang were discussed as the most generic representation of the dualistic force in nature. In turn, Logos and Eros symbolize more expatiated versions of yang and yin. Logos symbolizes the force which strives to bring and sustain forms in existence. Logos is the ultimate paternal principle. It corresponds to ideas such as intellect, judgment, discrimination, rules, order, movement, tangible reality, etc. On the flip side, Eros is the ultimate maternal principle that is specific in the female psyche. Eros symbolizes the force which places matters into relation, which acts as the opposite of Logos connoting the dissolution of discrimination, assimilation, stillness, chaos, mysteriousness, etc. If Logos shall correspond with the Will to Power, dare I say, Eros would correspond with the Will to Compassion, which contains the aspect of Love as mentioned in Christianity and Buddhism.

In a positive light, the Logos stands as the images of that of protector, guardian, security, and order, while in a negative light, it stands for one who seeks only to dominate and to merely exert power at all cost. Thus, an overpowering Logos becomes the image of a tyrant. Similarly, Eros also possesses two sides. As the maternal instinct that brings about connection, Eros represents that which is receptive, livening, nurturing, and fosters creativity and relationships, but in its extremity, it becomes a force that swallows all, where everything blends in with everything, no discrimination and isolated forms is allowed. Too much Eros thus becomes a case of unmitigated compassion that seeks superficially to nurture but ultimately brings ruin to all, via the complete assimilation of everything. In short, when Eros reigns supreme, Logos as the will to power shall recede into oblivion, and when Logos becomes predominant, there is no room for connection and relationship.

The ego of the male has a stronger tendency to manifest qualities embodied by the Logos and conversely, a female's ego the Eros'. However, the human psyche is far from being unidimensional. Within the depth of the shadow lives the counterpart to Logos and Eros. The masculine contains the feminine, known as the *anima*. The feminine contains the masculine, known as the *animus*. The representation of the anima and the animus are the synthesis of the experience one has with the intimate members of the opposite sex. Within them also lie the emotional impression, dependent on fondness or hatred, toward character traits from key family members or friends of the opposite sex in someone's life. The anima and animus have a direct influence on how an individual manifests the quality of the opposite sex in his personality, what he or she looks for in a partner, and how he or she reacts to and connects with people of the opposite sex.

Finally, there is the lesser known factor that is coined by Jung as the *collective unconscious*. Whether a person accepts the possibility of the collective unconscious hinges on whether he can accept that there is something "not of himself" in his own psyche, which contains content and values that are supra-personal to him and exists regardless of his acknowledgment. It is very hard to accept such a concept for the modern man who prefers to only accept that which can be processed intellectually and proven rationally. It is also hard to accept because having such an impersonal aspect inside also means that we are not fully in control, while the average modern person would like to believe in that we are fully in control. However, it is quite undeniable. As throughout life as a human, we continue to make decisions and develop skills and abilities that come to us seemingly without our conscious involvement and dedication. Sometimes we get a sudden moment of clarity and think of a solution that came out of nowhere. Sometimes we suddenly develop interest, maybe even obsession, in things and we know not why. These occurrences often provide great help in us adapting to our environment. Or, they lead our life in a completely new direction. That is the manifestation of impersonal content. These impersonal contents, embodied by archetypes and universal symbols, reside in a realm called the collective unconscious.

Jung was not alone in the description of such a realm. Within Mahayana Buddhism, there is a level of consciousness that is called Alaya-Vijvana, which is translated as "storehouse consciousness." It suggests a level of consciousness that is precognitive, also impersonal and timeless, that contains the seedlings of thought and sensation that is common across beings. Even quantum physics suggests a similar view, with new theory substantiating that the basis of materials is in fact immaterial. Summarily, it is based on the discovery that electrons, though widely known and thought of as a defined particle, in their natural movement in an atom exist as a wave. The nature of these waves is probability fields which implies a fundamental level of existence that is immaterial, in contrast to the idea of materialism in traditional physics. Such immaterial existence does not invalidate the materialistic notion because electrons are indeed material as observed on one plane of knowledge. However, per the alternative immaterial property, as developed in quantum theory, the parallel can be drawn with the collective unconscious and Alaya-Vijnana that a basic, common, non-empirical level of existence or consciousness is possible across all things. This befittingly corresponds with the discussion of form (permanence, materials, being) and formlessness (impermanence, non-being, void, emptiness, or sunyata) in Buddhism.

Returning to describe the collective unconscious with the previous understanding, the collective unconscious, consequently, is the resting place of potential, non-empirical human psychic content that is supraordinate and beyond the personal psychic realm. It is the pantheon of archetypes, or otherwise the substratum of historical experience, ancestral memory, and universal experience. It is the birthplace of spirits, gods, goddesses, mythical creatures that are the concretization of archetypes and other fantasies. It is the arena of all human potentialities, good and bad.

Within the vast realm of the collective unconscious with its timeless and incalculable content, there lies an essential archetype, symbol, image, or idea that Jung coins as the Self (though Jung denotes it as "self" with lower case). If the totality of being and existence, corresponds to Tao, God, Brahman, Ahura Mazda, etc. then the Self is the image of God (or any of the other names) in the human psyche, and it is the innate part of ourselves that represents the universal existence and also that which connects us to the whole. The Self is the part of the human psyche that is divine and holy (as in whole) and is analogous to the ultimate principle of wholeness, of universal totality. Its symbolic manifestation includes the mandala, circular ring, the cross, and other quaternity symbols, while its personification includes holy figures such as Christ, Buddha, Krishna. Otherwise, the Self also corresponds to Atman in Sanskrit, or the Buddha-nature (zi-xing, 自性, in Chinese). The Self stands for wholeness and is the imperturbable part of you. It is the true source of peace, steadiness, stillness that allows you to have a connection to everything else if you sincerely allow yourself to connect with it.

The Unconscious

Outside of talking about the collective unconscious, though the word unconscious was used, the concept of the unconscious was conveniently skipped in the last chapter. It is because I find it necessary to layout the "overall map" first. Frequently, I read and hear others speak of the unconscious as a necessary quality of some factors, such as the assumption that the shadow is always unconscious, but I find it inaccurate and incomprehensive to make such an assumption on a factor being unconscious. Rather, the unconscious covers psychic region partially that looks like below:

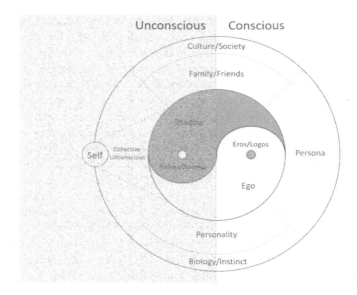

The fine line between the unconscious and the conscious will be called the unconscious veil, or more simply, the veil. Though the veil

is drawn straight down the middle, the amount and coverage of the unconscious region can have an innumerable degree of variability such as some of the impressions below:

Freud was the one who popularized the idea of the unconscious. He construed the unconscious part of the psyche as a reservoir of feelings, thoughts, memories, and other sense-experience that lies outside of man's conscious awareness. He further focuses on his theory that these unconscious contents result primarily from man's suppressed biological and instinctual urges from his sexuality. Jung later expanded on Freud's theory that the formation of the unconscious is regulated by man's disposition to adapt to the demand of life. That is to say, Jung expanded the scope of the unconscious. If the unconscious is an undiscovered basement, Freud discovered the entrance, opened the door, and took an initial look at its content. Jung as a successor followed the footsteps and performed more extensive exploration.

As Jung has observed from his studies and clinical experience, the unconscious' development in man's psyche exhibits a strong, proportional relationship to the development of the individual and his environment over the millennia. The development of the individual means the shaping of the ego, the shadow, and the maintenance of his persona in the environment. The relationship means that as the scale and complexity of the human civilization grow, so do the scale and complexity of the unconscious, the conscious, and their dynamics. In other words, the separation between the conscious and the unconscious has become more crystalized as civilization develops. Whereas in the past, the contrast and the separation between the two are much more blurred.

Our ancestors' lifestyle is much simpler and less hectic. It was also full of unknowns. There were immensely more things they did not know compared to modernity. However, though there was much they cannot comprehend, in the intellectual sense, their more direct, less mediated connectedness to nature and adherence to "natural flow of life" led to their disposition to embody the unknowns into their everyday life and belief system. They possessed a more instinctive approach to survival. This connectedness is what lies behind rituals, traditions, religious belief and other cultural artifacts, such as legends, myths, and fairy tales. So, they live their unconscious through direct incorporation into everyday life. Their prominent attitude, otherwise derogatorily viewed as "blind belief" by modern man, in a certain way of nature allows for the manifestation of unconscious content... In such a way, their unconscious force has an outlet and a neighborly dynamic between the conscious and the unconscious was therefore maintained. That supplied them a healthier level of psychic balance than their modern counterpart.

In ancient Mesopotamia, the meaning of life was to live in concert with the gods. Humans are to aspire to the will of their deities and collaborate with them to fend off the forces of chaos. There is a lack of discussion of after-life while the deities were presumed to be actual forces that roam the land, so one is to dedicate oneself in earthly duties as dictated by the religious edict. Tragedies and misfortunes are the deeds of demons and malicious spirits. The people were to enlist their gods' assistance with help from their priests, and by making sacrifices they regain health and balance in their lives. Even if some of the people are not "spiritual adequately", they would at least live their life in accordance with the beliefs. And if necessary, had help from priests and tribal medicine men that enable them to maintain a connection with the unconscious part of their psyche.

Similarly, Mongolians have their shamanism. Mongolian shamanism follows an animistic tradition that acknowledges living energy, or spirits, to be inherent in all things. Like the Mesopotamian, for the Mongolians who believe, the tradition permeates their mode of thinking and behaviors in daily life. The worship of the Tenger, their god, and rituals with the shamans are a means to strengthen their connection with nature and all of creation. Shamans who actively enter an altered state of consciousness by being possessed with ancestral spirit could be regarded as directly accessing information from the collective unconscious.

The development of civilization and cultural flow had greatly increased the scope of consciousness through the broadening of knowledge. The increase is most significant in the past century with the extensive application of intellect and flourishing technology. While that had brought prosperity, the usefulness of intellect has charmed people stuck in using a sort of hyper-focused attention that brings along the disadvantage. The usefulness is glorified, and we are so desperately in love with it. As a result, human attention has been kept away from looking at anything other than what is conscious. No attention is applied to care for what is unknown and unconscious. The discussion of Mesopotamian, Mongolian traditional and religious practice is not meant to drive home the point that their people were in a "better" psychic state than modern man, and that those belief systems and rituals ought to be readopted. Mesopotamian religion and Mongolian shamanism though may be categorized as religions, but they are much more encompassing. They entail more than how people worship their religions, like how to bow, or how to behave at a ceremony. They are the people's autocratic way of life. Living in such a fashion and without the hyper-emphasis on the intellect, the distinction between conscious and unconscious is in a much blurrier state within their psyche. This is in great contrast with the modern man.

Even just a little over a century ago, there was still a large part of the world population that believed in after-life, karma, heaven and hell, etc. The modern man of the recent decades that had rid themselves of such religious notions is truly a new phenomenon.

The deities, spirits, myths, and other similar notions in the category serve a great purpose. They contain wisdom that cannot be expressed directly. They are the distilled observation by the previous generations, channeled into personified images and pictorial messages. They contain information from reality that is always encroaching on the human species. They were man's amalgamated effort to grasp the unknowns of reality conjoined with man's effort to manifest his own uninterpreted unconscious content. Both kinds of effort worked in symphony to embed ancient wisdom in these cultural artifacts. In such a way, old myths, traditional stories, old society scripts contain wisdom that serves as guidance to people to weave their way practically through the external reality, while addressing the internal needs of their adherents. These were the inheritance from nature and our ancestors, through millennia of gradual development.

Modern people act as if it is the ultimate truth that we only live in the conscious. We may speak or think otherwise but our actions betray such an assumption. It may be even a strange thing to acknowledge and discuss the power of symbolism. In short, modern people reject the unknown and reject the unconscious. We so despise the notion of not knowing and thus always act in the preoccupation of knowing. We like to believe that we are under control. So, we behave as if among the many things and creatures, only human species live with consciousness. This becomes a strong contrast to the ancient's way of life that espouses the unknowns and the beingness within all that exist. With our passion for our conscious self and belief in control, we idolize meritocracy, productivity, and work ethics from Puritanism. Because working hard is what can always be controlled... and working hard is what we do. So, we work hard with our intellect and preclude all our other capacities.

In reality, there are many more forces outside the realm of consciousness that are influencing us, most or all of which outside of our attention and control. This is not a fatalistic view. This is the truth. And the only feasible, reasonable attitude to confront this reality is with the Will to Understanding, to shine a light on to that which is dark. Such an act includes applying both the intellect to digest and possess knowledge, and all the perceptions and senses we possess outside of intellect to know beyond knowledge.

It is only in recent centuries that people had cut ties with the concept of Gods and cultural myths... Much of the causation can be attributed to the Age of Enlightenment, which Immanuel Kant distinguished from an "enlightened age" which has yet occurred. Since the Age of Enlightenment, rationalism (intellectualism) bourgeons and had conquered human society since. That is demonstrated in the trend where what cannot be justified by rationality and what is not measured, proven by the scientific method is simply not true, treated as non-reality. What lies outside of that are ignored or perceived as useless. With such belief, we stigmatized and declared war on all deities and religious concepts. We turned them into mortal enemies, where all forms of old societal scripts, traditional roles, cultural milieu, and religious practices are systematically and consistently deprecated. Our actions may yet follow some traditions, our mouths may yet speak of them and some may sound like believers, but internally people are brimmed with doubts and disbelief and are mainly driven by the *fully automatic model* of the universe.

Perhaps we should have to do away with old practices eventually, but the reckless, belligerent, arrogant manner with which we abandoned them presents a strong case of "throwing the baby out with the bathwater." Their sustaining nature to us is overlooked completely. With such an attitude, such manner, the modern man had quit trying to connect with nature and with other things in existence. Now in the 21st century, people are proceeding gradually even to cease connecting with each other. Pretense is largely what remains, as many play the acting game of persona.

As humans had turned their back completely on the unconscious, the distinction, autonomy, and volume of the unconscious had increased accordingly, within the individual and on average across species. The following diagram probably more accurately represents the current status of man's psychic arena which is covered in unconscious more than ever.

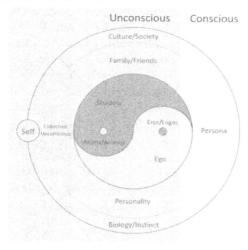

Modern man is unconscious of too much about himself. To such an extent that Jung once commented, "Man know nothing of himself." The situation had only gotten worse since his time. That is not just the result of man ignoring his cultural history and myths.

The unconscious is most receptive in its nature. It receives all of the individual's experiences and perceptions including sight, sound, emotions that were not consciously perceive. These contents of the personal unconscious, left alone, grow and mold themselves away from our attention. With all the consorted forces in modern life that almost prohibit a person from ever exploring the unconscious, its content – childhood trauma, hidden feelings, repressed memories, "non-right" thinking, etc. – is liable to turn into a monstrous untamed beast. On the other hand, if one is able to tame the beast, he can reap its benefits.

What lies in the unconscious cannot and will not remain hidden. What we do not pay attention to do not simply disappear. Forces that we do not understand will only influence more subliminally. The unconscious' rectifying effect from being ignored becomes apparent, demonstrated by the human world that had been running a counter-experiment.

The lack of light shone on the unconscious had led to strife in all inter-personal relationships, through displacement, projection, etc. These phenomena are presenting themselves in societies across the world at every level in the behavior and mentality of the people where polarization, tension, and conflicts continue to escalate. While we continue to quarrel with each other and consumed by the confusion, fear, anxiety from our own dissonance, the unconscious clandestinely extends its subliminal influence as we lack both the resolve and will to understand.

Why is it that the unconscious veil need be peeled back? That is because the danger of the unconscious lies not inherently but when it is ignored and hidden away. There exists in universe, in all things, a force that seeks to be whole, to reach balance, no matter what and how much time it may take (because in the perspective of the universe, time is irrelevant). If we only live in the conscious, if we never choose to integrate, an aspect of the universe has gone unexpressed. That is not only a pity, but we also risk a fearsome force from the unconscious that shall constellate in masses of man that will steamroll its way to expression. The personal unconscious (unconscious area of ego and shadow) affects the individual on a personal scale. But frightening is when a large sum of unconscious people begin to congregate. Together they will be seemingly possessed by the forces of the archetypes from the collective unconscious and incarnate them. Humans had already demonstrated plenty of examples in the 20th century. Is it wrong to call the wars and deaths acts of the devil? They were the acts performed by massive groups of humans as if possessed. The leaders did not act alone. They had the support from plenty and were able to commit their acts by harnessing the pre-existing forces from people's personal unconscious, such as fear, anger, resentment, jealousy, etc.

Eric Neumann provided a great analogy for archetypes. The human body has organs that perform their tasks, each with their own role, to sustain the body. Organs need to intake nutrition, secrete hormones, and excrete wastes. Archetypes are the psychic organs of the human psyche. When the body is healthy, there is no thought regarding the organs' operations. The body continues without a bother as it receives enough care and nourishment. But when the body is not well taken care of and falls to ailment, the organs' effects come to the forefront. And so is the same when we ignore our psychic health. Individual man's psychic health is dependent upon proper functioning and cooperation of Logos, Eros, anima, animus, and other archetypes and sub-archetypes. By giving the necessary attention, acceptance, understanding, one can receive the nurturing force to restore health to his psychic organs. In contrast, negligence leads to sickness, where some archetypes will eventually go berserk and wreak havoc in one's psyche, just like physical organs can do to the body.

Dynamics in the Psyche

With the now described unconscious, it will be easy to observe that the various psychic factors or forces fall into certain natural pairings, not strictly speaking:

Ego vs shadow, Eros vs animus, Logos vs anima, society (superego, morals) vs biology (Id, impulses), society(tribe) vs ego(individual), family(nurture) vs personality(nature), collective unconscious(eternal) vs persona(temporal), conscious(order) vs unconscious(chaos)

The fact is that there are innumerable details to read about the dynamics between the forces within the psyche and its influence in specific scenarios, if one so desires. This chapter will include discussions of a few ideas that I find relevant. One helpful thing to keep in mind is that the dynamics between the dualistic pairs and how each force manifests its behavior never fall outside the general ideas of duality described in Part 1. Duality. They will always remain true in the background.

The quality of ego per individual may differ in complexity, density, malleability, grounded-ness, and strength. It can be comparable to a building, as buildings may differ in size/scope, interior layout, structural sturdiness, foundation, and built-in technology.

Density – How much he retained within his ego framework, between worldly knowledge and numinous wisdom
Complexity – How many connections he makes between what he knows, highly associated with his intelligence and digested life

experience (non-digested being experience that one has not been processed thoroughly through self-introspection)

Malleability – Affects how easily a person can integrate new wisdom and knowledge. That may require the destruction of what he already knows in the process. This is reliant on the openness trait in his personality. Additionally, there is dependence on how deeply ingrained he is with certain ideologies, which may act as defense mechanism against new ideas, for better or worse

Grounded-ness – How much of the content is founded on truthfulness or falsehood, in the context of reality/wholeness.

Strength – Generically how well a person may hold up and adapt to the ever-encroaching social environment and natural reality. Dependent upon the combination of density, complexity, malleability, and grounded-ness

In a cultural milieu that promotes individual integration, the individual's ego shall contain conscious qualities of himself and who he thinks he is. In such a scenario his ego shall blend well with his persona, contains qualities dictated by standards of the society and simultaneously is informed by who he thinks the society wants to see. However, that is not the case for human society nowadays. With the contemporary cultural climate, modern man has adopted an uncanny ability, to a scary and unhealthy degree, to compartmentalize and decouple his ego and his persona. While the line used to blur between the two, the compartmentalizing trend is worsened with ongoing social engineering driven by a divisive attitude, and it renders an intensifying fragmentation between the ego and the persona. This trend reflects itself through the transition in the focus of self-help books, from 1960s through 1980s on the character-building (ego related), to the early 1990s until now on the importance of marketing oneself (persona related).

Disparity and imbalance between ego and persona will lead to anxiety and other negative emotions. When the disparity develops to a sufficiently severe degree, they become conditions known in psychology as complexes or disorders. Prior to the disorders and complexes that had been named in modern psychology, more generically, they are lumped together with the label of neurosis in milder level and psychosis in more severe cases. This applies also to the other factor vs the ego and is the coming apart of ego vs other pieces of the psyche. In other words, a person diagnosed with complexes is experiencing conflict(s) of a certain magnitude between his ego versus other factors (society, family, persona, personality, biological instinct). Like bodily pains that arise to inform us of health issues that require attention and do not happen by mere chance, complexes seek to inform us the necessity for new adaptation, usually some form of reshaping of one's ego framework but also perhaps the requirement to physically change one's external environment. A successful adaptation would lead to renewed vigor in one's life while the failure to attend would lead to stagnation, downward spirals, and inability to "move on." However, in the adaptation process, the useful qualities gain grounds in the ego while the opposing would recede into one's own shadow. An example may be a tug-of-war of values between what is acceptable in the standard of the society or family and what is acceptable to one's personality and biological nature. In such a conflicting scenario, if the social values triumph, then one's true personality becomes more recessive. If the personality is deemed more valuable, one may appear to become ill-adapted to his society.

In more recent years, there are frequent talks of trauma. It is like a psychological survival scenario where the ego is subverted. Examples may include… Horrific childhood experience. Job loss while one's identity is merged with the career. The sudden death of a family member or friend who one has come to depend on physically, mentally, and/or emotionally. Betrayal by a loved one. The sudden shift to a new environment where accustomed rules and beliefs are suddenly no longer applicable, such as a new soldier placed in a war zone. People who had been traumatized had experienced a strong threat that had invalidated a significant portion of their ego and in worse cases, the annihilation of it. Because the ego provides the frameworks and scripts for an individual to interact with his society, the traumatized person had lost his psychic tool to interact with his reality. He will be required to re-develop a new egoic framework to interpret the world. However, as the ego supports a person regarding what he "knows" so that he knows how to act, a traumatized person is confronted with an overwhelming amount of unknowns. Along with re-visitation of the instigated experience, a person may be submitted to a range of emotions, such as fear, guilt, sadness, rage, and shame. The ego may be further weakened. To surmise, such a person is facing complete chaos. One must learn to retrieve what he needs from the chaos, and that is only done by discovering new knowledge and revisiting the experience to learn what was destroyed. That provides him the materials, energy to rebuild. If steps are taken in such direction, that leads to understandings that allow the reconstruction of a feasible egoic framework that abides both his current environment and the traumatic experience.

While one typically needs to rebuild his world literally in the external world in the aftermath of a trauma, it is imperative to not forget the internal rebuilding process. However, people often ignore the internal aspect and get distracted in the external world. Regardless, when one is confronted with chaos, just as one does when dealing with the unconscious, it is easy for one to just feel helpless and be paralyzed, like a deer in the headlight. Shrinking back and retreating to certain haven is common. So, one may attempt to return to old routines and habits, but that will bring no progress in resolving the issues, especially as a part of the person's psyche knows that repeating old patterns will be futile. There may be a prolonged period of miring in denial, avoidance, blaming, and rumination. It is as if the individual is stuck in how he used to be (attachment to an ego) and unable to venture into the chaos. But, it is within the chaos that contains new possibilities. If we may call the ego a person's "sphere of reality", when trauma occurs, it ruptures or destroys the sphere to a degree that demands severe overhaul or rebuilds. Unless that happens, the person cannot make lasting changes to himself and his situation, whether mentally or physically.

With such descriptions for trauma and complexes, it follows that they are not to be viewed as illnesses that are merely burdensome and to be suppressed or eliminated. Instead, they are expressions from our psyche in reaction to a life event or some on-going troubling experience that requires our attention. They are allies that bring with them messages and not enemies. They need to be treated with an accepting and understanding attitude, instead of a combative one. In such a perspective, trauma and complexes can be conceived as part of the healing process.

Whether a person can advance past his trauma and complex, in the end, depends on happenstance and perhaps his support network. But much of it also relies on first, if the person realizes and accepts some existing issues that need to be addressed, and then, how much will he possesses to push forward with the right attitude and the right mindset. Does he have the resolve to take each small step forward repeatedly with a Will to Understanding?

This leads to the next question, what is there to generally understand about the ego?

The archetype of Eros (the great feminine) and Logos (the great masculine) provide the general orientation and prominent traits for an ego. Eros and Logos are also the archetypes from which more granular archetypes arise from. For Logos, there are father, emperor, hero, hermit (wise old man), joker, fool (child), and many others. For Eros, there are the mother, empress, maiden (virgin), priestess, witch, etc.

Below are some traits that are associated with the feminine and the masculine, along with the extremely imbalanced, negative side of each trait.

Eros/anima/feminine quality:

Free, spontaneous	Unruly, maniacal
Sensitive	Hysterical, melodramatic
Tactful	Fainthearted, cowardly
Compassionate	Lack of boundary, unassertive
Holistic thinking	Lack of order and details in expression
Intuitive	Illogical (dominated by feelings)
Caring	Obsessive
Nurturing	Overprotective
Open (to the unknown), mysterious	Ungrounded

Logos/animus/masculine quality:

Authoritative	Dictatorial
Confident	Arrogant, narcissistic
Protective	Domineering
Logical, linear thinking	Divisive, hostile, narrow minded
Ambitious	Machiavellian
Assertive	Combative, defiant
Grounded	Rigid
Physical power	Harsh and abrasive without thought
Dynamic	Restless
Order, security	Loss of freedom, confinement

A person with a healthy development for a character trait would demonstrate the positive side of the quality. An unhealthy imbalance would then cause the outward expression of the negative side of the trait while the opposite side of the trait falls into the shadow. For example, a very powerful person would have "vulnerability" in his shadow. He would loathe having to display any weakness and will react to others who are weaker than him with disdain. He so dislikes the idea of himself being weak that he would rather see others as the weak, whether it is true or not. That is an example of projection where an individual cast his own sins, guilt, or other negative emotions and qualities upon others.

The flavor of the shadow, like the hue of a picture, is the opposite of the ego's archetype. That is the animus(male) in female and the anima(female) in male. How the animus and anima manifest rely on the balance between the ego and the shadow. For someone who is integrated with a healthy balance, such a person would be able to display positive traits from both the male and the female because he is conscious, knowledgeable of both forces to utilize them properly. However, when the balance is off, such as when the ego is ill-developed and Eros/Logos is not allowed to function properly (due to factors such as social or family values), one may have difficulty to behave with the ego's archetypical positive qualities. Moreover, the negative traits of the shadow will also begin to show. A traumatic event may also lead to such result. For a female, she will lack a sense of femininity. She will be possessed by a strong interest in the intellect. Her rational drive thus may lead to an obsession in maintaining control and an insistent imposition of categorization and ranked order in all things. She may become overly argumentative, excessively critical, and hostile. For a male, he will lack a sense of masculinity. He may be overly sensitive and lacking in drives. He may yet seem to resolve matters with reasoning when in fact he is mired in emotions and cannot seem to become resolute in addressing problems.

Another possibility is a worse scenario called *possession*. When someone's shadow falls completely into the unconscious, there is a likelihood that such an individual may fall under the possession by the anima, if male, or the animus, if female. The identity of the person has been assumed by the opposite sex's archetype. It makes for a worse and confusing scenario than mere imbalance. In such a scenario, the animus and the anima will lose their appeals but manifest traits at both extreme ends simultaneously. The animus could be dogmatic for orders, dictatorial, arrogant, Machiavellian, domineering, etc. but will seemingly possess ungodly power and charismatic charm. The anima could be unruly, hysterical, cowardly, unassertive, obsessive, etc. but visibly compassionate as if can protect everyone, shockingly intuitive, mysteriously appealing. However, in such a case, for most, women will turn into inferior men, and men will turn into inferior women.

Another way to interpret possession is by using the analogy of parents being dominated by their child. Although the typical authority in the relationship should be in the hands of the parents and others still assume the parents to be the authority, the child is instead the one pulling the strings behind the scene like a puppeteer with his marionette.

All that only testifies to the old wisdom that all that begin to fall out of balance is headed toward a downward spiral, unless wisely intervened. The word "wisely" here being the tricky part.

Additionally, it is important to note that the animus and the anima are heavily informed by the intimate figures of the opposite sex throughout a person's life, such as mother, grandmother, aunt, etc. They take on the flavors and values of those important people. A vague ideal imagery is then formed. The anima or animus will then, in a subdued manner, play an influential role in subsequent interactions later in life with other people, especially of the opposite sex. That leads to man and woman pedestalizing members of the opposite sex who possess qualities matching to the image of the ideals. Over the eon, men would dutifully serve and protect woman who emanates great female qualities, and woman would willingly yield themselves to man who personifies certain exhilarating male traits.

Consequently, the anima and the animus play a major role when one seeks a romantic relationship. The ideals within the anima or the animus may become the greatest hindrance in developing a long-term relationship. Because after all, a relationship is established with a living person, not ideals. If the ideals are properly understood for what they are, illusory, and thus understood to not be fully expected of the partner, that allows the partners to compromise in the relationship. However, as our shadow contents are frequently not well understood and remain in the unconscious, intimate relationships create about some of the greatest challenges in an individual's relationship with himself and the other person. Because of the physical, mental, emotional closeness with someone with the opposite sex, such a relationship provides ample chances for one to observe and reflect on his anima or her animus. That provides many opportunities for the integration of his or her own shadow. However, the surprise and sudden confrontations make the experience scary and uncomfortable, where previously unaccepted ideas, denied thoughts, fallacies, weaknesses, and dark emotions that were under the rug are thrust in front of one's face. Though that makes an exceptional opportunity, it remains a monumental task. However, if there is at all any success, it is in this sense that marriage can make a person whole – *You complete me* – not that another entity's presence may simply do so. It would be the metaphysical marriage between the masculine and the feminine within each person.

Finally, the area of the psyche that is most relevant in the formation of the ego that has not been discussed is the personality. The personality sits in a reciprocal position to family and society. Personality traits by themselves have no intrinsic values. Certain traits only become more valuable than others due to the value systems from external contexts. If the characteristics of personality are homogenous to the values of the contemporary family and society, there will be notably fewer disputes during one's development and an easier adaptation both internally and externally. For example, since the advent of the 20th century, extroversion has become more and more valued, so on average, someone with an extroverted personality would have less internal conflict and an edge in gaining social grounds. On the contrary, an introverted person will have a more difficult time to assimilate and excel.

There exist different methods to appraise personality. The trait extroversion was already mentioned. That is a common trait in the well-known personality taxonomy systems of the Big Five (OCEAN) personality model and Myer-Briggs. The Big Five is the currently accepted and popular scientific model for its validity(predictability) and reliability(precision). It evaluates five traits which are Openness, Conscientiousness, Extroversion, Agreeableness, and Neuroticism. Myer-Briggs appraise personality with four categories, which are Introversion/Extroversion, Sensing/Intuition, Thinking/Feeling, Judging/Perception. Depending on the traits, the personality will have one of the four primary functions as the dominant function. Those four functions are sensing, intuition, thinking, and feeling. Beneath the dominant function, there are auxiliary, tertiary, and inferior functions. There are many other models for personality assessment. Another one is the Herrmann Brain Dominance Instrument (HBDI) which is also commonly used. It gauges personality by evaluating a person's preferred modes of thinking, which include Analytical (technical), Practical (organized), Relational (emotional), and Experimental (holistic).

Before diving further into talks of personality development, there is an important matter pertaining to the role of the persona in modern society.

The Game of Persona

Shakespeare wrote in his famous poem, "All the world's a stage, and all men and women merely players." So, all of us play on the stage of the world, of society, acting with a projected identity that is our persona. Before the most recent decade, the demand to sustain such acting was limited to the social circle within one's physical reach. The stage was relatively small and the audience that a person necessitates to entertain was also small.

The world is a stage. With the advent of social media, the entire world has become the stage for everyone as long as they partake in social media. The allure is irresistible because who does not want to project a happy, cool, successful identity for all others to see and prove ourselves to everyone else? Even the small inkling of such desire within an individual would beg to perform on the world's largest stage. And so, all the digital platforms are welcome with open arms and open hearts, in the name of better connecting the entire world's population.

But do we really connect better? All digital platforms are tools. Tools improve efficiency. Conversely, social media becomes an amplifier of who we are for better or worse. Digital platforms provide more convenient, wide-reaching channels to communicate. But before that, there was already a lack of self-understanding among people, even about the ego, neither do most possess the will to self-reflect and understand. A person who lacks self-understanding to maintain a properly functioning ego, cannot maintain a balanced connection with another person, and can be easily influenced by others. Specifically, that is the result of the poor functioning of Logos or an un-honed animus, which leads to the overactivity of Eros and anima that by nature is relational and tempted by

149

groupthink. Consequently, social media has only made the situation worse by providing everyone at their fingertips the grandest stage ever. The low-effort investment, convenience, and speed at which people can "perform" on the stage had the majority gravitating toward it. In the future, the title of the "grandest stage" may only be usurped by the world of virtual reality, where one can practically manufacture a brand-new identity or simply indulges their shadow in the creation of an alter ego.

As social media gains prominence, it has crept into all facets of interpersonal relationships. As it has become the medium that drives commerce and social interaction, it forces almost everybody to participate. Because marketing and projecting who others want to see is *the* game, who we are no longer matters but time and effort are all being consumed on maintaining the superficial shell, the mask, the persona. Also, because almost everyone uses it, if you do not, it may be difficult to even have some low-quality connections with others.

The ego and persona are inevitable elements for humans living in society. It is important to note that the danger lies not in the game of persona. Society establishes the hierarchy of values that are the right morals and correct choices. The individual shall observe the values and hopefully integrate them into his egoic framework. That enables people to interact and behave in groups. But due to current civilization's sophistication and technology, the integration step may be overlooked, which allows the individual to engage only in the acting and pretending. So less and less vision is shined on the formation of ego, understanding one's self, sincerely questioning where we came from and where we are going, and more and more attention is affixed on the maintenance of a suitable persona. Without a properly formed ego and integrated understanding, and time to think, more and more behaviors are derived immediately from social pressure or personal instinctual impulses.

Society provides shelter (with its infrastructure) and also guidelines (with its culture) for the individuals. Society mandates the generals. Meanwhile, the individual commands the unique. The persona is the individual's abidance to the generals. The individuals, in turn, refresh the social infrastructure and culture by each realizing their sovereign will. Without such will, the individual will fall slave to conformity and generality.

The individual is considered an acceptable actor on the social stage to the degree he satisfies the qualifications demanded by a crowd consisted of managers and audience of the stage. The bigger the crowd, the more generic the set of qualifications become to suit the demand denominated from a common set of populous desire. Such summation becomes contemporary caricatures and stereotypes. That is why, when the caricatures become the norms, the standard, among people rather than the exceptions, it signifies the decline of the culture. It is the failure of the individual to withstand the onslaught of social, peer pressure to fit in.

Peer pressure may come from the audience such as parents, teachers, friends, partners, etc. Managers, which include entities such as governments, corporations, other institutions, religious leaders, and demagogues. They desire to exert absolute influence on both the actors and the audience. They have their agendas that necessitate to inform us who we "should be," be it for intentions and purposes honorable or malicious. That is the significance of propaganda and other subliminal psychological manipulation techniques, to gain control over the crowds. By boasting the desirable qualities and humiliating and denigrating undesirable qualities of the individuals in a crowd, the individuals will bow together to the values of the group and become dedicated zealots. Unless the individual possesses a strong will, or his family imparted and infused in him a firm moral structure countering the common values, he will likely succumb to the pressuring force to conform and act as the society dictates.

The process for the transformation may be slow, but for the majority of people, the result is guaranteed. The message for required action is always for the greater good, higher ideals, and other selfless acts. Who can argue against such rhetoric? Not easily at least. So, the individual instinctively approves the required delegated act and call them good, which will prove useful to those who called for it. The individual may also reap usefulness and attain approval, and he becomes further entrenched. But soon, the individual forgets the source of action and approval, and he performs the act habitually. Each step one takes to cater his persona to follow the preferred social image against his own genuineness, the further diminished(unconscious) his personality and ego become versus the perceived values of the tribe. After all, it is in the name of the greater good, and instant gratification certainly feels good. With social media and other digital platforms, the individual learns that as long as he controls and manipulates the flow of information, he can construe his deeds and spin them in the light of the right morals to achieve desirable outcomes within his social circles.

When the individual prizes the validation from everyone in the crowds, the entire world becomes one's stage. In persisting to appease everyone and pander to the tribe, the individual voluntarily renounces his individuality and subjectivity. He denies his own will if it ever tries to speak. As everyone is trying to appease everyone else, the lowest common denominator becomes the standard. Everyone will embody the most cliché and generic behavioral blueprints, or the easiest ideological thought patterns the social authority advocates and provides. Ultimately, everyone becomes like hollow beings. They appear as if clones of each other, devoid of individuality and authenticity. He is not even living in his own ideal. He is living the fantasy borrowed from others. The appearance, the persona, without corresponding personality and egoism as support is non-substantial, fragile, and merely false. Because that is what each person depends on solely for survival, the persona becomes indispensable. It is also fragile, so it requires immense protection. While the person becomes a cipher and loses his individuality, the persona becomes the purpose in life. Any perceived threat will trigger a defensive response. The greater the pressure from society for specific traits, the more emphasis the average person will place on forcefully building precisely a persona with those traits. They will forget personal values, genuine desires, innate personality, and biological instincts. They will over-identify with the persona and be entirely self-serving. It is all about "me, me, ME" for the sake of self-preservation.

This is an extreme case of living only for purposes given from the outside and conformity driven by fear. "I can't be wrong because everyone else is doing it." When the populace falls under such spell, the majority's behavioral patterns can be identified to fit under the few ideological umbrellas that are prominent and trendy in their contemporary setting. They act, talk, and think in a regurgitating manner as programmed robots. That is the meaning behind The Matrix Reloaded scene where Neo re-encounter the revived Agent Smith, accompanied by hundreds of copies of himself and who was able to infect anyone else who approached him. In greetings, Agent Smith continues to fixate Neo with his persona, calling him Mr. Anderson even though Neo had shed that identity long ago to awaken to his individuality. So, Neo as the personified integrated being comes in direct conflict with Agent Smith who represents the ultimate generality driven by so-called purposes. Their physical battle instantiates the ever-existing conflict between individual sovereign will and infringing tribalistic force.

Living only for the purposes of the persona is self-defeating. While people receive the influence from external sources on how to mold their images, they are acting on the belief that they control their own destiny with their own sheer will. They believe they are free, but they are being governed by the influencers. They are acting in behest from others. Such an occurrence will not go unnoticed in their psyche. Over time, individuals would have exerted such a large amount of effort to uphold the decreed purposes and ideals. If the act eventually fails to amount to any fruition, usefulness, or rewards, the only feasible reaction is to blame others, blame society, blame anything else but themselves. They are obligated to project their misdeeds onto others or risk having to re-examine themselves. They never had ownership after all. They can only believe that they had acted per the instructions from outside. Together they constellate a will against life, their actions devolve to be counter-productive to the nurturing of himself and his surroundings. The consequences will be fundamentally perverse to their high ideals. They will even laugh and cheer in excitement as they watch the world burn as a result. These are the Last Man of Nietzsche, or mass-man of Kierkegaard warned about.

Relating more specifically to the social context in 2019, there is an unmistakable emphasis on the image of wealth, fame, and vanity. Unfortunately, those are not always readily accessible to all people, nor the pretension of it viable. The next best option is the act of playing "victim" which is a quick and easy way to obtain instantaneous validation from others. It is as if we have instinctively placed and learned victimhood as one of the highest virtues in recent years (in 2020). Namely, whoever suffers more from sexism, racism, or some form of inequality shall win sympathy, fame, and some reparation. That leads to an overabundance of offended individuals, and some go as far as to manufacture crimes against themselves to soothe their need to play the role of victim. On the other hand, one may also gain social standings by appearing to stand up for the victims. That leads to the act of "virtual signaling" and "moral grandstanding" where everyone is trying to out-moralize the others, standing up for some other victims. All these acts should hopefully grant them the social status they desire, or at least, grant them labels with certain groups. And by association with the group, they will also gain moral high grounds or financial benefits, which if successful, further feeds the persona.

The assumed triumph of human rationality swept our individual subjectivity deeply into the unconscious. But, that which is buried deepest in the unconscious exerts its force in the most unforeseeable way in greater potency. Hence, we have the modern age of tribalism that is irrationality disguised under a thick skin of rational ideology. This is *enantiodromia.*

The degree that one's ego stands in contradiction to his persona will lead to psychic repercussions. So perhaps one suffers from self-loathing because deep down one knows he is unable to uphold his sovereignty and manifests his authenticity. He is a betrayer of himself. Perhaps one experiences depression which may be mitigated by the prescription of never-ending thrills and pleasures. Perhaps anxiety disorders occur because the persona is no solid ground to stand on. Neurotic and psychotic episodes are very much within the realm of possibility after some time because the disassociation between one's ego and persona cannot be hidden forever. These disorders and episodes are always to be temporarily but consistently suppressed by more thrills and pleasures, or various chemical cocktails.

All in all, modern humans already lack a general understanding on the egoic level. As we further divert our attention to the game of persona, our self-understanding, psychic fragmentation, and the unconscious condition continue to exacerbate.

Stages of Psychic Development

There are different seasons throughout the year. At each geographical location, the weather and ecological patterns are all distinct in each season. For that reason, residents in each area must learn and adapt to them to survive. At least, that is what people used to do before our modern lifestyle. It is just like bears living in harsh cold weather. They must increase their food intake before winter and accumulate sufficient nutrition to sustain through hibernation.

For human beings to navigate through life, it can only be helpful to have some ideas about the seasons of life. As the old saying goes, "For everything there is a season." Knowing the season tells one how to act, when to act, and when to not act. One big mistake for the 21st century moderners is to have seemingly forgotten that, and they act as if each person is simple, easily categorized, replaceable, and static creatures, no matter the personal differences, no matter the age.

There are countless models to assess personality, beyond the mentioned Big 5, Myer-Briggs, HBDI models. They vary in reliability(precision) and validity(predictability) with the Big 5 standing at the top in the psychological community as of currently. One may even include the various cultural, esoteric methods such as the Chinese "four pillars eight characters" method, "Zi-Wei" astrological reading, and the western astrological system. There are people who are averse to these readings. It is as if there is a fear that arises from the attitude that people are merely static creatures. The results would be deterministic (and thus knowing may kill joy and ruin the thrills in life). Or they are afraid of being superstitious. Regardless, though the accuracy matters, the most important use of personality assessment lies not in the result but the self-reflecting process that comes thereafter.

If the individual possesses a sincere desire to reach a level of understanding, any of the personality models can be informative. That is the case even if the individual fails to answer the questionnaire accurately, or if the result is inaccurate. Because if he is genuine, in the end, he will honestly get to a point where he honestly compares the results to his experience to discover new insight about himself.

No matter which personality measurement is discussed, in every era, there is a set of traits more preferred and compatible with the demand of the environments. An extroverted individual has an advantage over an introverted one currently in modern society. Fortunate are the ones born strong in traits that are conducive to success in his time and social context. He will have an easier time growing up. It is not an easy thing to happen because the demands may also vary from one environment to the next. There are also sub-environments beyond social standards, such as ethnic culture, community rituals, familial religion, and wishes of parents. The more the distinctions between those and the individual's personality, the more likelihood of tribulations during one's development. An example could be a teenager just over the age of ten in an immigrant family. He would have developed to a certain degree accustomed to his own culture, and that which is also what his parents desire him to retain. However, in a completely new environment, he must also adapt and internalize other traits for him to socialize and fit in, against the discouragement of his parents if they are not open-minded.

Even if one gets lucky and has an easier time in youth, that does not guarantee success later in life. Traits considered superior in a time period are the ones the average person learns, internalizes, seeks to portray and accentuate, even if just mere projections as part of the persona. Because of that, a side of the personality matures, while other aspects are suppressed. Those aspects of the person become the shadow and may fall into the unconscious. But life has different seasons. What one needs to do and the aspects of his being that need to be cultivated and applied will change over time.

Jung proposes four stages to describe the progression of an individual's psychic development:

Athlete phase – This is the stage where one focuses on his physical appearance and external accomplishments. This coincides with the physiological growth, getting used to one's own body through the adolescent period during which the mental capacity is also in rapid development, acting as a sponge to adapt to the environment.

Warrior phase – This is the second stage that does not necessarily fully happens. From adolescence through mid-life, the individual forms personal goals such as in a professional career. This coincides with the matured formation of one's ego (shadow also) and to the degree that it is well developed with appropriate strength and skills, the individual may achieve high social standing and gain material success.

Statement phase – This is the phase where a person may run into the colloquial "mid-life crisis." Despite social achievement and material satisfaction, even if they provided fulfillment for a period, one becomes unhappy and bored with life. One may have developed all the strengths necessary to allow success, but it is of no use in resolving the unhappiness and ennui. The utility of the strengths and the knowns are exhausted at this point. This is when the question "Is there more to this life?" is asked.

Spirit phase – This is the final phase in life, and this is arrived at after one put in some effort in new studies, self-reflection, and integration of the unconscious. Afterward, the individual realizes all previous efforts and successes do not define his person. A new perspective is gained where the persona, the ego, material gains, family, friends, country, all previous conceptions become of little significance. One learns of what is larger than life. One sees himself, what is within himself, and the world for what they really are – one in the same.

Confucius proposed a very similar flow and stages in life:

20s – one is undeveloped and must focus on studies to obtain external knowledges

30s – one has obtained adequate proficiency in skill and in developing himself (self)

40s – with aggregated life experience, one can adapt to many life changes and not be lost

50s – one begins to gain insight into the natural flow of time and reality

60s – one can observe wisdom and essential elements in all encounters

70s – one understands the rules of nature and can freely manifest himself in the flow

The largest percentage and most rapid development of ego and the incorporation of personality occur between childhood and through the mid-20s. It is interesting to note that such occurrence coincides with the physiological development of the neocortex in the human brain. It finishes maturing around age 25. The neocortex includes the prefrontal cortex which is the central hub of modern man's self-control, execution processing, and rationality. And it is easily observable that people rarely demonstrate any substantial change or deviation in character beyond.

If one is lucky to possess temperaments that match the demands of his time, he gets to strengthen what is innately strong in his personality. However, that may lead to a greater imbalance in his character later in life. His weaknesses shall remain weak and may appear as obstinate handicaps later in life. On the flip side, a less lucky individual will have to overcompensate on traits unnatural to him to fit in socially. He may have to push aside his genuine personality, talents and hide his natural tendency. However, such individuals may become more well-balanced individuals as he was forced to learn skills and habits to amend what he was not naturally strong at. He possesses hidden strength in his personality that, though temporarily set aside, can be of great use in later moments in life. On the contrary, such individuals may fail and writhe in misery. If he fails to amend his weaknesses and acclimate to his environment, he builds up resentment and other negative emotions. That could become a downward spiral. All in all, there is simply no perfect path or guaranteed methods for success in life.

To further simplify the life stages from Jung and Confucius, human's psychic development can be summarized in two halves. The first half involves the development and fortification of qualities and psychic content across ego, shadow, persona, and what lies in the conscious and unconscious. The second half necessarily involves the integration of what was undeveloped, neglected and had become unconscious. That often requires an overhaul, reshuffling, and reassembling of what had been fortified in place in the psyche. If one accepts the responsibility of the second half, one comes to the *Spirit* phase according to Jung, or what lies beyond the age of 50s according to Confucius.

One does not look at sunrise at the dusk with the same mood and feeling when one looks at the sunset at the dawn. Carl Jung wisely pointed out that one cannot use the same attitude and strategy to treat someone who is in his 20s and rising in life as someone who is past his prime in his 40s, 50s.

The strength and values developed in the first half may serve one well for periods of time through life with no certainty. It may be the case for a small percentage of people that no adjustments are necessary for their entire life. But for most people, it is most likely the case that one ultimately hits a plateau or crisis around mid-life, perhaps before, perhaps later. When the previously honed strength and values no longer suffice, one may choose to look for answers beyond what one already knows. Or one may remain in denial. It is within this scenario that makes it helpful to have some ideas about stages in life so one can adjust one's attitude and choices accordingly. Like playing any game, fighting any war, there are times for attacking, times for cultivating resources and strength, and time for playing defense. One should be flexible in adopting strategies.

In Myer-Briggs, the proper developmental path is to find ways to grow the capability of the four functions – dominant, auxiliary, tertiary, inferior - in one's functional stack at corresponding stages in one's life. Having all of them developed and working in coordination is an aim. In HBDI model, understanding the preferred modes of one's thinking provides one the awareness to consider the usage of other modes when necessary and take advantage of the strengths and weaknesses of each mode.

For those who become cognizant of the subtle differences and begin to ask questions pertaining to the later stages in life, they had unwittingly chosen the path of conscious individuation.

Individuation – The Circumambulating Hero's Journey

In the last few chapters, there was quite a bit of discussion on my conceptualized map of psyche and its various parts and their dynamics. They are just one more possible mapping to reality, just as there exist many other guiding principles and other mappings from ancient times to present days, mystical to scientific. They are all propositions. In the end, the comprehension of these contents can only be digested and realized through real application and reflection in one's life. The validity of this kind of knowledge and wisdom accumulates only if one continues to maintain a sincere investigative attitude with his own experience, while eluding the usual troupes of psychological escapism – denial, displacement, projection, repression, regression, sublimation, etcs. On the other hand, there is also physical, sensory escapism. The learning reinforces application, and the application reinforces learning.

Individuation is such a process, whether one relies on Jungian terminology or not. Individuation is the process of becoming a sovereign entity, with the integration of all of one's innermost uniqueness and the reconnecting with the Self. It is worth repeating that *Self is the goal of individuation* because the Self shall act as the root, the foundation, and the guide in the process.

While we think we have gotten smarter, while we revel in our intelligence, while we marvel at our technological accomplishment, our underlying *modus operandi* has not changed for millennia. In the arrogance of modernity, people had forgotten that man and his consciousness are yet shrouded in complete mystery. We incessantly dig for solutions on the outside.

If the problems we face are as grand as we construe them to be, should it not be even more so that we apply all the senses, abilities that we possess? Why the adamant rejection of the possibility of anything beyond intellect and its byproducts?

What myth do we live out? What stories are we trying to write? We simply do not care. We have forgotten the past. We do not contemplate thoroughly regarding the future. We seem to know nothing else, except to gain money, fame, and "more."

What we already know we know. What is within consciousness cannot reinvigorate nor innovate. Rehashing what we know to solve problems that arise from the knowns will only shift the problems around. That is why humanity sits at an impasse. But it does not have to be. It does not have to be for people to over-rely on our intellect. It does not have to be that people over-identify with their ego. And it certainly also does not have to be that they continue hoofing blindly to the tunes of the social cacoethes. Except we do, and our reality becomes a travesty of nature.

One key to resisting that is detachment. It is the realization that my ego is not me. My personality is not me. My thought is not me. My emotion is not me. My reputation, social status, career, relationships, money, etc. all are not me. It is not that we have to abandon and destroy those things and knowledge that was learned. When un-identifying with them, we put space in between us and them. That gives room to obtain a new perspective. By letting go, we gain. We can begin asking questions. That is the beginning to genuinely investigate life.

The journey of individuation, or self-actualization, may have started with the passion of the ego. The tricky step, perhaps the greatest hindrance, is detachment from the ego during the process. Sometimes people inadvertently apply an "ego is bad" and thus combative attitude, where the ego is something to be subdued or destroyed. But that is doomed to fail because the intention and thought to destroy the ego arises out of the ego itself. Like an eye cannot see itself, the ego cannot understand itself from a yet egoic perspective. One must be able to step outside of his "self." That allows one to venture into the unknown.

What will be helpful lies in the unknown. The unconscious is the fountain spring of creativity. Chaos gives birth to new creation. Opportunities arise when order is disrupted. Sometimes even learning common knowledge can cause angst and be quite painful. Our physical body freezes when there is a sudden surge of overwhelming stimuli causing a "deer in the headlight" moment. Facing the unconscious greatly increase such possibilities in the psyche. That may be why people invariably have instinctual fear and resistance to anything of the unconscious. Modern people are simply not accustomed to it. As Jung and Nietzsche had both pointed out, the *depth* and *abyss* are, justifiably, to be feared. The emotions, repressed memories, and trauma that linger in personal unconscious may turn the stomach. Forces within the collective unconscious are far-fetched and nebulous, causing them to be even more frightening. The fears are proper and legitimate. But preparation always helps. Knowledges, without being attached and blinded by them, are crutches and armors against dangers. The more one understands, the less scary the world is. The emergence of the unconscious is disruptive but if interpreted properly and successfully integrated, one reaps healing and developmental benefits.

Human artforms contain many symbols. Those symbols are the product from the unconscious. Symbols exist as perfection, and the values of the symbols lie in the formless content behind them. So long as one has not understood and integrated the value and meaning behind a symbol, a symbol remains a perfect existence and will exert influence over the individual outside of his conscious perception. It is just as scenery that appears magical and picture-perfect from afar, and thus incur awes and yearnings. One cannot perceive blemishes and imperfections from afar. Only by examining closely clears away the alluring fog of perfection so that one does not bow to the lionization of the symbol.

Arts, myths, folklore, cultural ceremonies, religions, alchemy, other forms of rituals are the means through which symbols and unconscious content are transferred. We garner minimal benefits through superficial experience with them. They are equivalent to useless when people had forgotten their process of formulation and only treat them literally. The connection is lost and the meaning at creation is no longer stimulated. If traditions and rituals are merely maintained for their forms, they will serve as balls and chains. Therefore, holding on to traditions for their own sake is detrimental. On the flip side, it is the duty, the responsibility of the individual people of every age to replenish their culture through the rediscovery of the meanings behind these symbols. In this spirit, Kierkegaard wrote, "The Truth lies in the subjectivity (Sandheden er Subjektiviteten)". In light of postmodern attitude, the meaning is reversed to "subjectivity is truth." Such interpretation leads to the view that each deconstructed, personal thought (maybe disguised feeling) can be treated as standalone truth. There can be endless deconstructed thoughts and if each fight to be the truth, there can only be endless power struggles between factions who hold differing thoughts. That is a perversion to the original idea. Truth is to be translated and manifested into forms and beings through the spirit of the individual, as opposed to the individual manipulating the Truth.

Those who investigate the symbols are the seekers who dare to attempt to relate to the metaphysical meanings from their labyrinthian origins. It is an even more arduous task for those who attempt to give form to the metaphysical content once again. It is an undertaking that requires both voluntary and involuntary functions in one's whole being. It is like learning any discipline intensively, such as painting or playing a musical instrument. Despite the effort, pauses and rest are required as progress is contributed to with passing time as if the brain or the inner being has its own will. That is the work of an artist. By consciously choosing the individuation process, one is choosing to be the artist for his life. And by consciously choosing, one is answering the call to adventure in the hero's journey. It is the will to leave the status quo, to venture into the unconscious.

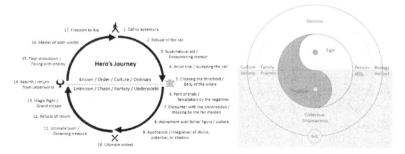

Easier it is to never answer the call to adventure. In real life, we can often witness people who perform actions but somehow not "get anywhere" with their life. Or sometimes their life is stuck in endless repetition. Mentally, it is easier for one to absolve himself from responsibility by blaming other things such as handicaps and trauma originated from parents and family. Other times, they devise reasons that originated from his society and culture. Technically, he would not be wrong because those factors are always exerting their influence. And certainly, no one can convince him otherwise. If he persists, such thought will turn into habits, personality, or pathology that will be rooted in one's psyche. And he, makes no improvement with his life.

Jung has often used the symbol of the dragon to represent psychic challenges. To the ego, the shadow is threatening. To the conscious part of ourselves, the unconscious is ghastly. The dragon is the summation of those fears and the experience behind – rejected ideas, hidden past, undesired memories, repressed emotions, etc. One who has never met or choose to avoid the dragon is no hero. A hero must dare to gamble his life and not be overcome by the fearsome creature. Only if he conquers the dragon and come back with the treasure did the hero complete the journey.

Individuation involves an endless number of iterations of the hero's journey. Every step in the journey, every iteration, one is circumambulating. Circumambulation is the act of devotion, typically in religion, where one moves roundabout a sacred object or statue. Metaphorically, the same movement is required. That is what leads one eventually toward truth, light, understanding wholeness, and re-connecting with the Self within.

The most direct way to puncture the unconscious veil is by going through the deepest, darkest, most pernicious part of one's self. That means the one thing that one would always like to purge immediately from his conscious mind the moment he sniffs its presence. The moment it pokes its tiny head out, one would hammer it down. The one thing that is denied, avoided and repressed at all cost to not be talked about, felt or thought of. The most fearsome dragon represents that personality trait, experience, memory, knowledge, idea, or emotion. And that dragon is fearsome and powerful. The more one tries to avoid and seal it away, the stronger it grows. The hero is one who chooses to deal with it, but that dragon can be too overwhelming.

Likely, one will not succeed at once in conquering the dragon. Fortunately, in the individuation process, one may continue to make attempts, and one can always prepare through self-study and hopefully with the guidance of an experienced, wise counselor. Without a counselor and self-study, it is easy for one to get lost in the process. In Jungian terms, one may succumb to the inflation of the unconscious part. It takes over one's ego operation as the ego is not grounded and too weak to counter the pull of the opposing force. Repeated failures can further weaken one's ego. The risk for inflation and possession is to be noted, as Nietzsche wrote, "He who fights with monsters should look to it that he himself does not become a monster. And if you gaze long into an abyss, the abyss also gazes into you."

During the process, one may experience an even more difficult time. Preparation may seem exhausting. The end is nowhere to be found. There is a part of the self that will want to stop, just because it would be so much easier. It is easier to not answer the call. That is even more so for modern people as there are infinite possibilities of distraction from doing anything useful.

If one chooses to rest on one's laurels, one avoids the dragon. But one's life comes to a standstill, boredom and other psychological phenomena probably soon follow. To fight the dragon, one cannot avoid sacrifices and injuries. That means the destructive part of the process is inevitable. Baggage that weighs one down on the journey and in the fight will need to be disposed of. There are previously conceived notions that must be discarded. There are belief systems within the ego that need to be shattered. But if one pays close attention, there is always a will within that urges one to make each cycle of the journey. Maybe that is what we call the conscience, or maybe it is the siren of the Self. One cannot help but feel deep down that there is something to be achieved in life. That is the transcendent function. It is part of the universal force that seeks reunion, that facilitates one's transition to realize and reunite all the opposing forces within the psyche.

For individuation, one is to heed the "Sermon on the Mount" to always aim and move toward one's perceivable highest good, whatever it may be in the moment. One is to maintain the Will to Understanding. There are adjustments and redefinitions to be made in that personal "highest good" along the way but that is normal. There may be common, helpful practices but there are no strict paths that are applicable to everyone. Remember it is a circumambulation.

There are infinitely more ways to visualize and model reality. There can be infinite ways to describe the path, infinite crossroads to choose, and infinite aspects of reality to study. But that precisely corresponds with everyone's uniqueness. Everyone is as different a being as can be. They need to choose to follow their own path, nothing preordained. They need to be able to let go of what one "should do." That is how one's true interest may thrust forward.

Ego is contributed to by all the factors surrounding it, it really does not matter which field one chooses to dive into to deepen one's understanding of his self and his world, insofar, one can maintain his resolve and a sincere Will to Understanding. Driven that way, anyone shall encounter his metaphysical dragon eventually. One can put his head into subjects such as archaeology, history, linguistics… One can apply a cold eye on observing social and historical trends… One can study the collective social psyche, the generation of a normative amalgamation… One may delve through the layers of desire from the ego and the shadow… One can spend effort on the understanding and development of his own personality… One can learn about man's behaviors and instincts from fields such as psychology, philosophy, medicine, and evolutionary biology… One can learn discipline in an artform… One can do all these things in parallel or one at a time. After all, the key lies in the choice to adhere to one's highest aim in the moment. So long as one is heeding the siren calls of true interest, the learning will be deeply personal and not merely informational. In such a manner, one will go all the way with the learning. That turns the learning into deep knowledge that interweaves into a web of relations that allow more accurate introspection on one's self, one's own psyche.

Eventually, that way of self-study, self-learning will lead up to the facing of the unconscious, the limitation of what is known to the individual. In this case, one encounters the unconscious with some preparation, as opposed to the sudden exposure through trauma. One can fix small flaws and issues each time, in response to one's slightest calling each time. Instead of facing a gigantic dragon at once, one practices by slaying smaller monster at first and just keep moving forward, navigating toward his highest good while holding true to one's choice and maintaining the Will to Understanding at all cost.

Due to choices that lead to the resolution of trauma and complexes and the knowledge of certain natural order to things, one gets to a level of peace and stillness that permits proper observation on himself. The same purpose is served by the discipline, rites, and habits that various religions enforce on their adepts, to remove or resolve mental distractions and blocks. Simplifying one's life is often advised. There are reasons for the warnings by the Buddhist five hindrances and the Christian seven deadly sins. This kind of improvement can continue to happen, thus starting the process to understand the eventual reconciliation of the different opposing parts within his psyche... and perhaps, and only perhaps then, one may reach a state of stillness to let the Self shine through. The persistent effort is about creating a quiet state, synchronizing as much as one's body, mind, heart, and energy. That provides the right conditions and the space for the "highest aim" to organically materialize. The higher the aim becomes, the deeper one needs to go within himself, just as a tree that grows tall requires roots that reach downward deeply.

The truth is that individuation is always happening for everyone regardless. In the last few paragraphs, the common themes that are repeated are, will, aim, and choices. Those are the distinctions that lie between an unconscious individuation process and one that is done so consciously. It is by this choice that at the end, much more of the darkness, the unknown, and the unconscious will be understood.

Let us suppose the human intellect, together with its conscious attention, acts as a flashlight. An unconscious individuation process is like someone holding the flashlight consistently in one direction. Occasionally life throws a curveball at him which briefly forces the light to shine on another area. However, frequently, the person will quickly and habitually snap the flashlight back to its original direction. Despite the new area being shown, one pays no attention. Rarely does it amount to any significant personal change. He is none the wiser.

On the other hand, an individuation process that is consciously chosen is akin to someone actively shining his flashlight in as many directions as he can. He pays attention each time as he wants to understand. Even if randomly, such an act alone reveals to him much more what lies in the darkness each time. He gains more understanding and integration of the unconscious than the unconscious process. The more areas that light had shone upon mean the more clues one gathers as to where one may shine his light on next. With some luck, and if the person continues to strive, he may stumble across a central lighting system to the psyche. That central lighting system is the Self.

The Self is the luminous nature of the psyche. The light can be blocked but is incorruptible. A person who reconnects with the Self walks in the light, and he also becomes incorruptible. The Self now serves as the root, the foundation, and the guide. With it, one can read all kinds of text and he will be able to gather the essence of the words' meaning. He can be in any situation and be unperturbed. Without ever rediscovering the Self, everything will forever feel elusive, like trying to escape from quicksand.

Famous Taoist poet Bai Yu Chan from Sung dynasty wrote:

四大威儀皆是假 – The four postures are of no importance
一點靈光才是真 – An inkling of illumination is the true reality
晦藏靈明無多照 – Maintaining and channeling the sparkle within
方現真如不二身 – The real "you" shall appear

The "four postures" cover the four main movements as a human - walking, daily living, sitting, and sleeping. In Taoism, technical guidance for both physical and mental aspects are provided regarding these four postures to help adepts to further their Taoist practice. However, master Bai Yu Chan clearly points out that as much as one endeavor in practice, the key remains that it is about finding that "illumination." That is the true realization of Tao.

The goal of individuation is the Self. Buddhism has Prajna paramita as the highest aim. Christianity discusses the Wisdom of God. Kabbalah interprets Chochmah (Wisdom) as the first aspect of the Creator. Wisdom is the highest aspect of the Self. In the end, the naming does not matter. All these practices share a sense of aspiration that is essential as human beings. Without such an aim, one can endlessly swim in the sea of philosophical text and religious scrolls. One can spend an eternity mired in the endless interpretation of words, words, and more words... It is equivalent to the fact that within Hinduism, one relentlessly struggles in the wheel of samsara, never realizing that moksha(liberation) lies outside of samsara. If one yet seeks moksha, that means he has not attained it.

Even if one comes to reconnect with the Self, it does not mean that it is the end. One's experience with it and the understanding from it will continue to deepen. The Self is merely the central lighting system. It is yet up to one to continue to investigate, rediscover the beautiful and the ugly in the new light, and recalibrate one's paradigm of good and evil. One's view and behaviors based on the level of experience and understanding of wholeness will be everchanging, just as the external environment will be everchanging.

> To change with change is the changeless state.
> -   Bruce Lee

The Self and content from the collective unconscious are of the generality. It is the role of the hero to repeatedly contend with nebulous content and bring forth the values into his reality. He does not do that if he misidentifies himself as the Self and becomes possessed. He does that by articulating and giving forms to the Truth, through his being, his subjectivity. He does so despite the falsehood and illusions that will fight him in his world. And he does that repeatedly. Every age of humanity requires the people in it to act out such role of the hero and resolve the conflict of their generation.

No one else can command anyone to do this, tell them what

should be done or should not be done. The result is teleological... only with personal choice and sacrifice will one realize Truth and find proof intrinsically through the manifesting act and attitude in his own life. "If you know it, you know it." It is evident of itself but perhaps that is why it is difficult for the linear, rational mind to accept. Logically, it must be that there is a separate doer and then there is the doing. Without letting that go, one cannot see that the doer and the doing are one in the same. But it is also precisely why Kierkegaard makes the point about a necessary *qualitative leap*, commonly known as the *leap of faith*.

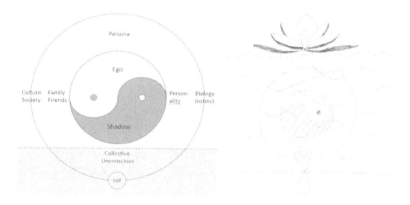

The lotus flower has been a lasting symbol in Hinduism and Buddhism. It is also featured as the seating on which the Buddha and other enlightened deities reside. The lotus is synonymous with the idea of enlightenment, the transcendental existence of a being who has awakened.

The seed of the lotus lies dormant brewing beneath the bottom of a lake. Despite the mud in the soil, the debris in the pond, the murky water, the lotus eventually rises above and blossoms into its refreshing beauty, untainted by passage through the filth. Therefore, the lotus is also a symbol of purity. The growth of the lotus seed provides a perfect illustration of the accomplishment from the process of individuation.

One who has rediscovered the Self has awakened. He has risen above the illusions of the world. With that he possesses an unfazed awareness, as close as possible to what may be called unprejudiced objectivity, to perceive the world. He does so as someone who is pure, but who maintains a clear understanding of the filth, dirt, chaos, darkness that remains part of his being, as a nurturing force like manure that fertilizes the plant. He knows, deep in his bone, that there is no good without evil, no benevolence without malevolence. He comes to see past duality. Therefore, he has what it takes to reconcile and unify the opposites in himself and manifest behaviors outward that may assist the world to a more balanced state.

Much more simply, he knows the falsehood of persona, a façade contributed mostly by what others want. He knows the illusion of the ego, which is just who he deems himself to be in the moment. He knows the unconscious that is the source of what he may be. He knows that he is he yet he isn't he. He knows ultimately the real ground of being lies in the Self.

> This universe is a tree eternally existing, its root aloft its branches spread below. The pure root of the tree is Brahman, the immortal, in whom the three worlds have their being, whom none can transcend, who is verily the Self.
> - Upanishad

-

Satori

During the discussion of Jungian psychology, the map of the psyche was laid out and factors were divided for the sake of discussion... reality is not so obvious. Such as, who is to say the manifestation of archetypes is not part of our biology, as evolved cognitive structures that help govern our emotions and thought? Are the ego and persona so clearly distinguished? More generally, when we speak of feelings and thoughts as if isolated things, are they really? Because when we feel angry, or think of something irritating, our body becomes tense and perhaps may sweat. Can it still be said then that a feeling is only emotional or mental? Where does the feeling end and the physical or physiological begins?

During the learning process, one must pick up categorization, labels, and names to further comprehension. But at a certain point, to come back around the entire circle, full comprehension is arrived by the letting go of them. They still serve their purpose, but they are not the totality. This is the inkling of a happening that is sought after in the Zen practice.

Satori is the momentary suspension of one's egoic perspective. Sometimes it is called the ego loss or the ego death. In a wildly different perspective than our common daily one, the ego is not real. In such a state, one realizes the meaninglessness of the egoic attitude and the purposelessness of nature. In such a sense, life is whole and the totality of being is as it is, without one's needing to control and assert power. This seemingly random occurrence are often accounted for by people who had a stroke (like Jill Bolte Taylor who wrote *My Stroke of Insight: A Brain Scientist's Personal Journey*), soldiers who survived a non-exploding bomb, people who had other kinds of near-death experience, people who had gone through mystical experience, sometimes through the use of psychedelics. Finally, there is also a slim chance for people who experience life tragedy that completely uproots one's ideal and blows the ego structure into smithereens... if one survives and not be completely broken by the experience.

Convey differently, satori is a glimpse of the Self, the luminescence in a mental atmosphere where all of one's existing intellectual constructs and categorization take a backseat. As such, one sees beyond words and pre-conceived notions. In psychoanalysis, methods are proposed to try to circumvent the intellectual layer, man's stubborn rationality that hinders exploration of the unconscious content in the psyche. These methods include free association, active imagination, and dream interpretation. Outside of psychoanalysis and under private settings, people who seek spirituality and perform self-integration work had used lysergic acid diethylamide (LSD), psilocybin mushroom, ayahuasca (dimethyltryptamine, DMT), salvia divinorum, and other hallucinogens. Put differently, they are tools that serve to "dropkick" a person from his everyday consciousness into exploring the psychic realm beyond it. However, the person can just become disoriented or addicted to a maze of visualization. The aim and the will need also be combined with adequate knowledge and life experience to observe and digest the vision. Otherwise, the imagery may simply remain imagery. Perhaps that is why sometimes the glimpse is just a glimpse and does not produce meaningful changes in a person. It is similar to the difference between unconscious individuation and conscious individuation.

Satori, is a glimpse into the door leading to the realm of enlightenment. It is the crackling of possibility, of potentiality. It is yet up to the person to walk through it and deepen his realization. The beauty of the satori is akin to the moment where a joke was told and you suddenly get it. The excitement and ecstasy of the moment would be completely ruined if the joke has to be explained to any degree.

In Zen practices, a method to create doubt in one's intellect and an attempt to incite satori is called the koan. It is presented as a story, question, or dialogue. One such story is the dialogue between the

Han dynasty Emperor Han Wu Di and Bodhidharma.

Emperor Wu asked Bodhidharma, "I have built temples, copied holy scriptures, ordained monks and made donations. How much karmic merit have I earned?"

Bodhidharma said, "None what-so-ever."

Emperor Wu asked, "What is the first principle of the holy truths?"

Bodhidharma said, "Emptiness, nothing holy."

Emperor Wu asked, "Then who is standing before me?"

Bodhidharma answered, "Planting flowers to which the butterflies come. I know not."

Zen

Continuing the story of Huike and Bodhidharm from the chapter Resolve...

After Bodhidharma accepted Huike to be his student. Huike said to Bodhidharma, "My mind is anxious. Please pacify it."
Bodhidharma replied, "Bring me your mind, and I will pacify it for you."
Huike said, "Although I've searched for my mind, I cannot take hold of it."
Bodhidharma said, "There. I have pacified your mind."

Koan is Zen and guru's way to place a student into an impossible or illogical situation, to try to jolt the student out of his habitual mental routines. It contains a hope that by some natural stroke of luck the student will have an illumination that the situation is to be "solved" in a completely different paradigm. A solution or proper view on the situation cannot be reached as long as one holds on to his common intellect. Attachment to the intellect is a persistent blockage to a more natural mode of being.

How does one see and experience totality if one is always concentrated on minute things?

Language is powerful but has its limitations. As a student, it is important to process text and sutras for their meanings but also not be hung up on words to grasp what lies beyond. Though the role of a student is to learn and apply methods, techniques, and discipline, uniquely in Zen, it focuses keenly on a breakthrough, the sudden enlightenment. In the role of a teacher, a Zen master is to apply what is called *upaya* which literally translates to "convenience." The nuance of *upaya* conveys that the master is to use any expedient means to spur a student to his own realization. Therefore, it is a mistake to expect a Zen master to fit any stereotype and follow conventions, though he may. He may behave or speak in a manner, without boundaries but guided by his wisdom, uniquely suitable for a student in a specific moment.

One may think of a Zen master as a proxy of the totality of being, who is trying to throw everything at the student to break the hardened mold in which he has confined his life. Like a skillful entertainer, the Zen master will adapt his message to the audience, even if it is counter-intuitive, even if it contradicts himself and his doctrine.

Modern man is stuck in one mental modality. He is attention driven, which is a state of intense focus, typically with a desire or goal in mind that pushes forward with force. In extreme, such a person's perspective becomes narrower and narrower and is akin to being permanently stuck in "fight or flight" mode physiologically. That is in contrast to the state of mind Zen seeks to cultivate. If one is willing to step back, detach from his desire, one becomes relaxed. In such a state, one regains his peripheral senses and wider observation. Attention mode is detail-oriented while awareness seeks out patterns. One carries the weight of seriousness while the other more playful. One is akin to linear processing whereas the other parallel. People who are acquainted with and habitually use attention mode fear awareness because linear processing allows for control, while with parallel processing, one must accept there being unknown background processes beyond one's control. Is the problem one or the other? No, the problem is being stuck in one. A young student went to a master with a question:

> Student: If I work very hard, how soon can I reach enlightenment?
> Master: Ten years.
> Student: Hold on. If I really work at it, how long until – [master interrupts]
> Master: Twenty years.
> Student: No no, wait. You don't understand. I'm – [master interrupts again]
> Master: Thirty years.

Attention, intellect, ego, persona, the conscious are elements that can be lump into a game of trying to control things and that is the game society plays. If we can use a more playful attitude in looking at life, maybe we can shed the mantle of grim seriousness and explore the axioms we have adopted in life. Ideas and rules that we have learned since baby, almost none of them are absolute ideas that approach Truth, yet they become discreet gospels. Most of us live through our lives without ever putting many thoughts into them. "That's just the way things are," we think, if we ever get to thinking about them. Absent-mindedly accepting that, people yield to society's ways. We are perpetually stuck in one mode of consciousness and comply with these unexamined thoughts. And too many do remain stuck, in comfort, until they experience extreme hardships in life that exceed what these rules provide guidance for. Under the scenario, their reality bubble bursts. With a lack of goal, desire seemingly meaningless, and amidst mental turmoil, a percentage of these people snap out of the attention state and begin asking questions. This is when they may tune into the awareness state to explore beyond what they already know and also turn the awareness inward for introspection. It is no wonder that people who hit bottom can often become very creative. Their worst fears are already in front of them.

Just as Wisdom is an aspect of the Self that is within, awareness is another aspect and exists in all of us. It just requires us to let go. Throughout history, it was already difficult enough to urge people to beware of spending all his attention on ambition and other basic desires. Not much headway is made in addressing that. Now we have mobile devices that are basically "attention black hole." Every mobile app is trying to steal a part of people's attention and absorb them further into the black hole. Facebook, Instagram, Whatsapp, Snapchat, TikTok, Youtube, text messages, emails… And every other company creates an app to get a slice of the individual's attention pie. Furthermore, every app is programmed to capitalize on man's primitive psychological circuit and cater to the more basic emotions. Notifications, likes, in-game currency, etc. Outside of mobile apps, there are also myriads of entertainment options and millions of shows available on streaming services. Every option tends toward sensationalism appealing to baser instinct and trying to continuously capture people's attention. Eventually, emotions and thoughts appear inseparable from ourselves thus clouding and burying our awareness.

What we need to do is to step back from such culture to uncover, relearn the awareness that is always there. If the culture, the society is wrong, the individual needs to be strong enough to repudiate it (with clear understanding).

Unprocessed thoughts and feelings distort reality and prohibit us from seeing reality as it is. Seeing things with a pessimistic point of view is a distortion of reality. Seeing things with an optimistic point of view is also a distortion of reality. Sadness is just sadness. Pain is just pain. Happiness is just happiness. Passion is just passion. But we do not experience life like that. We categorize each experience as "good" and "bad" and desire preferential treatment to only have the "good." We label that being sad is bad and being happy is good. We dramatize the good and the bad.

Awareness is breaking free from those habits and finding space from our thoughts and feelings. It is about seeing the truth, unclouded and without the interference of thoughts and feelings. Awareness is like a silent observer with a third-person perspective. Thoughts and feelings thus become passing scenery that leaves room for us to decide its significance.

What hurts now may become beneficial for us later, and what gives us pleasure now may induce pain later. A painful, struggling past may handicap one's future progress but the painful experience could be the factor that propels one to his ultimate success. The past influences the future, but the future also redefines the past. An attention-driven modern man often knows the former but fails to recognize the latter.

There is no need to suppress sadness or try to avoid it. Same for pain. Same for happiness. When you are sad, you are just sad. Likewise, when you are happy, you are just happy. There is no need to perpetually drown in the sadness, nor there is any need to capture and perpetuate the sense of happiness. There is no need to worry about how this happiness will eventually disappear. There is no need to punch people in the face when you are feeling angry. It is okay to just feel and experience the emotions fully, without suppression, without dramatization. Fully experiencing is a silent act. In such a way, it is much less likely for the feeling to overcome you.

The same can be said regarding thoughts. There is no need to suppress thoughts. Instead, when you are aware, you simply see the thoughts that linger in your mind purely as they are, and hence you may come to see the truth within yourself.

Put in other words, awareness is simply being. Walk when you walk. Eat when you eat. When we see a beautiful sunset, we can simply watch and be in the moment of watching the sunset. That is simply being. When we try to capture the sunset, that is not simply being. When we force ourselves to exclaim, "what a beautiful sunset!", it is not simply being. But there is no restriction on not saying such things. To say or not to say, neither is right or wrong. It all depends on whether one says it with an ordinary mind. Nansen tries to direct Joshu to the ordinary mind in the following dialogue:

> Joshu asked Nansen, "What is the Way?"
> "Ordinary mind is the way," Nansen replied.
> "Shall I try to seek after it?" Joshu asked.
> "If you try for it, you will become separated from it," responded Nansen.
> "How can I know the Way unless I try for it?" persisted Joshu.
> Nansen said, "The way is a not a matter of knowing or not knowing.
> Knowing is delusion; not knowing is confusion.
> When you have reached the true Way beyond doubt, you will find it as vast and boundless as outer space.
> How can it be talked about on the level of right and wrong?"
> With these words, Joshu came to a sudden realization.
> -   The Gateless Gate (Mumonkan), Case 19

Living in society, we cannot be without attachments. What we can achieve is being aware of our thoughts and emotions. Awareness is inside all of us. But for most of us, it is like a mirror that has been covered with a thick layer of dirt. We will need to uncover it to once again to use it in life.

The more time one practiced spending in awareness, the more

time one can sustain it. Going back to the mirror analogy, the process of practicing awareness is like polishing the mirror. Next in the progression is when you become the mirror. After this step, one must make the final leap to enlightenment, a state where even you and the mirror both dissolve, a state of awareness that may be called no-mind. There is no mirror. This is the key that leads one to see emptiness, oneness, and connectedness in Zen. Polishing the mirror may help a person to get to the moment to make the leap, or it may trap you forever. The final leap is the difference between the poems by the future Sixth Patriarch Hui-Neng and his senior Shen-Xiu during a poem contest proposed by the Fifth Patriarch to select his successor.

Shen-Xiu wrote:

身是菩提樹– The body represents the Bodhi[enlightenment] tree
心如明鏡台– The heart acts as a mirror that reflects reality
時時勤拂拭– Man must polish consistently, diligently
勿使惹塵埃 – So that no dust shall gather

Hui-Neng wrote:

菩提本無樹 – Bodhi[enlightenment] emerges from no tree
明鏡亦非臺 – Nor is the luminous mirror found on any stand
本來無一物 – All was no-thingness
何處惹塵埃 – How may dust even gather

So long as one insists on attention on a particular object, one misses the point. So long as one insists on a specific idea, even if that idea is enlightenment, one misses the point. To come to one's Buddha-nature (Self) is to regain the perception of the Tao, the interconnectedness, inter-relationship of everything.

Fundamentally, most people live as if there is only existence. Survival at all costs is embedded in behaviors. Striving for material security is the common goal, which in modernity, that has even been promoted to be the common good. But fundamentally, being cannot be without non-being. Happiness cannot be without sadness. Because non-being, sadness, evil, death, etc. all the negative sides of nature are what we come to be deeply unaware of, emphasis to become aware of them again and again appears as the stable of religions and philosophy.

The practice of Zen is also a practice to be in the moment. With self-consciousness, human beings gained the perception of time. It is the ability to divide, and in this context, dividing and remembering things in terms of past and future. Frequently do people lose themselves in thoughts of the past (regret) or into the future (worry), especially how much analysis we can perform now. Attention to these thoughts removes us from the present moment and from being aware. We overlook that the past and the future are always occurring now in the mind. So, Zen also promotes the concept of being here and now. The world is one process, and everything is always happening now. To quit being fixated in the past or the future. Detached from any thought and any feeling. No goal. A silent mind. Simply be. Finally removing even any concept of awareness and Zen.

People often turn to Zen when they run into obstacles in life and would like to "try out" Zen as a solution to their problems. The same can be said about other religions and secular belief systems. Regardless, by working and practicing Zen, it is as if people want to earn the right to be rid of the pain and suffering. While the methods and practices may alleviate pain and mitigate the problem, they are not to be mistaken as the solutions. Though by practicing awareness, one will obtain a sense of calmness that allows for better observation, judgement, and decision. It does not provide a right or wrong answer, but it most probably allows you to make more optimal choices that are more optimal for the situation and more desirable to your being.

Irrespective of the benefits, it is worth reiterating the notion of Satori and a sudden, instantaneous awakening process in Zen. One is to detach from preconceived notions and take a leap. It cannot be earned by virtues or study because it is an inborn aspect of our being that we seek to reconnect with. But because this aspect is such an unknown in contemporary society, it is like an alien object. For it to reveal itself, one must be willing to give up everything he already knows.

Traditional Buddhism provides a progression that fosters the conditions for the "last leap". First one comes into stillness. From stillness, one becomes aware. From developing awareness, one finds his "ground" or his "root." With grounded-ness, he can sense emptiness. Letting go even of emptiness, he reaches "annihilation." He may circle round and round and round in front of the door of annihilation. If he can leap into annihilation, he reaches a state that may be called enlightenment/moksha. But to him, there is not even enlightenment.

Consequently, Jiddu Krishnamurti echoed and maintained that: There is no "I". There is no center. For what is left, when every concept has been washed away?

An ordinary mind.
The attainment of no attainment.
Just the simple moment, here and now.

No center. No mind. No self.
Just this.

> To see nothing is to perceive the Way, and to understand nothing is to know the Dharma, because seeing is neither seeing nor not seeing and because understanding is neither understanding nor not understanding.
> - Bodhidharma

Transcendence of Opposites - The Middle Way

Religions and philosophies, they are fingers pointing at the Truth. The fingers are not the Truth, but generally, people only see the fingers. They hold on to it dearly for comfort, even though the fingers seek to guide us to see past the original sin – the development of a self-conscious mind. It was the moment humans come to notice self and other, good and evil. From there, humans had further divided up nature, both abstractly and physically.

As a species, humans have grown accustomed to their many material things. Technological advancement now further enabled the division into the virtual realm. Convention teaches people that these things are what is real. Hinduism labels them as *maya*, which means illusion. *Maya* has grown impregnable in modern society. Not being aware of the origin of the separateness of things, man suffers from illusions and can be easily fooled. We believe there is a truly separate individual, and that the isolated ego is indeed real. We endeavor to maintain happiness persistently while mundaneness and suffering are inevitable. We act as if we can control the world when we scarcely control most of our brain's functions. Instead of becoming aware of the reality behind the curtain of illusion, human has become a species of amnesiacs. If not that, we are at least purposefully ignorant. Because the condition is worsening, we are ever more becoming one-sided bigots because we think almost absolutely in black and white. That leads to attachment to one side and inability to comprehend people on the other side.

Even the "fingers" had been subjugated to propagate *maya*. Fortunately, the many "fingers" available to us continue to point at the Truth if one can break the spell and dare to look.

The convergence of Depth Psychology and Zen/Buddhism can be observed in the last few chapters. Terminology differs but the intimation is shared, such as Self and Buddha-nature, wisdom and awareness, unconscious and unexamined thoughts. There are other religious texts, models, principles formulated by wise ancestors that sought to describe the essence of reality uncovered due to their religious spirits. In the end, they are all fingers pointing at the Truth, if only we spend our efforts on excavating the common wisdom behind languages, names, and terminology instead of trying to compete in the reinvention, creation of new definitions to win merits and accolades.

In Tao Te Ching's chapter 42, it is written:

道生一	From Tao, one emerged
一生二	From one, two arose
二生三	From two, three arose
三生萬物	From three, all things were born
萬物負陰而抱陽	All things bear Yin and carry Yang
沖氣以為和	Flush with breath (Qi) thus reaching balance

Laozi laid bare the creation of the world and the role for human beings in six sentences.

Reality (nature) is but all together oneness
Oneness gives birth to duality that is the foundational forces of existence
Duality gives birth to a third force that drives the circle of life
Through the dynamics between three forces (trinity), existence blossoms into many things with their beauty and complexity
Despite things arisen are seemingly separate, all behave according to the pattern of duality
It is with the energy of our beings that the duality is brought to balance

Is that really so different than the Christian myth? God first created the Garden of Eden. In the garden, God gave life to Adam and Eve. Adam and Eve ate the forbidden fruit, thus gaining consciousness. So, the now-conscious couple had to leave the garden, but with consciousness, they were able to move on to form the budding human society with the development of myriads of things thereafter.

Many fingers are already pointing at the moon. The idea of the trinity (one but three, three but one) is common among mythology. In Christianity, they call it the Father, the Holy Spirit (Mother), and the Son. Going further back in time, Zoroastrianism's Gathas of Zarathustra venerates Asha (Truth and Righteousness), Vohuman(Pure Thought and Love), and Khashathra (Strength and Will). Yang, the Father, Asha, and many other deities are the formations from a basic archetype on one side of duality while Yin, the Mother, Vohuman and, again, many other deities are the formations from archetype on the other side of duality (See Part 1. Duality). The Son and Khashathra are the formations from the archetype of new generations.

Guiguzi, a mysterious Taoist author, provided another perspective for Yin and Yang. Yin is still and passive. Yang is movement and active. Energy and man in their behavior cannot be, nor should try to be, permanently bound in one state or the other. An individual should be active when a situation calls for. Otherwise, he should be still when necessary. This is the gate to the Truth. The power can only be harnessed when one is not "hung up" on either side. That is why Taoists maintain the highest "good" (good as in the act of approximating Truth) is to imitate the behavior of water. When others are high, water flows low. When others are low, water flows over, eventually covering it. Water nurtures all living things without needing praise. Water slams with force in mass when it can freely flow and trickle in drips slowly when the path is narrow and blocked. Such movements are part of Yang. Water sits in absolute stillness when contained and is receptive of all that falls into it. Such gentleness and calmness are part of Yin. A man who can command these virtues/attributes, Yin/Yang at will, without unnecessarily, is a man with strength. The *meek* is such individuals who can wield strength with moderation and shall be the ones to inherit the earth. So, be like water.

Human beings' role in existence, in the perspective of the universe, is represented by the Son. Man, with his gift of consciousness, needs to develop the awareness of duality and learn to be the mediator between these implicitly symbiotic forces, inside and outside of himself. He must go through trials and tribulations, with strength and will, inheriting the power from the Father and the Mother. In other words, he needs to embody the hero archetype. If he is ever able to master his strength, to embody the paradoxes, he shall accept full responsibility of such a role and continue to contend with and mediate the dualistic forces of nature – good and evil, life and death, etc. – within the grand scheme of oneness. If there can ever be said of an ultimate task as a human being, it would be the understanding and reconciliation of opposites. Earth's people will need to realize and accomplish this to contribute to sustaining balance and harmony. Some will fail, become consumed by the horror of the unconscious, unable to see beyond the tragedy of life and his inner demons, and become resentful of existence. In other words, he will turn toward nihilism, wishing to have never been born and seeking to return to the "original" oneness through destruction. The majority simply slumber through life and continue in the endless cycles of samsara.

As babies, we were born into the world knowing the world as a whole. Developing into infants, we were taught to see the world in parts. The parts continue to divide and multiply in number throughout one's life. The last stage of this game of life, if one cares to reintegrate, is to return to again seeing of the world as a whole, while simultaneously containing all its complexities, the beautiful and the ugly.

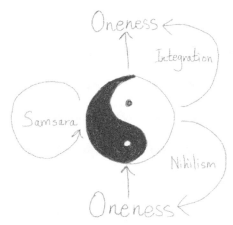

In Buddhistic terms, a man is to awaken to his Buddha-nature and walk the Middle Way. The Middle Way echoes the role of the tight rope walker and can only be trodden by one who possesses Wisdom (Prajna), without which, man is liable to be too attached and unbalanced. One will try to impose order over chaos. Action through such intention will result in more chaos. It is like trying to smooth the surface of water by ironing it.

As universal laws, these patterns play out on all levels of reality. Universe is the macrocosm. Human is a microcosm. Going further granular yet, the same laws can be observed. In an atom, the electrons that hold negative charges exist around the nucleus. The electrons remain in space around the nucleus stably because there is positive charge in the nucleus due to the protons. The protons' positive charge would have repelled each other and destroyed the nucleus, but the nucleus stays intact because of the existence of neutrons. The neutrons provide the mass, the binding energy to hold the nucleus together. Without neutrons, the atom is destroyed.

The role of human beings in relation to his environment is akin to that of neutrons. Applied this idea on top of the original trinity, the symbol of quaternity, like a mandala, is formed. Removing the Son, you have a flipped version of trinity where *one gave birth to two* just as myths around the world depict creation story beginning with a primordial masculine force (yang) and feminine force (yin).

Incidentally, the idea of man's path to navigate through duality, in aspiration to know God can be drawn to form the Caduceus symbol that represents peace within the quaternity. According to Greek mythology, Caduceus is the staff carried by Hermes, the divine trickster or the god of boundaries and transgression of boundaries. On the path of awakening, some trickery and crossing of boundaries are desideratum. Hermes is also known to have the ability to move freely between the mortal and divine worlds. He is a very appropriate symbol for the individual who is to accomplish a hero's journey.

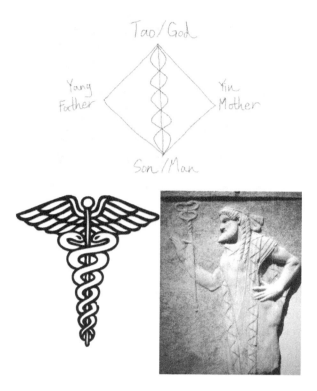

Human games are all founded on dichotomy that floats out of the foundational duality. On any spiritual path, individuating path, one inevitably initiates by learning many divided concepts. Also, because practicing paths are managed by human beings and still under the influence of people's egos, it is easy in pursuing these paths to end up being confounded in illusory human games again. If that is the case, one may be trapped in the last and perhaps the worst ego trip of all. If one does not break through, one may be entangled forever. For example, on the path of asceticism, even though one continues to deprave oneself and suffer pains to dwindle the lower self and to reinforce the higher self, the seeking of the higher self is the affirmation of the lower self. The lower self can never disappear as practice continues because it is always the lower self that seeks the experience. If one believes one has adopted the higher self, that means the lower self is yet inside and may take over any time. To prevent that and suppress the lower self out of fear, one may overinflate the higher self and become possessed. In a different scenario, as one strives to eliminate all desires, the desire to eliminate desires yet remains and grows stronger. It is all around catch-22, but one may continue to feel like progress is being made and become none the wiser.

The eventual final step to be taken is to realize that they are all false dichotomy, and ultimately oneness is inherent. Higher consciousness, lower consciousness… are both inaccurate. They are one in the same. Language is cumbersome and ineffectual because the everything-category is ineffable, which is also why sometimes wisdom that emerges from such understanding is called the silent knowledge. Any conception of God and duality are to be abandoned. Anything and everything are also false dichotomy. In the Heart Sutra it says "no birth, no death, not defiled, not immaculate, not expanding, not shrinking…" and also "No avidyā. Thus no ending of avidyā. No death. No elimination of death."

The etymological roots for the word religion is re-ligare, meaning to reconnect or to reunite. Modern people are generally focusing only on gains, pleasure, and happiness. Even though it may seem grim, it makes sense that religions emphasize grim themes such as sin, suffering, and death. Reunification can only happen when both sides are properly recognized. Hence, even outside of religious context, it requires that one experiences terror, despair, perdition, death deep in his bones before he reconnects with the true light that lies beyond.

Each individual must find his own path back to the infinite, through his own quirks, his own uniqueness, his own personality, his own will, his own understanding, and his own choice, if he so sincerely desires. This will be a hard game of chance because more than ever this is simply not the way of modern society. Many boundaries imbued by our analytical mind that need to be crossed will be too unconventional.

Society is purposeful. Nature is purposeless.

Is society wrong? No.
Is nature, absolutely right? No.

Is *maya* bad? No.

Ego loves meaning. Life is meaningless. Is one or the other wrong? No.

Society is the human game with man-made rules. Nature is the being game with universal laws. As an integrated human being, one would need to be able to freely and seamlessly traverse in and out of both games and play both games simultaneously – the game of playing both games. Kierkegaard wrote more eloquently, such a human being situates himself perfectly in "the simultaneous maintenance of an absolute relationship to the absolute, and a relative relationship to the relative." Such a person can enjoy playing the game without becoming attached. He can play if he wants to. He can stop if he wants to stop. He knows how to play the game. He knows he does not need to NOT play the game. He no longer strives but acts in the flow with peace, levity, and without bondage.

He is in the world, but not of the world. He is one who has transcended the opposites.

Part 3
Independent, Short Writings

This section contains standalone essays. Some are newly written. A few are past writings that fit the theme of this book and provides my thought in other areas. I will mark those with a date.

The Limitation of Language

One must keep in mind that language is of high significance and irrelevance at the same time. Language is significant in so far it is the carrier of messages beyond the words. Words are carefully crafted by people such that the underlying messages are understood by the audience. The true value lies in those messages. If the audience can understand the message regardless of the words, then language is of less significance. Also, language becomes irrelevant when too much emphasis is placed in specifying, defining, proving, and expostulating in the superficial meaning of the words. Then the message gets ignored.

The message content behind the words is of utmost importance.

When reading classic texts, a reader is to commune with the heart and spirit of the author. As such, the reader is making an attempt to approximate the essential spirit of the author and the truth of mankind's late sages. When too much attention is directed to definition and semantics, the essence and truth will be inaccessible. When instead language is manipulated with the intention to abrogate the truth, language itself ceases to carry any real values and communication becomes meaningless. And when people focused on only words and ignore the meaning, context, and spirit behind them, they can be easily deceived.

Human is more than just our thinking process. Thoughts and other intangible psychic content reside behind the words of languages. Language is the bridge that spans the chasm and allows the connection between individual human minds. For two individuals to truly connect, they must each remain open to thoughts beyond their own and contribute to building the connection together. They must have trust in each other and be able to risk offending the other person. If offense does occur, they can remain hospitable to each other to resolve the issue through further discussion. Communication is only about superficial data. Connection occurs when a mutual understanding of the values and meanings behind the communication is allowed and prioritized.

Given the explanation, it becomes automatic that language and free-flowing communication are essential for the bringing forth and construction of the best ideas. Without such freedom, the best talents are to be buried along with people's individuality. Connections are blocked as free thoughts and words are censored within oneself and between people. That is why the ingenuity for the United States' founding fathers to put the protection of the "freedom of speech" in the first amendment of the Constitution.

House Analogy of Psyche

The individual human psyche is like a house, with an assortment of rooms.

An unexplored psyche is like a house that an individual had just moved into. He easily becomes familiar with the general areas that he uses constantly. For other areas, those represent the many unconscious content. Even in familiar areas, there are more minor locations and details that may remain unknown and overlooked, representing more minor unconscious content.

If the person is willing, curious, and thorough, he would take the time to pay attention and explore the unexplored areas. He will begin cleaning up rooms that were unused. For the areas that he had already learned, there may still be places like the back of the drawers, dark corners of the cupboards, under the carpets that may require cleanings. If he continues, he will shine a light on the dark areas. He will see and tidy things up. He will claim true ownership of the house.

On the other hand, the person may just be lazy and ignore the unfamiliar territories altogether and maintain only the general areas that he constantly uses. The unexplored areas remain there. They will consistently and subliminally affect his mood living in the house. Fears and doubt may lie in the back of the new owner's mind. Over time, those areas may contain problems that worsen and suddenly cause damages that spill over to other parts of the house. Perhaps some creaking noise begins to be heard from those areas. Perhaps there are rodents or harmful insects growing in the dark corners. With enough unknown areas in a house, it may even resemble a haunted house! Such people may for unknown reasons frighten others away. Continuing to live in such a condition will certainly cause some disturbances in one's mind until one finally decides to do what was needed to be done from the beginning.

When two people meet and become attracted to each other, they are drawn together by intrigue and admiration in each other's window dressing, the exterior look of the house. So, they initiate contact. They will eventually visit each other's houses. If either one of the parties has yet fully explored the full extent of his or her own house, then shall the insecurity and fear from the sections unexplored begin to cause problems in their interaction. But it may also be the case that both parties have a similar amount of explored and unexplored territories in their houses that makes them a match. It is not so much because they had explored the same quantity but the fact that they had applied similar amount of effort in the process of exploration that allows them to share and connect on an equivalent level.

The number of people who had fully explored their houses are far fewer in numbers than people who hadn't. It is always a small minority who chose the hero's journey and made it back from the "underworld." They will have difficulty in finding people who had gone through the experience and capable of mutual understanding to develop a friendship. One like that has estranged himself from the masses. That is inevitable. For these people:

Be cautious in choosing companies. Do not cast pearls before swine.

Forgiveness

There are two sides to forgiveness. One is forgiving the other person for yourself. The other side is forgiving the person for that person.

That means in one way, having a deep understanding that in many ways, we are all doing our best; however, that best may be malevolent, evil, and destructive whether deliberately or unintentionally. Such malevolence is a potentiality within all of us given certain sets of circumstances. So, the acceptance of evil within yourself is vital, akin to the Christian idea of the bearing of the cross, aka bearing the sins of the world. With such understanding, you can let go of what the other person did to you.

The other side is a waiting process. You forgive the other person when there is observable action, expression, or behavior that demonstrates that they had undergone an internal process of understanding regarding their past action. They came to realize about the harms that were done from various perspectives. Sometimes a deep sincere apology accompanies... but sometimes not. The apology may be irrelevant as sometimes the corrective behaviors are much more subtle gestures. It is more relevant that the newly reached understanding would cause a shift in a person's attitude.

The best scenario is that both sides of forgiveness happen. But nowadays, it is somewhat rare for people to have introspection. So, often time one has to suffice with the first side of forgiveness.

Levels of Perspective
(from May 2010)

Our attitude toward life has a direct relationship with the level of perspective one can adopt. In turn, our perspective has a direct influence on our behaviors, our relationships with all things exist, and our ability to react properly to situations in life.

Capability to see from higher levels of perspective allows for balanced human behaviors, optimal reaction to situations in life, and harmonic relationships with other living things.

An analogy for the effect of a difference in perspective can be the comparison of the view of a caterpillar and the view of a butterfly metamorphized from the caterpillar. If you ask a caterpillar to talk about the view of a butterfly, he will not have a single clue. If you ask a butterfly to convey to a caterpillar its point of view, such communication is a seemingly impossible task.

Regarding perspective for mankind, I find it silly that we have neglected our potentiality. In fact, we undermine it more and more. By that I mean, we are free and given the capability to adopt many levels of perspective, unlike caterpillar and butterfly and other insects and animals. Yet, we fail to develop it but become increasingly short- and narrow-sighted. Our education system does nothing in terms of developing perspectives and enforces mere teachings and memorizations of information that prevent such growth.

A possible break up and definitions of the levels of perspective could be, from low to high: Individual — Family/Friends — Local community — State — Nation — Multi-national alliance — The entire human society — Earth (the entire ecosystem) — Planetary system — Galaxy —

Universe/Cosmos

In communication, sometimes someone is stuck in a lower tier of perspective. It will be very difficult to try to tell him about ideas from a higher perspective. You can also have a blast boring the heck out of someone if you try to convey an idea, say, at the national level, when he only allows himself to view, let's say, within the individual level.

The emphasis is on "they only allow themselves to see" from whatever perspective they want. You cannot force someone to understand unless that person wants to go beyond and see from a different perspective.

I sincerely believe, for us to get anywhere in solving any world issue, we need a good percentage of people, at least enough of them in positions of power, with the understanding and capability of seeing from the "The entire human society" level at least but maybe "Earth" level, without forgetting about the lower tiers. The answers will appear only to those. Until then…

It is very apparent that currently, most people with power and influence at best can see from the "multi-national alliance" level on some occasions. Meanwhile, it remains true that many of these people are frequently operating for the benefits relevant at the lower levels.

I offer no solution to make people see with a higher level of perspective. Because, no one can force others to do so. It can only happen when they genuinely seek to understand on their own. The trick lies in the ability to let go of the belief and idea from the other levels of perspective before one reaches higher.

So, maybe the initial question was, how far and wide do we let ourselves see?

The real question is, what beliefs and ideas are we willing to let go of?

People who seek spirituality and enlightenment are really seeking the cosmic perspective with an indescribable understanding that in so far as interconnectedness and relationship go, that universe is everything including us and thus we are also the universe. To get it, one would need to be able to reach a state where all human ideas become irrelevant, including the words that may lead you to get it. When a person is restricted by no idea, he is free to see all ideas.

Another saying we have is that "true love can save the world."

Now I say, true love arises out of the knowing, allowed by higher levels of perspective. It is like knowing that another organism is a part of me as much as my heart is a part of me. And because our hearts exist as a part of us as much as we are a part of our hearts, all is connected and is one.

Update December 2019: I would like to add my theory for the time units corresponding to the levels of perspective:

Individual – days, months
Political – months, years
Sociological – years, decade
Psychological – decades, century
Philosophical – centuries, millennium
Astrological – millenia, aeons
Cosmic – eternity

Money Solves Money Problems
(from June 2012)

I was sitting down with a few friends at dinner. We had some discussion about money and the many things that we can do if we have more money.

Is money important? The answer is yes, given our social context. Money is so important due to the importance our society has placed on it. One can say money is not real. It is just numbers. It is just a mean for trades. But money looks as if real in the context of our society and civilization, especially because of how much power it grants you these days. Despite originally created as a bartering tool … it has become a very powerful tool that we almost solely focus our life on it now.

Despite the poor getting poorer and the rich getting richer and supposed "class warfare," the only attitude to money I can see is, for us to accept it for what is and understand how it is a useful resource in living in society.

Don't hate it, and definitely don't hate people because they are rich… Dislike them for their characters if you really want to dislike them. It is good to be precise.

Realize, money does not solve all problems.

Money solves all money problems. It solves many problems only because we had chosen to involve money in all the aspects of our life. But if you find important things that do not involve money and if you can reduce the footprint of money involved in your life, you can reduce the number of money problems.

Never say money is not important, which I don't think anyone can say unless they "quit" living in civilization. I want to manage it now, save and invest diligently now because I do not want money to be the primary factor in the many decisions in life.

Relating money to serious relationships such as marriage, it seems to always be the last straw that completely kills the relationship. Not having money in a marriage is like not having the number 2 pencil when you need to take a written exam. The pencil won't help you ace the test but without the pencil, it doesn't matter how smart you are or how well you know the materials.

Money is a resource to be utilized to solve our money problem so we can enjoy life and give our best to improving all the other (more important) aspects of life.

I like to write about money and personal finance sometimes [on an old blog] because it is a practical side of modern life. That makes it a relevant topic to explore. While exploring, deeper questions would come to the forefront. Writing these thoughts remind me of what a sign in Einstein's office says, "There are something that counts that cannot be counted, and there are things that can be counted that don't count."

I suppose I also want us to explore what cannot be counted and to reach the exploration of what cannot be counted through what can be counted. In another sense, we take care of what matters less so that we can focus on what matters, and not confuse what matters less as top priorities in the process.

In short, manage your financial health such that you can prioritize and have energy on other major aspects of your life: physical, intellectual, family, social, and spiritual. And do not lose sight and accidentally place money as the highest aim.

Ordinary Mind

Two parables, worlds apart, bear the spirit of the ordinary mind.

Story of Job from the Bible

Job was a good man. He served the Lord and prayed to God every day. He provided offering to God's altar and endeavored to live his life as God's will. He was always kind and gentle. When his children would misbehave, he would pray to God for forgiveness on them.

God was aware of Job's devout behaviors, but Satan was suspicious of Job. Satan theorizes that Job's faith would falter when his blessings from God were taken away from him. So God wagered Satan to test Job, without harming him.

First, Job received news that he lost all his sheep, camels, oxen, and asses, which numbered in the thousands.

Next, Job received news that his sons and daughters met their ends together in their oldest brother's house that suddenly collapsed on them.

To what had happened, Job kneeled before the Lord and said, "Naked came I out of my mother's womb, and naked shall I return thither: the LORD gave, and the LORD hath taken away; blessed be the name of the LORD."

Satan was not yet satisfied with his test. So God wagered him again, as long as Job's life is spared.

So, illness struck Job and ugly boils enveloped his entire body. Yet he speaks no ill of the Lord. His wife griped, "Do you still persist in your integrity? Curse God, and die." To which Job responded, "You are talking like a foolish woman. Shall we accept good from God, and not trouble?"

Then three friends visited Job, intending to comfort Job. Upon seeing Job, they commiserated with his sufferings for several days. But finally, they believed that the tragedies had come upon Job as forms of punishment for some great sins unknown and could not hold their silence. They tried to question Job as to what evil things he had done. Job insisted that he had done no wrong, even as his friends continue to pester him to confess his sins. While Job was grievous and angry about the situation himself, he did not say that God had done unjustly upon him with unnecessary suffering.

Finally, the Lord appeared before the men and told the friends, "You have not spoken the truth about me." But Job asked God for forgiveness for his friends and He forgave them. Then the Lord returned Job his health, doubled his wealth, and granted him a long happy life.

Taoist farmer story
Once upon the time there was an old farmer who had worked his crops for many years. One day his horse ran away. Upon hearing the news, his neighbors came to visit.
"Such bad luck," they said sympathetically.
"Maybe," the farmer replied.

The next morning the horse returned, bringing with it a group of wild horses.
"How wonderful," the neighbors exclaimed.
"Maybe," replied the old man.

The following day, his son tried to break-in one of the wild horses. He was thrown and broke his leg. The neighbors again came to offer their sympathy.
"Oh no! Such bad luck," cried the neighbors.
"Maybe," answered the farmer.

The day after, military officials came to the village to draft young men into the army. Because the son's leg was broken, they left him behind.

"You are so lucky!" congratulated the neighbors.

"Maybe," said the farmer.

The Loss of Stories

Depression, loneliness, anxiety, anti-depressants usage, suicide rate, alcoholism, and illicit drug abuse are all tracked statistics that are increasing at an alarming rate in modern times. Just what is happening?

Since generations long past, people had lived their lives by following scripts, and milestones that are laid out by their customs and cultures. Between the gaps uninformed by available scripts and milestones, people were also able to flow through life by acting out implicit meanings that are intrinsic in religions, myths, and archetypical stories.

The common set of scripts can vary generation to generation in details but for the societies in stable settings, the basic ones can be:

Leaving the family, moving away from parents
Be a virtuous person
Find a partner and have a family
Be a good wife/husband
Be a good parent
Find a stable job, have a good career
Be a loyal, loving friend
Maintain a balanced life
Maintain a healthy body
Contribute to the greater good of the society
Patriotism
Buying one's own place (American Dream)
Filial piety (strongly promoted in Confucianism)
Aspire for deeper understanding into life (spiritually, religiously motivated)
Become filthy rich

When society is stable, a large portion of the population will be able to find various forms of success by following through with many of the scripts. There will always be ones who had strived but failed and became disenfranchised. Their number will be low to not generate enough force to disrupt stability. However, what happens when the authority and the managers of society lose sight and become foolish?

I find this is another way to view modern days problems. The problems spring from a loss of scripts, a loss of stories.

Culture used to supply the scripts, but we have dismantled too much of it. A cynicism was developed and fostered toward existing societal and cultural scripts. So, a systematic rejection of anything from the past had pervaded and enforced across modern social milieu. People come to believe that the old ways had been forced upon the people as tyranny and must be overthrown.

That view is not completely wrong. Society has to set rules, manage expectations to maintain a sufficient level of homogeneity among individuals. That makes us tolerable for each other in community settings and able to function in groups. Citizens will be able to contribute to the maintenance of the society, joining in common goals. However, the opinion that society, or most parts of it, is only tyranny has become the extreme opinion that many people possess. If that is their sole belief, the only response is to get rid of it, which is the dismantling of the system from the highest level.

Because of the cynicism and hostility, people believe the old ways are simply bad and must be destroyed. The flip side of that is, anything new is simply better. Because the old ways are destroyed and new ones not being well thought out, fewer and fewer scripts are workable or possible paths. As the society destabilizes, more and more people become frustrated and resentful with life, aimless and mired in hopelessness, and feeling lonely and rejected.

We are living in a time where the pursuit of happiness is held as one of the most important goals. That further makes the disenfranchised feel worse about themselves and resentful of others. Ironically, scripts that had been undermined were able to provide people a good chance at happiness.

Everything seems to be coming together to create a vicious cycle. Things got bad. Society and cultures were held responsible for the majority of the blame. Further erosion of cultures causes things to get worse. More and stronger the blames are cast upon society and culture. The process is accelerated also with the arrogance that we can manufacture new rules based purely on our intellectual capacity.

Currently, it is as if only the accrual of fame, money, power is important and defined as success. This is promoted incessantly and fanatically through the telling of the immense success of entrepreneurial pursuit, e.g. young college dropouts turning into billionaires. There are also the rise-to-fame stories of celebrities which further promote the importance of money and fame. News reporting frequently focuses on social media celebrities who suddenly stroke fame out of thin air. We are quickly reducing the only values in town to be chased after to be power and power only. And power is what fame and money boil down to. If you don't subscribe to chasing money like others, you are considered out of touch with reality. Anyone who does not tune in to the money-earning-related script is akin to being excommunicated, a stranger, a queer to the majority.

As sufferings increase, those disappointed with the status quo will fall prey to the demagogues who promised radical changes with a paradisal future and be stirred into a frenzy crowd, or mass movement, or perhaps even a revolution. Such a revolution promotes not the creation of a new society but mostly the destruction of the old. The fear of the mass demands it. It is about the destruction of whatever scapegoat is appointed as the source of their suffering so that the appointed leaders create one in place of it. The question is whether the leaders selected by such a mass are the ones to be trusted to lead the charge for a new tomorrow.

The culture is not what is making people feel lost. People are lost because they are rejecting and destroying the culture from which they came from. For those whose family and community retains a strong sense of tradition, that becomes a great source of mental tussle, turmoil to struggle against the flow of the greater society.

Imbalances are all around us in our external and internal environments now. Western god is beaten down. Eastern spirit is buried. Messages and meanings are lost on both sides. The cultural stables of East and West - Confucianism and Christianity - exist as mere skeletons without substance. With both east and west's cultural zeitgeist sunken to new low...

> Darkness will be preferred to light, and death will be thought more profitable than life; no one will raise his eyes to heaven ; the pious will be deemed insane, and the impious wise; the madman will be thought a brave man, and the wicked will be esteemed as good. As to the soul, and the belief that it is immortal by nature, or may hope to attain to immortality, as I have taught you, all this they will mock at, and will even persuade themselves that it is false. No word of reverence or piety, no utterance worthy of heaven and of the gods of heaven, will be heard or believed.
> -   Thoth's Prophecy of Egypt, As Transmitted Through The Hermetica

As possibilities dwindle and because of societal and peer pressure, the populace reduces their vision, drudges through the days, ignores intrinsic calling... The culture begins to decay from within... Rejection of any objective unifying principle... "What is" does not matter. Facts do not matter. Truth does not matter. Man will be stuck in relying on rationality and logic that continues to innovate unsuccessfully in creating more technologies, more new rules. As these new creations fail, more is demanded and instantiated. As all of them come to fail eventually, there is little man can rely on but to fight each other to uphold his illusory reality and his minuscule self, among the infinitely many other... It is an all man for himself scenario, with random alliances forming, that results in violence and power struggles. It will be a fight between each other that has no quarter, no compromise but only ends with the annihilation of the "other side." It is through this pattern that more and more scripts are debased and subverted.

As successful scripts are reduced, people's choices in behavior become limited. More and more, people and things shall tend toward the generic because only a few qualities are held in high esteem, and everything else is considered bad. Nuances and uniqueness become lost, both in external reality and internal in people's inner thinking. Because those are lost, people neither possess nor care about the narratives, the experience, and little details about each other. On top of it, we do not want to hear about what is "bad." Negativity be damn. The substance, the authenticity in the connection between two people are precluded. People are stuck with relationships that lack understanding and lack depth. With the internet and social media, the physical social dance that happens when two people meet and mingle is trivialized. Without this, people are unable to foster deeper connections. All these factors combined removes the narrative we may learn about each other in a relationship. Without narrative, there is little to no meaning behind the words we speak to each other. We become no more than labels to each other. Consequently, modern relationships are more contextual than ever. Family, friends, lovers are all replaceable.

There was a time in the past where neighbors know each other, and friends see each other without planning weeks ahead. But now, people hardly meet up. When they do, they are often doing some activities. We hurry to meet and we hurry to leave. Friends no longer sit around a table, sometimes talking, sometimes in silence, letting thoughts and emotions organically arise, expressed, and molded into something more than just data. Without that, the joy from the serendipitous surprise that may occur during these times of idle company is also gone. These chanced happenings are part of the beauty in life. With mobile devices where we can get everything almost instantaneously with the flick of a finger – entertainment, thrills, sex - what does it mean that we can skip all the steps and processes in between to always make new "friends"?

The abilities and skills for connecting are diminishing in people, and such gathering is a lost art. The fact that humans are turning to robots/AI for companionship is symptomatic of the state of affair regarding the loss of scripts, stories, and narrative (or more generically the psychic condition in modern man). Lacking the social skills and abilities for connection, people demand the removal of all gray areas. But life involves risk. It is always about the surprise and potentiality of chanced outcomes. That is aliveness. Without the potentiality, there is no life in beings. But man has grown too fragile to handle the risk. He cannot handle surprises. It explains the rise in robot relationship promotion, where humans play controller, almost God-like, to dictate how much aliveness they prefer in these robots. In such a way, it is only foreseeable that mankind's emotional, mental, philosophical readiness to intermingle with his reality will continue to recede.

Without scripts and narratives.
We have ourselves a mental crisis.

Without stories. Without risk. Without possibilities. Without each other.
We may as well be robots.

The Art of Doing Nothing
(from January 2010)

I think we are under a kind of illusion about life. Or should I say, modern life?

It is all about productivity.
It is all about technological advances.
It is all about the newest and greatest.
It is all about moving forward. Progress!

And in the name of progress, our successes have become failures.

Maybe we ought to take a minute and pause to do nothing. More than the question of what and how to do, NOW. Perhaps it is time to consider what not to do. It may be a good idea to do nothing than to do just anything.

So many of us, coming out of the mothers' womb and from that moment, we are to take off and start running, metaphorically. We say, "Life is short."

So therefore, we are to learn to eat, pee, poop, talk, walk, run, and then to get educated, to become successful, to contribute to our community and the world... as fast as possible. Meanwhile, we assimilate our parents' and elders' ways of living, friends' advice, social trend, marketing information, and whatnot. Over the years, we accumulate and assume more and more identities and expectations.

Life has a purpose.
Ah, so many things to do and accomplish.
From birth, we ought to never stop.

No matter what, we just gotta keep doing.
ALWAYS.

And so that is how humans had been for the past couple hundred years.

As a result, we are incapable of knowing when not to do something. Or rather, we suck at doing nothing.

So there is always supposed to be a point. But what point exactly is that? That we *must* have a purpose? We are *always* to be productive? There is a mad dash to keep productivity on the rise. So much for free will.

We spellbind ourselves into the illusion that we must always be doing something. Resting is for the weak.

Despite all that. I find that in life, most people need only to do a few things right in life to have a decent time while avoiding mistakes. That much is the truth.

However, because we must do something always, we do a lot of things that create messes and troubles, and then we spend the rest of the time fixing them. And we'll probably be making more messes and troubles in the process because we are not very good at doing nothing.

If we are able to do nothing, there are much fewer things for us to set right.

Doing the right thing in life is about knowing in your bone who you are, what to do, and what to apply at the right moment. You simply do it. And you know exactly when to act because you are not busy doing something else.

Like a beast attacking its prey. Attacking at the exact right moment means there is a meal. Any slight error means nothing to eat, perhaps for days.

However, the case for us modern people is where we not only

have all the daily routines, we also overdose ourselves socially, mentally, and emotionally to obtain, to accomplish more, to succeed more. It is no wonder that we all end up with social, mental, emotional indigestion. Well, and we often end up with physical indigestion too.

When we cease to do nothing, we never get the chance to be with ourselves. We never learn to live with ourselves. We never come to understand ourselves. We never give our brain and body a chance to recuperate. We cannot be creative.

And most of us don't even sleep enough.

So, do more nothing. Allow yourself to pay attention. You can see wider and further. There will be fewer mistakes. Relax more. You will have less stress and improved health in the long run. With a less crowded mind and schedules, you can be more creative too!

Agenda Mentality
(from March 2009)

Everything we have these days seems to be designed to be fast and easy for us to get somewhere, to have done something – always having a destination in the mind. We shall herald all conveniences!

Everything we do have become a means to an end.

When we make that our sole mentality, we render the means meaningless. By the time we reach a destination with such mentality, we will most certainly regret, or be in denial, because we have forfeited so much for this end. Only that, this end... this moment you have hoped and wished and dreamed about is no more special than all the other moments you have sacrificed. Even if it feels special, the excitement and exhilaration are so fleeting, so anticlimactic. The moment leaves you as quickly as they arrived. The hunger and desire that had grown and multiplied many folds over time are not nearly satiated. This serves to only exacerbate the empty feeling. So immediately, you move on to find a new end to chase.

Everything is a means to an end. For modern people, the end is a moving target. As such, everything becomes a mean, and there is never an end to the pursuit. The present moment is perpetually overlooked. The end will never arrive. Little respect is paid for all elements of joy in the moment while the eyes are focused on the end in the future.

Such mentality brings perversion to virtues. The notion of virtuous behavior is no longer because of the virtuous behavior itself but because you can get something out of it. This agenda mindset has seeped into most aspects of our daily life and has led to the perversion of everything that we do. The rampant desire for an end has overwhelmed the quality of the means.

It is not wrong to have an end. Just that the means always become perverted (aka, unintended consequences) when one is concerned only about the end because he is willing to do anything to get to the end. That is how desires make us do bad things. If the end always justifies the means, you have made yourself unaware of what you would have sacrificed in the process.

For examples...

An important virtue of frugality lies in its non-wastefulness, not only because you will have lots of money and may become millionaires.

The value of a relationship is the relationship itself, not because you NEED to network, or that you will become happy, or you will get something out of the relationship.

The best reason to create quality is for the quality itself. Treat everything else as side effects.

Meditation, is not really about meditation
(from January 2013)

A long time ago, I wrote the post The Agenda Mentality.

Meditation is directly related to that. Because...

True meditation means for a person to arrive at a "no-agenda state." So really, the goal of meditation is not meditation.

Meditation is unlike anything else that we do normally every day and all that we had been taught to do. That is, almost everything we learn and do follows the mentality that can be sum up as "getting from one place to the next."

But to meditate is to be completely here and now. There is no agenda to chase. There is nowhere else to go. There is nothing to be done.

To be completely here and now is to realize and simply be your whole being. And that involves your body, your mind, the sensation from five senses, and your surroundings. Ultimately, it involves everything – inside and outside of you. Your perception is wide open and accepting of whatever your senses tell you.

This is the state of being, which we are all capable of. Meditation is simply a mean for us to practice it and eventually, be in such a state of being without trying.

To fully immerse yourself in the experience of meditation, you cannot be doing something specific. If you try to arrive at "using all your senses," you have obstructed your ability to do so.

So, in a way, we could qualify meditation as a practice of doing nothing. And to do nothing, it is helpful to first be able to observe and re-discover that you are doing something. Learning through negation.

Therefore, we are provided with guidelines and steps to meditate. But keep in mind, to meditate is not to meditate, that is, the act of following steps and guidelines.

The easiest way to meditate, at first, is by sitting because in sitting, you are at least not doing something physically distracting. Sometimes it is called "Za-Zen," which means sitting Zen.

It will take many of us a period of time to relearn the ability to simply sit.

After that, we move on to the mental part. It is irrefutable that modern people are addicted to thoughts. We find our logical minds so useful that we cannot stop using it. Therefore, we are to sit and simply observe our thoughts. And we do not try to stop thinking in meditation. If we think, we let it happen and simply notice what we are thinking. Eventually, it will go away. If we try to forcefully stop thinking, we just end up thinking about trying to stop thinking which is another thought.

Beyond the mental part, we have the body. While we can watch our thoughts, we can also watch our bodies. We can observe all the sensations at the various parts of the body. Feel where the tension is. Feelings and tension happen hand-in-hand. Similar to the instruction about dealing with thoughts, we do not try to relax because trying to relax is itself an effort that causes tension. Simply pay attention.

After a while, we will notice the intermingling relationship between our mind and body. When we think different kinds of thoughts, we cause different kinds of sensation or tension in our body. So, we learn to pay attention to both, which including the openness, reception of our five senses and our surrounding, are all part of "the whole experience."

There are other techniques involved, such as lots of breathing exercises, but that is a different topic. One tip is for us to re-learn belly breathing (aka deep breathing), which assists in relaxation both physically and mentally. One can learn to focus on breathing to help practicing meditation. A specific tip that is very useful, is that it is impossible for us to pay full attention to our breathing and to think at the same time.

Learning to be here and now. Not another agenda-thingie to do to achieve peace. Meditation is a practice of a state of being.

Or… start with letting go of that goal-setting mindset.

And you start by rediscovering your innate awareness and letting it be free – by paying attention. Pay attention to your mind. Pay attention to your body. Pay attention to your surroundings. Pay attention to things you cannot see. Pay attention to everything.

Meditation is as easy or as hard as you make it.

Thus, the story of a master's answer to a student asking what is the secret of the practice of Zen…

"Attention, attention, attention."

On Breathing

Breathing has a lot of likeness to how life is. With our bodies, there are many functions that happen either under control or completely outside of our conscious control. Breathing is one that occurs autonomically without conscious interference but can also be manipulated through conscious control. In life, one can do very little and let things occur to them, or one can choose to exert control on many aspects of himself to change the outcomes. Perhaps that is why there is such a tight correlation between someone who is in touch with his life, himself and how well he can control his breathing.

Breathing is an integral part of many disciplines. Meditation is one, but outside of it, breathing techniques are taught for sports, martial arts, yoga, tai-chi, qi-gong, and even just basic working out. Breathing is a fundamental skill and can be a mastery on its own.

That is an opposite view of how most people see breathing. People assume they already know how to breathe. It then gets neglected. That coincides with how many modern people had lost touch with himself. Most people go through every day not giving a thought about his breathing. Slowly they became habituated to a shallow, quick, chest breathing pattern.

I personally find breathing practices an essential part of self-discovery and coming to a balanced state of mind. If I purposefully slow down my breathing, my mind also begins to slow down. It is important to maintain breathing through the nose and allows the breath to reach deep into the belly. That is called diaphragmic breathing. That is easier to achieve if one imagines letting the air sinks down into the belly than trying to control the muscles around the nose and belly to do the work. Otherwise, more tensions are generated in those muscles which in turn hinders breathing. By inhaling through the nose and then exhaling for a longer duration than the inhalation, the muscles and different parts of my body begin to relax also. What I also enjoy is the moments between the inhalation and exhalation. I feel a unique clarity and focus in my mind if I maintain those moments for a while. If one can be consistent with the breathing practice and let the turbulent mind slowly settles its thoughts, a sense of calm and contentment naturally arises from within.

Another useful tip for breathing during exercise is to inhale through the nose and exhale through the mouth. Such a breathing method increases the amount of oxygen intake while helping the muscles to stay relaxed for optimal movement. If more air is needed during exercise, one should inhale through both the nose and the mouth at the same time.

Beyond anecdotal reasons, there are many scientifically proven factors that support the importance of slower, deeper (diaphragmic) breathing. Quick, short breaths inform the body's nervous system to trigger or stay in the "fight-or-flight" mode, otherwise known as the sympathetic nervous system. Hormones such as adrenaline and cortisol are released in this mode. They help the mind to focus and the body to attain high energy to react more immediately to threatening situations. However, prolonged exposure to these stress hormones leads to symptoms such as hypertension, weight gain, irritability, and fatigue. To trigger the parasympathetic nervous system, which is the mode of relaxation and rejuvenation, a person needs to intentionally slow down his breathing and take longer breaths. This leads to the reversal of many of the effects under "fight-or-flight" mode, such as slower heart rate, improved blood pressure, and lower anxiety.

Beyond triggering the parasympathetic mode, science has offered other clues as to why deep nasal breathing improves health. Research has found that within the frontal cavities of the skull that connects to the nasal passage, the paranasal sinuses produce nitric oxide (NO) that mixes into the gas during nasal inhalation. NO helps kill bacteria so its one function is to sterilize both the sinuses and the passage way to the lung. Moreover, NO is a vasodilator. That means it increase the surface area of alveoli, which are the branches in the lung that absorb oxygen from the gas we breathed in. That leads to more oxygen being absorbed into the bloodstream.

It is important to practice nasal, deep breathing because of its relationship to the maintenance of both physical health and a healthy mental state. Even just a few minutes a day practice will help to turn shallow, chesty breathing habits into better habits of deeper breathing to reap its benefits.

Living in the Moment

(from February 2008)

Living in the Moment...
What does it really mean?
Does it mean to live it up, festivity and party every night?
Does it mean to live like there is no future and seek pleasure day after day as a hedonist?
Does it mean to spend all your livelihood on a trip to the Bahama resort at a whim?
Aren't we living and breathing every moment? Aren't we already living?
What exactly does it mean to live in the moment? It sounds so... cliché.

Living in the moment means having awareness in the here and now. Not letting our egotistic thoughts and emotions dominate. Stop regretting the past. Stop worrying about the future. This helps us to appreciate each moment, along with all the small things within each moment.

Sounds simple enough? Not so fast... Not so easy...

What happened is that we learn NOT to live in the moment as we are growing up. When we are kids, we cannot wait to become teenagers. When we are in high school, we cannot wait to get into college. When we are in college, we cannot wait to be working and making money. When we are finally in the corporate world, some of us want to go back to school and some of us get bored and can't wait for retirement. When we are single, we want to find a girlfriend or boyfriend. When we finally found a partner, we want our single life back. And we are always bombarded by advertising that endlessly tells us this "one more thing" that we need to be happy.

If only I buy this LV bag, I'd be happy...
If only I afford this Lamborghini, I'd be happy...
If only I own a house, I'd be happy...

As it goes, we are constantly thinking about and longing for the next place we want to be, the next thing we want. We constantly chase these ideals that are thoughts in our heads instead of doing what matters.

On the other hand, we need to be cautious about our memory, as our past can become another form of ideal or baggage where we hold on to the happy times or stuck dwelling on the bad ones. Your past has contributed to what you are today, accept it and do what you can with what you have now. What you do now will redefine what was.

Living in the moment is simply sitting if you are sitting. It is simply doing whatever you are doing. It does not involve thinking about the past. It does not involve thinking about the future. It only involves awareness. It is whatever that you are doing and whoever you are here and now. As described above, our behaviors have been trained to do just the opposite, myself included. We need to practice in order to get better at it, just like everything else in life – practice makes perfect.

Meditation is a pronounced method to practice living in the moment. There is also awareness. Living in the moment and awareness go hand-in-hand. Moreover, I'd say awareness is a prerequisite because it lets you see your thoughts as you start thinking about the past and future. Now, it is not that you cannot learn to live in the moment if you do not meditate. Meditation is a method that allows a faster pace of learning because you are only sitting during meditation instead of being in motion. Sitting removes the habituated distractions. The stillness of just sitting makes it easier to practice awareness and notice your thoughts. As you sit, you maintain awareness and pay attention to your body, its tension, and the emotions and thoughts that appear in your mind. As you let the body relax and the thoughts come and go, you learn to simply sit, and you come to understand better what it means, and feels like to live in the moment.

Of course, there are other things we can do to practice living in the moment. In fact, things such as listening to music, playing the piano, dancing, drawing, riding a motorcycle, etc., we are inherently able to do them as if we are living in the moment after enough practice. As I listen to music, it is easy for me to simply listen. In my fencing days in college, when my opponent is in front of me, I simply fenced. In those moments, the only things that exist are my opponent, myself, and our blades. There is no room for external thoughts. It is easy to be in the moment doing our favorite activities. Now we must do so in the other ones.

You can practice living in the moment by applying this "simply doing" concept on other things. For example, when you are talking to someone, you listen and focus solely on the conversation partner, instead of thinking what to eat for lunch, or what you want to say, or which candidate you would vote for president. Even if your thought starts to drift, your awareness will let you see that you are thinking about something else and then you can shift your focus back to your conversation partner. As for me right now, I am writing this post and it is my only focus, which should allow me to write it to the best of my ability. In other words, an analogy can be drawn between "living in the moment" and "doing the best in what you are doing in the moment."

Do not mistake "living in the moment" as in giving up thoughts, past memory, and plans for the future. Living in the moment can provide a new sense of appreciation and enjoyment in everything we do every day. If you learn to live in the moment, you learn also to find peace and joy in every moment. You think and worry less about the past and future.

And why else do we want to find peace and joy? Because then we can have a good time without chasing material goods and learn not to be dependent on external means to be happy. It is kind of like knowing how to have a great time without being drunk.

Let each of us examine his thoughts; he will find them wholly concerned with the past or the future. We almost never think of the present, and if we do think of it, it is only to see what light is throws on our plans for the future. The present is never our end. The past and the present are our means, the future alone our end. Thus we never actually live, but hope to live, and since we are always planning how to be happy, it is inevitable that we should never be so.

-    Blaise Pascal, Pensées

Wu Wei – The Way of Non-Striving
(from June 2009)

Directly translated, Wu Wei means no action, or non-action. But that meaning is lacking in that translation. It may lead people to think that it is some sort of fatalism. Wu Wei is NOT merely not doing anything.

A better English interpretation for Wu Wei would be "the way of non-striving."

The following questions are why this is very very relevant for our everyday life. Ask yourself, are you struggling? Are you trying very hard to achieve or become something? Do you feel that you deserve that special something because you work very hard? And when you do not get it, you feel sad and suffer?

Is life about working hard? Sometimes, not always.
Is life about relaxing and play? Sometimes, not always.

The key is to know the timing, acting in the flow.

The following may sound mad and completely contrary to common sense that we are taught. My realization is that when we try so hard, try too hard, often we do not get what we want. And even if we do get what we want, we soon realize how big of a mess we have on our hands that will require much more effort to clean up, more than what was exerted to obtain what we want.

Therefore, I think it is important for us to understand Wu Wei. They always tell us to innovate and think outside the box, right?

Wu Wei – the Way of Non-Striving. It is action without striving, without trying. It is more like natural action - action that fits in the flow of a situation, is appropriate to the objective reality, and harmonizes/supports/balances the many dualistic relationships here and now.

Stop trying.

When you try, you don't do. (you are not 100%)
When you stop trying, you simply do. (now you can be 100%)

Sound simple? It is. Is it easy? Not really. It requires much practice.

Whatever it is that you want to do, you continuously pay attention, learn, understand, practice, and repeat the process. At some point, after enough practice and repetition, you can let it go. Then you simply do.

Some examples base on personal experience…

Like a pianist who needs to perform a piece, after much practicing, he knows exactly which keys he needs to hit and how exactly he wants to hit it to convey his emotion. When he performs, he simply does it. However, if he has to think about it and tries to hit the key the way he wants, he will miss or play the note differently than the original intention. He may also lose his flow to finish the whole composition.

Same thing for a vocalist. The mere act of trying to hit a high note will obstruct his ability to do so because of the muscle tension that is generated from trying. He needs to simply do it.

The same thing goes for a basketball player. The talk about being "in a zone" or shooting "in rhythm". Do you think the player is thinking about how he wants to shoot the ball when he shoots the ball? When he is in the zone, he does not. He simply does it, something that happens after hours and hours of practice.

We always say we must be free. But the mere thought that we must be free binds us to a concept that limits freedom.

We are always told that we must be happy. But the mere thought that we must be happy makes us try so hard to find happiness that we become unhappy.

Our overzealous effort to control all things in life is but self-defeating proposition. This "fighting" mentality is one such common sense that can be let go.

One cannot ALWAYS be happy.
Things cannot be perfect.
There will always be ups and downs.
People come and people go.

See things as they are and then simply react. Can you do it? Or do you have doubt about it? Then you will keep striving.

There is nothing you can do about the problem because there is no problem. Much drama in life is created in the mind. Yes, it is very real when you have created it. But can you not create it? Can you live without drama? Can you resolve the problem without causing new ones? Do you need to be excited, surprised, elevated all the time? Then there will be no end in sight. It will be a moving door.

There is not an end to strive for. That does not mean you do nothing. That means whatever you do, with the realization of Wu Wei, you do your best and act in the flow... you are held back by no ideals nor desires. If you must conceptualize, it is doing for the sake of doing, for that moment of greatness. That is being in the flow. That is "playing in a zone."

Without striving, you stop trying too hard.

There is time for movement and time for rest.

To win any war, one needs to know when to attack, when to defend.

You act when it is time to act.

You don't act when it is time to not act.

How do you practice? For most of us... Slow down. Stop. Allow silence. Be Still. Embrace solitude. Breathe. Pay attention around you. Repeat. Thousands and thousands of times.

Because of this realization, I am very wary to use terms such as "fight for", "to defeat", "to beat"... how we claim we need to "fight for peace," or that "love and compassion can defeat suffering."

When you are aware, realize how all things are connected, you act without striving – Wu Wei. Love and compassion arise from within, not forced. We simply do it because not that it is good for us, but that things can be so much worse.

Additionally, in the act of fighting, attempting to defeat negativity, we validate the very negativity we want to defeat. We emphasize the negativity. We make it an important thing in life. Is negativity what you want in your life? If not, then let go. Not saying they are not real. You decide for yourself if your pain, depression, problems are so important that you MUST fight to remove them. When you do that, are you not putting more emphasis on them instead, and with emphasis, are you not keeping them in your life?

The negativity may be very real and it may take some time. But slowly, we can let it go bit by bit. You do what you are to do. Through practice, through time passing, you simply let go. You act without striving.

But if you are a courageous soul, perhaps you can just let go immediately. That is also possible. In an instant, you would have realized Wu Wei. You are free. You no longer need to try to be free.

You stop making a mess by trying too hard.

You act or not act without striving.

You simply are you.
You just be.

In simply being, there is no you.
When there is no you, there is no one to worry.

Seeking nothing, he gains all;
Foregoing self, the Universe grows "I"
-    Sir Edwin Arnold, The Light of Asia

Spirit of Play vs. Seriousness

The concept of play is important as part of understanding the game of life. From Hindu text, the Sanskrit word *lila* provides the most suitable meaning. There is no simple translation, but it embodies the idea of the world being a creative play by the divine energy, *brahman*.

If one can indulge the imagination on how the universe (Brahman) playfully shapes existence spontaneously, one can get close to the spirit of play.

We pay lip service to this idea of play these days but most of us do a very poor job of it. In America, many people schedule a vacation to take a break from work. By going on vacation, one becomes fitter to return to work, but getting back into better shape being the purpose of having the vacation is just the opposite of the concept of play. You do not play when you do it for a purpose. There is to be no reason for play.

We can think back to the time of our childhood. We spent an inordinate amount of time playing. Adults may qualify those times as learning motor skills or developing social interaction capability with peers. While the children play, and while we used to play as children, we were thinking of no such things. If there is clay in front, we mold them to our desires. If we have crayons in our hands, we draw freely with our imagination. Even if there is no toy around, we make toys out of random things, or we play make-belief with our fantasies. All of those are precisely creativity.

Imagine the mood, the attitude of kids shaping clay into various objects. The moments were open-ended. It was about spontaneity. No one told us what to do. No one told us we *must* play. No one told us what to make. We were not playing to get somewhere. But when we flip the switch, as we grow up to be adults, we meet up with *lila*'s opposite, seriousness. We gradually grow from being playful to being serious. We become so serious about life and everything we do must serve a purpose.

Unable to tune into the spirit of *lila,* we become stiff. We forgot that we *can* do something for the sake of itself, and that, we can simply enjoy the moment.

Can we recall the moments when we are the most creative? In those moments we were probably not being very purposeful. It is serendipity. How about the moments you were the most joyous, experiencing something that can only be described as revitalizing to your spirit? You were probably not acting or thinking about gaining something down the road during those moment. Each of those moment is significant of itself.

When we allow ourselves the spirit of play, life can blossom. Otherwise, the seriousness, the weight will hold us down in the long run. And life, becomes a drag.

Two ways to "succeed" in this world

The success discussed here is the conventional belief where success means having fame, money, power, or the likes.

There are two ways to arrive at success in the modern age.

One is through the cultivation and continuous activation of a very strong and complex ego. Someone like that plays the game of human very seriously, but they may do it very well. They had the intelligence and were able to learn the rules well. They are willing and able to maximize the limits, the kinks, and the loopholes in the rules. Through great control and strong ambitions, they can avail themselves with great gain. They are superb players of the game of human. But despite all the success, something probably feels missing inside these people, which leads to their relentlessness, endless ambition. Despite all the success! They only have partial sight in the game of life. To win the game is to see that the game of life is to be played on two levels. When they are trying to "beat" the game, they are not aware of being. And because only through extraordinary control can they maintain their standings, they become spiders trapped in their own webs.

The other way to be successful is achieved by maintaining awareness. This path is usually more gradual because of disinclination to be overzealous or to apply exploitation. Additionally, it is also rare to occur because people with awareness know what is enough. They have a low baseline of need and keep life simple. They have a sense of infinite connectedness and simply go with the human game in the flow. They can enjoy the little moments every day. They do not over-strive and seek to find what they truly enjoy to do.

The way I aim for is the latter – to live with awareness. I wonder where I will head sometimes. How will it become of me, if I can succeed amidst illusions as if I am part of the illusions among people, remaining aware and just flowing within the Tao? It goes back to the fact that if simplicity and authenticity are what I have come to enjoy, they are already there, or rather here. So, to gain more success is of no great concern after all. Even if I "succeed" but if in the path I sacrificed simplicity and authenticity, it would really be a failure. What a dilemma!

Learning, Teaching, and Being a Teacher

Teaching and learning have a lot more to it than what we call education today. When we say we have an education problem, the true problem lies in the fact that the older generations teaching children what are thought to be practical, what life ought to be, while what is truly practical, what life really ought to be is something else.

It must also be clarified is that the existing form of education by modern institutes mostly involves the lower form of teaching. That is the transfer of data and the passing of information. Additionally, schools currently behave as an entity that enforces conformity in demeanors, demanding a certain level of blind belief in what is being taught. That would be a detraction from the more pure intention of teaching, which is to encourage students to learn (not just the soulless memorization of information) and to cultivate an investigative mind. As a consequence, we are coming up with some new generations that are lacking in both substantial knowledge and adaptability.

The new generations are young, so the onus falls on the adults in not being so great at teaching. For that, I distinguish teachers in five tiers:

Horrible teacher – bad at teaching information, perhaps even fail in transferring the correct information. Not even interested in teaching, not interested in knowing the students.

Bad teacher – teaches correct information. At least some interest in teaching. Still no interest in the students. Therefore, no extra guidance beyond the passing of information.

Good teacher – teaches correct information. Interested in teaching and the students. That motivates the teacher to provide proper guidance about the formulation of the information into knowledge, based on his style.

Great teacher – does everything that a good teacher does. However, a great teacher helps the students to turn the information into knowledge in a style that is catered to each student's uniqueness. He will also try to provoke within his students an investigative mindset.

Excellent teacher – does everything that a great teacher does. The best teacher is an occurrence that happens when the style of the teacher and the style of the student are complementary to each other.

The first three levels of teachers are involved in teaching on the level of knowledge, that which can be grasped by intelligence. They teach abstract patterns and data that had been collected and formlated to deal with specific situations. However, we know that in real life, there is an infinite combination of situations possible. If we are only taught a very small subset of strict patterns, those patterns would fail to help us in many other cases and new situations. We will render ourselves stiff, unable to respond.

The best way of teaching is that despite the need to teach rules and patterns, on top of it is the need to teach student fluidity. Instead of strict patterns, the teachers seek to foster what may be called colloquially critical thinking. With critical thinking, the student can independently make his own observations, develop his own knowledge, and form new connections between existing ones. On top of it all, the teacher, in this case, will not only transfer knowledge but pushes the student, who in this case is also open to the possibility, of conceiving a level of understanding that is in principle beyond the level of knowledge and intelligence. The teacher will consistently test and sharpen student's abilities that will help to give birth to his own view on life, his own system of thinking, and his own wisdom. The teacher aims for the student to learn through himself, instead of teaching the student to become like the teacher.

Ancient text and scriptures never explain clearly what to do.

There is a good reason behind that. They tell stories and maintain ambiguity because that invokes in the readers, the students the desire to find in their own hearts that which need to be known and to be done. Hence the phrase, follow your heart. It is not about following impulsive feelings and compulsive thoughts but finding an answer that finally comes through after introspection.

Such a teaching and learning scenario is opposed by most education settings nowadays. Efficiency and curriculum are prioritized. Outside of education institutes, people who want to succeed scramble to get from books or lectures quick tips and straightforward methods. They want to get rich or famous quickly. Millions of volumes are written mostly with quick tips, 10 steps this... 9 ways to that... 5 reasons to do something..., where if the readers only follow, they can get rich, lose weight, find their dream partners or success, or whatever it may be. I find there is a level of irresponsibility when people simply provide tips and prescribing strict methods, with the promise of bringing about great changes.

Transferring data and teaching of knowledge are unavoidable but causing people to be entrenched in following strict patterns is detrimental in the long run. It is like in basketball if you try to teach Lebron James to play only like Magic Johnson, or Kobe Bryant, it will not work.

Instead of teaching predefined ways to use the mind, we are to teach people that the analytical mind is a tool. There is a time to use it and there is a time to set it aside. Meanwhile, understand that we need to let others walk their own paths. Teaching is fine, but people may not be ready to learn yet, just like yourself before a critical point. There is no forcing information, knowledge, or wisdom down others' throats. It is impossible to force others to change. That will only push them further away from learning. This is especially important with the people who we care about because the urge to teach them, to get them to change will be even stronger. Be extra careful not to alienate them by forcefully trying to change them if you want to keep them around. It is important to know when to wait, stand aside, or walk away.

This is part of being respectful and compassionate toward your fellow human beings. Although it can be painful to watch as they make mistakes and get hurt, people need to make their own mistakes. That is part of life's journey. Without tripping and falling and getting back up, people do not grow. Although it would be better to learn from watching others' experiences or reading books, not everyone is able to do that right the way.

Therefore, it is important to notice when you begin "playing hero" and try to "save people" because you are hurting them in the long-run and not helping them to learn. People can only save themselves when they are ready to learn. We all have our own responsibility to learn, so leave others with their responsibility.

What you can do is to make yourself available. You provide them the support and kind words in their endeavors but keep from lecturing them. Be present to share their joy and tears. And because you did not push them away through "force-feeding", when the time is ripe and they are ready to learn and to change, they can take full benefits of your being.

Part of being an excellent teacher is knowing the timing to teach and the right words to say. A teacher can only teach if there is a student. He must also protect the students from himself such that the student has room to develop his own way and style.

Being a teacher is a learning process in itself. Once again, all of us can never stop learning.

As Bruce Lee said:

> I'm not a master. I'm a student-master, meaning that I have the knowledge of a master and the expertise of a master, but I'm still learning. So I'm a student-master. I don't believe in the word 'master.' I consider the master as such when they close the casket.

The Fate of Artists

The life of an artist is a life of expression. What does he seek to express? After all his training and arduous effort to progress in his discipline, he must muster all his will and creativity to bring forth into the physical realm a sliver of the ineffable, so long as he desires genuine creation. Such is a monumental task. The risk of undertaking this task is the possibility of the artist becoming the exact opposition to the life of an artist – a nihilist. If enough obstacles, if enough failures, if enough tragedy shall befall the artist to unseat his confidence on his goal, then he may turn on himself and become an enemy of existence. He will label it irredeemable and rail against it. Secretly or subconsciously plotting its erasure.

Music: Imitation of life

Music imitates life in more ways than any other thing.

Symphony and orchestra provide hints for a balanced, realistic attitude on life. A symphony has a beginning and an end. The beginning and the end of each piece of music is different from each other. Some start very slowly and some with gusto. Some end quietly and some with a bang. The musical notes are like the days that string together. Some flow nicely but some isolated with silence. Some go high and some reach low. The orchestra that performs the symphony involves many musicians and instruments. For the sake of the symphony, each instrument is unique. It could be argued that positions such as the first violinist, the pianist, or the conductor are the most important. But to assemble the music performance properly for a composition, all instruments are equally important. During the performance, the musicians are to wait for the precise moments to come in and out, synchronizing with each other. In between, there is to be silence. Mistaking the timing, the performance is ruined.

Being a music performer can provide guideline for learning and the build-up of a discipline. I had a few years of training in classical singing and just under ten years of lessons in piano. There are many fundamentals that require endless practice to master before one can perform at an adequate level, such as breathing, posture, basic fingering, arpeggio, etc. Those fundamentals are built on top with more complex techniques over time. That takes persistent practice. However, resting between practice is essential. It is better to practice in short intervals with rest in between than the same amount of time in one bulk. Somehow nature took its course and the brain did its magic while I was resting, while not conscious. There were also multiple times where I hit a plateau. No matter how much effort I put in, improvement remained elusive. However, upon persistence in mindful practice, suddenly after some time, things fall into place and it "clicked." I was able to move on to try to find my next plateau. Finally, simply being able to hit the musical notes with the right timing based on the sheet music does not mean one can *play* music. This goes back to the idea of *lila*. During the moments of playing the music, one is to perform as if all the practice, skills do not matter and let the music flow out from the fingers (or the voice for singing) with personal genuine emotions from deep within, while simultaneously without compromising the technical aspects. The best performers are able to play on demand.

In music composition, there are major chords and minor chords. Major chords tend to sound "happy" while minor chords tend to sound "melancholy." There are certain chord progressions that naturally sound good as if they are meant to be together. For ones that do not quite match with each other, there are still less obvious ways to arrange them to create different flavors of music. Always using the same progression would become monotonous eventually. Every chord in a key has its nuanced flavor, like the dreamy IV or dominant V. Major and minor chords in a key are mixed together to create the ebb and flow of moods in a piece of music. Let's not forget the diminished seventh that has a sound fitting for a horror scene. There is almost an infinite amount of combination of flavors. As the saying goes, variety is the spice to life.

Finally, it is about listening to music. There are varying degrees of immersion when listening to music. One can listen to music very superficially, mostly hearing the melody and the beats. Some people prefer to enjoy an overwhelming level of bass. But there are many more aspects that can create more immersion. Knowledge of music theories and skills in playing various instruments can help one develop sensitivity to hear harmonizing notes (voice or instrument) and pick out hidden accompanying instruments. It can become a kind of play to listen to those rather than the main vocal or leading instrument. Suddenly hearing a new sound within a piece that one has heard many times before can be quite exciting. By zooming away from the main melody and listening to "all" parts, I find myself able to feel and hear the "entirety" of a piece of music more than other ways. However, sometimes that is not so and trying to listen to the lyrics and imagine the feelings may instead lead to better immersion and connection to the feelings in the music. Beyond that, my mentality and emotional mood also come into effect when I listen, which is different every time. Conversely, each time I listen to the same piece of music is a unique experience by itself.

Mysterium Coniunctionis

Alchemists from the past are the predecessors of modern scientists. The alchemists were pushed with the spirit of inquiry to investigate into the nature of matter. However, lacking knowledge available now, they could only act out with their best effort what came into their imagination to fill the gap in knowledge. They projected man's collective fantasies into their discovery process and findings. As a result, the discovered processes and operations contain archetypical patterns that can provide guidance and insight into how any man can explore his own psychological realm. The goal of the alchemical process of integration translates to the aim of individuation.

Calcination is the first step in the alchemical process. This step involves the use of fire and Vitriol, usually sulfuric acids, to reduce the initial substance into ashes. Psychologically, this signifies the detachment from worldly attachments, known paradigms, and the ego. This can be the result of a series of trials and tribulations that gradually erode the arrogance of the individual. He thus comes to a humble state of mind and begins self-evaluation.

Dissolution is the second alchemical step. This operation involves dissolving the ashes from calcination in water. The effect of the water on the Vitriol creates iron oxide, a new ingredient to be used. Psychologically, this represents the individual's venture into the unconscious. As he was able to detach from his ego, let go of control, the content of the unconscious can bubble up. That provides the individual with new ideas, previously unknown parts of himself to work with.

Separation is the third step. This is the isolation of useful components from dissolution, discarding others that are impure and nonproductive. Psychologically, this is the conscious processing of new content from the unconscious. One needs to review the newly discovered materials and understand what needs to be reintegrated and what should be thrown away.

Conjunction is the fourth step. This step is the recombination of the chosen materials from separation. Psychologically, this is the beginning of the understanding and reuniting of opposites because previously the materials from the unconscious are now exposed to the conscious. The various opposites and their content (prima materia), such as categorically the conscious and the unconscious, the masculine and the feminine, are to be reunified into a new intuitive principle, a fluid system in the individual.

Fermentation is the fifth step. This step is to foster the growth of bacteria in an organic solution to spur the development and combining of materials. Psychologically, this is the gradual process of development that happens as one allows the exposure to opposites and unconscious contents with consciousness. Between the contribution of his will and personality and the said exposure, integration and new growth occur gradually and organically in this marinating process.

The sixth step is distillation. This step involves the boiling and condensing of the fermented solution to increase its purity. Psychologically, this means the eventual connection with man's highest ideal – the Self – the metaphysical philosopher stone, that which is most pure. The essence of the individual is finally discovered after a prolonged period of contending, understanding and resolving of the opposites, assisted by the removals of all the unnecessary and excess.

The seventh step is coagulation. This is the final bonding, sublimination of the purified material from distillation. Psychologically, this step represents the culminated integration of all the opposite within the individual. The parts inside him become cohesive and are all parts of the whole. He is connected to the Self and can manifest his understanding at will.

These are the seven main steps in the alchemical process. Carl

Jung exerted extensive effort into exploring alchemy, its significance and detailed symbolism, and wrote *Mysterium Coniunctionis*. Between the alchemical steps and the steps in the hero's journey, we can observe a strong correlation.

Enantiodromia in the Age of Pisces

Before I write about the age of Pisces, I would like to first discuss synchronicity.

Our typical mental process to understand disparate events that may have a connection are based on a strict cause-and-effect theory. Synchronicity proposes the possibility of acausal events having a relationship. Colloquially, people sometimes call them coincidence. An individual may experience an external event that informs about an internal thought or feeling while there being no observable, no causal relationship between the two. If one is able to pay attention and notice synchronous events, he may be able to retrieve messages that serve to guide him on his path.

The key when dealing with synchronicity is the intention to understand. This is not to allow random external events to make decisions for you. In place of superstition, the proper mindset of wanting to understand is foremost in studying astrological theories and factors.

Earth is surrounded by many stars and constellations. As earth rotates and simultaneously revolves around the sun, it appears as if the stars and constellations are moving around the earth. The constellations surrounding the earth in a band become the basis of zodiac astrology, which gives us the well-known twelve zodiacs. As earth does not rotate in a straight axis in reference to the sun, at the spring equinox, the sunrise appears to move across the sky into different zones divided up into twelve sections, each marked by one of the zodiacs. The sun's movement across each constellation takes an average of 2160 years each. The length may differ because the constellations each span different length astrologically, but astronomers maintain a system that considers them in equal length. For the sun to precess through all twelve constellations at the spring equinox, it takes about 25920 years.

We are currently approaching the end of the age of Pisces and transitioning into the Age of Aquarius. Some may argue we had entered the beginning of the Age of Aquarius because exact calculations are not readily made, and that leaves room for interpretation. Using astronomical measurements, we have roughly the following timeline of the recent ages: the Age of Taurus (4320 - 2160 BC), the Age of Aris (2160 BC – 0), the Age of Pisces (0 - 2160 AD), and the Age of Aquarius (2160 - 4320 AD).

The theory is that the zodiac's characteristic provides synchronous insight into the people and the flow of events of a given age. Perhaps astrological patterns can provide a glimpse, a theme, and perhaps a different perspective into humanity's history and fate.

We cannot deny that Christianity has gained prominence and had been the hallmark during the Age of Pisces. Pisces' symbol contains two fishes. Jesus and his disciples are called the Fisher of Man. The fish has developed from originally a hidden communicative symbol from the beginning to now an essential symbol in the Christian religion.

We can further see the manifestation of Piscean characteristics looking over the course of the past two thousand years until now. As the sun moves slowly through the constellation, we can view the age develops according to the traits of the zodiac. Just as the individual psychological development can be divided into stages, the progression of an age can be divided into three phases. The first phase fosters the various prominent traits of the zodiac, coming out from under the shadow of the previous age. The second phase involves the zodiac growing into power and stability, leading to many of its positive aspects. The third phase involves deterioration into imbalance and the zodiac's struggle against the coming of a new age, causing the manifestation of the downsides of a zodiac's traits.

Pisces is known as the sign of arts and poets, in other words, dreamers. Naturally, Pisces's strength is imagination, creativity, sensitivity, gentleness. Indeed, the development of religions and other artists from many centuries ago had brought about prosperity and enjoyment of life to many people thereafter. However, as the age of Pisces enters its last phase, we can begin to see more of the negative aspects of Pisces.

The opposites of Pisces' good aspects are over-sensitivity, over-compassion, confusion, delusionality, hysteria, escapism from reality, and deceptiveness. People who are affected by this can be easily ruled by emotions, deceived, attracted by superficial glamour, and willing to pay for any escapist experience (entertainment, pseudo mysticism, alcohol, drugs, sex, etc.). Because dreams and illusions are so important, people may do anything to look good while ignoring or falsifying the underlying reality. They also want to force others to believe in their good dreams. This urge can be so strong that they will do anything to project outwardly the image of a saint while denying ever having a dark side. People will speak piously but act in the opposites. Driven by the dreams of goodness, their compassion will know no boundary and become extreme. They would be over-protective and smother others with love that causes more problems and damages in the long run. It is the story of "giving a man a fish" continuously instead of "teaching a man how to fish."

The defining words for the last phase in the age of Pisces are "illusion" and "fantasy." If you look around the world at the present time in 2019, do you not see signs of Pisces everywhere and its "illusion" and "fantasy" influence becoming stronger?

Interestingly, the age of Pisces' transition into Aquarius corresponds to the ending of the Hindu calendar's age of Kali Yuga. Kali Yuga is the last age of four, the darkest age of all. It is otherwise also known as the Iron age and the Age of Conflict. It is stated that during Kali Yuga, religion, truthfulness, tolerance, and virtue will slowly dwindle into disappearance. Society is run by lies, manipulation, hypocrisy, and ignorance. Wealth alone will be used to determine one's character and qualities. Relationships are only skin deep. More detailed descriptions can be found in the in *Bhagavata Purana, twelfth canto, chapter two.*

I find it fascinating how these old calendars, systems, and text coincides in their knowledge and description, corresponding to the occurrence of our time. If for no other reason, it is useful to give these ideas some considerations so one can reflect on new possibilities and not remain blind with a myopic perspective. People can be so myopic that only considers the tedium and materialism of the human society.

Last Words

The game of life as human being involves playing the game on two levels.

The game of human is the role we play every day to fit into the social system we live in.

The game of being is the inner life of the individual and the inquiry into universal laws and patterns.

Currently, the game of human is the sole focus for almost everybody. We apply our technological prowess to manage and manipulate every aspect of our life in the social system. We can neither criticize nor refuse its advancement. Technology is a byproduct of our logic, rationality, intellectual capacity. So our firm belief in technology is underlined by the assumption that rationality and intellect can overwhelm and bend the fabric of reality to our full desire. Meanwhile, the "other side" to life, the game of being, is mostly overlooked by everyone, exacerbating the trend of generating even more new technologies, abstract rules in society that neglect universal law.

Carl Jung wrote a book called *Modern Man in Search of a Soul.* The soul is the energy in us that yearns to look beyond what we already see, what we already know. It is that which can connect the individual to the Self, the atman, the image of God, the Buddha-nature, and what have you. By over-identifying with his social identity and his tribe, modern society's individual has lost his soul. They are the walking sleep. The soul now sits in the shadow of our consciousness. It is there if we choose to observe carefully. We can wake up if we choose to.

Previously our ancestors lack the technological advancement, thus they had comparatively inferior intellectual infrastructure and were compelled to live out phenomena unknown by listening to their intuition. Knowingly or unknowingly, they drew power from the unconscious. Today's man is a newly formed man. Today's man is allowed and content to live only in the conscious, under all the protective mechanisms from his tribe (society). It is a new progression for human beings to put entire emphasis on social games with almost complete ignorance of what lies beyond. The level at which human beings turning their back to culture, rejecting traditions, and living in godlessness is a new paradigm. The modern world with its technological and scientific advancement stands at an impasse when it comes to matters in the arena of the heart, the psyche, and the soul. What needs to be discovered and bring forth cannot be brought forth because the matters lie beyond the reach of the contemporary accepted mentality and scientific precept. And despite movement forward in niche scientific communities regarding consciousness and spirituality, the movement seems almost too slow to be of any compensatory usefulness. Meanwhile, humanity seems to be in dire strait and in need of a more feasible way forward, a light at the end of the tunnel, some applicable wisdom in life to mitigate the insufferable misery and unruly insanity now sweeping across the world population physically and mentally.

As nature is a process, perhaps this is a necessary progression.

Man's evolution to possess consciousness, with the development of intellect and the development of the ego, as a prominent attribute, appears to provide a perfect impediment to having an inner world. It is almost given that one would sever connection to the Self and have to find his way back, if he realizes. Perhaps this is the trial... the rite of passage, which is something the historical youth must endure and pass to signify the growing into an adult, his individual. So, humanity is no more than a teenager yet as a species after five, six thousand years of civilization.

Can we make it past this progression?

Perhaps we must transgress to progress.

The Self, without it we are rootless, and we operate without foundation, with no ground underneath our being. Without grounding, we will be overwhelmed by the surmounting force of society. Overcome by the force, we cannot understand and become who we are, each with his own individuality. Without all of that, we have no compass to guide us in wielding the ever more powerful technology, to know when to use it, when to use it not.

If one becomes an amnesiac of his past, becomes divorced from his historical issues both personal and global, and acts hostile against his cultural roots, he is an orphan. It matters not by happenstance or with intention. He has no foundation to build on. He may appear strong but inside weak. The power of the will, knowledge, and wisdom of his ancestry will not be behind him. He has no real power but the illusory ones from his diminutive ego in the face of nature. How does one hope to withstand suffering like that? His belief in his tiny individual isolated ego makes him weak. He will remain weak while his real power is entombed in the unconscious. And the unconscious feeling of weakness, further drives and condemns him into the thirst for power and a hardened, cold attitude to life.

There is always a great danger to make sweeping statements regarding man's problem. The flamboyance of such an act is prone to reap criticism, but I do not find it needlessly reckless. It is important to rule out "what is not" in pursuit of "what is." If the changes we have made in personal lifestyle, and across society and culture are suitable, if there are proper mechanisms to regulate the energy of our beings, should it not be the case that we become less and less disturbed, our well-being healthier and healthier? We would not be bothered by so much doubt. We would not quarrel so much with each other. We would not be so conflicted on the outside and also inside ourselves. We would not be so weary, so anxious about life. We would not speak so much about mental illness. The atmosphere in human society is far from peaceful. Enough people are scantily carried forward with endless distractions and entertainment, or chemical and ideological crutches. Without them, they would not know what to do with themselves. We are the walking blind.

When a man disparages his culture, ignores his soul's calling, and lacks the will to move forward, he separates himself from nature. He blocks the ingress and the egress of the manifestation of the Self. The Self, if let through, like a light that shines brightly, shows one the experience and the infinity of an inner world, thus also the outer world. It grants him the receptiveness and sensitivity to see the richness and observe all the details of his experience. One can come to accept and see opposites as separate and as one simultaneously. One knows that the counter to chaos is not order, and the counter to tyranny (extreme order) is not chaos. He knows that there is no perfect system. The key lies in the individual. He knows that there is not one skill, one method, one way that guarantees success. He can freely find balance but also accept and apply imbalance when necessary. He knows that peace is not the absence of conflicts but proper coordination, like a dance, between dualistic forces.

Until we grow, self-transform, or have something to shock us out of the current impasse, we are stuck in the morass of "nothing-but" or "either-or" mindset. For we still argue, is it fate, or is it will?

The Nordic myth offers insight into the question. The Norns are three mysterious beings who live in the Well of Urd, or the Well of Fate, at the bottom of Yggdrasil. There they spin the threads of fate for all beings of the Nine Worlds, including the gods. However, what the Norns create is not the absolute future but a spectrum of possible destiny. All beings have some degree of influence over their destiny and others around them, through the will. Remember Odin attained great wisdom from drinking from the Well of Urd after sacrificing an eye, that connotes how sacrifices for wisdom also play a role in steering one's destiny. So according to the Nordic myth, there is no absolute free will, and there is also no immutable fate. Life is a mishmash of both. Fate and will make destiny.

Unfortunately for all of the inhabitants in the Nordic worlds, their worlds inevitably culminated in an epic battle between good and evil leading to the cataclysmic destruction including the gods, in the event known as the Ragnarok. Odin, despite his superior magic power and wisdom, could not prevent the Ragnarok. However, the Nordic lore of Odin describes him to exhibit characteristics and psychological flaws much like humans do. Perhaps that and the

Ragnarok can serve as a warning. Besides the Ragnarok, the Bible's Book of Revelation also prophesizes an eventual battle between good and evil that will result in destruction across the world. If we can avoid taking the prophecy too literally, can we not see that the polarization and conflicts between our worldly forces, communities, nations as the obfuscated demonstration of such battles? When people band together into a frenzied mass, combining their fear, resentment, disgust, anger, jealousy, and other emotions into a single unit, claiming themselves as good and others evil, and then clash with each other, is that not the incarnations of the evil spirits, demons, and devils?

We are at the state where the more we try to control, the more we seem to lose control. I cannot help but share the sentiment expressed when Robert Oppenheimer says, "It is perfectly obvious that the whole world is going to hell. The only possible chance that it might not is that we do not attempt to prevent it from doing so." So perhaps there is nothing to be done about the errors of humanity. That could also mean that we do not know wu-wei. We are simply trying too hard, scrambling around, reacting too haphazardly about everything. Perhaps the only thing that may hold us back from complete destruction is the doubt in our heart, the thought of "I don't know" or "Maybe I'm wrong." With doubt, perhaps then we spend more time in idleness and contemplation.

And if we cannot change direction and move away from the path of mayhem… perhaps it is nature's intention after all.

If people can bother to pay attention to the shaping of human history over the ages and development over the last century, it is not hard to see the trajectory the human species is taking. But, everyone is too busy these days.

What is attempted to be conveyed is circumscribed by man-made languages and their limitations. That is why myths across cultures and religions are largely parables, filled with subtle patterns and hidden symbolism. They are treasures for those who care to dig deep. The more words are written, the more the meanings seem to get lost. The more information is out there, the more people seem to get confused. And as I write… Am I being too verbose? Or am I being too concise? Hadn't all of this been said? I cannot be sure as I wrote. Too many messages had already been written to either serve as a piece of the puzzle of the whole, or to be the finger pointing at "the moon." What needs to be written had been written. What needs to be said had been said. It feels like that. The essential spirit has been traced and echoed across time and cultures for those ready and want to see. Those who understand it would come to understand. Those who do not yet understand will have to wait. It is said that man's extremity is God's opportunity. They await more experience to enrich the soil for the seed to germinate… by *the grace of God*, only after which he will begin his pursuit for the hidden treasure.

The pursuit of the inner world requires someone with paradoxical traits… someone strong yet can be weak, brave but not brazen, meticulous but not beholden by voluminous information, determined but calm, strong-willed but not inflexible, prepared but not entrenched, with haste but patient, steadfast yet fluid, confident but humble. He can dream high while keeping his feet on the grounds. In short, part of him already accepts the opposites and embodies their unification. He is because he is. And if he is not, it is because he cannot see past and is holding on to what he is not.

As I wrapped up this book at the beginning of 2020, the hysteria, the neurosis across the world are not subsiding. But there is always still a chance, just as the runes on Yggdrasil do not dictate fate absolutely. The society is not the instrument through which humanity will be saved but rather it is the opposite. The sovereign individual's duty is to first recognize and accept "the duty", and secondly understand, resist, and rejuvenate the society simultaneously. It is the creative power and influence of integrated characters and enlightened individuals that will save the collective. Their experience from their encounter, reconciliation, and a piercing understanding of reality almost demands that. If an individual had adequately developed his individuality, he inevitably influences society through his natural manifestation.

It is important to remember to see and accept that it is not about people are acting wrong or that they should not be doing what they are doing. It is the opposite. People are acting exactly how they humanly should. From there, we can understand the individual experience, the driving force behind the actions of each other. That which you cannot understand, accept, forgive, and integrate is that which you cannot help others to do the same. To accept that evil is as likely in us just as in others is the first step toward resolution. Of course, that sounds simple but simple things are often not easy.

Carl Jung was quoted by Gerhard Adler to have lamented:

> I had to understand that I was unable to make the people see what I am after.
> I am practically alone.
> There are a few who understand this and that, but almost nobody sees the whole...
> I have failed in my foremost task, to open people's eyes to the fact that man has a soul and there is a buried treasure in the field, and that our religion and philosophy are in a lamentable state.
> - Gerhard Adler "Aspects of Jung's Personality" in Psychological Perspectives 6/1 (Spring 1975)

In the process of researching and writing this book, I do not think that people had gotten closer to understanding, sadly. Perhaps the time is not yet ripe. Jung wrote, "If you do not succeed in producing the greatest evil out of this war, you will never learn the violent deed and learn to overcome fighting what lies outside you" with reference to World War I (Liber Novus, p.254). The bloodshed from World War I should have made it the war to end all wars. That did not happen. World War II and much more that came thereafter should have acted as extra propulsion for man to learn, to gain further insight into himself, to mitigate further conflicts. That did not happen either, despite the extent of mayhem, destruction, and deaths even if counting only those in the 20th century. It appears inevitable that a more colossal blood sacrifice is yet needed to drive man to relearn his mystery in the soul and on the path to the Self.

People now lack self-understanding. They are lost and intolerant, and thus they become easily sensationalized with anger, hatred, and fear. And it is with that, they are mobilized by self-interested individuals and groups to erode what had been created. We had torn down religions. We had turned our backs on cultures and traditions (social, economic, inter-personal, and familiar, etc.). Those were supposed to act as the moral high grounds for the citizens. Without them, that means the legal system becomes both the moral high grounds AND the low grounds at the same time, but we are also in the process of undermining the judicial system, the rule of laws. Because laws can be manipulatively written and interpreted in manner best suits people's special interest, where people perform superb wordsmithing, mental gymnastics in a gigantic choreography that undermines facts and truth.

It is foolish to think any of us can save the world single-handedly. But if there is ever a path where we can avert disaster, the only path forward is in the internal work to be done by each person. Call it a spiritual journey, individuation, Zen practice, what have you.

Scientists at the Rensselaer Polytechnic Institute did a study that suggests that if 10% of a population is committed to an idea, it will become the predominant idea in the entire group. That is a certainty if that 10% is committed thorough and thorough. What kind of changes will we see if enough people did the self-work and act with a new attitude toward life? I do not know. Will things surely change for the better across society? I am not sure. However, what human beings are doing is unsustainable. Maybe it is time for some creativity, real innovation? Aside from scientific technology, we need to also develop psychic technology.

In the end, even I wonder why I wrote this? But why do birds chirp? Why do clouds float? Writing this book feels kind of like that. Part of me does sincerely hope that this can provide guidance to a few people, or maybe bits and pieces end up being useful knowledge or wisdom for others. But perhaps as an ordinary human, there may still be traces of arrogance and hubris that compelled me to leave my traces, some written words to the world, my legacy... At any rate, I endeavored this to be the fruit of my research, investigation, and delineation of the Truth, as best as I can muster in my current state of being. In completing this, I feel that I had already received the prize. I also feel that this is my prayer for humanity, even though I foresee it being none more than a silent whisper in the perpetual tide of chaotic screeching. Anything additional that comes of this writing will be icing on the cake.

I possess no certifications on any subjects or disciplines for the materials that I had touched upon. Due to the topic I was trying to articulate, as I was writing, I tried to contain the feeling of *Indignus sum Domine*. On the flip side, being authority on nothing, but simply someone who has strong, genuine interests on the subjects and disciplines across the board, I think maybe that makes me a decent candidate in trying to consolidate and blend disparate ideas from disparate cultures', religions', other disciplines' main points into one vision (perhaps blasphemously, and perhaps poorly). No one can fault a credential that was never there. But consequently, it would be perfectly okay for others to write my book off as incoherent babbling of a buffoon (sometimes as I was writing, it feels like that to myself).

And I feel, that is quite alright.

Just, do not feel that that one must be any kind of expert to find *this*. *This* is available to everyone.

We are all human beings. And we are all playing the game of life. It is to be your choice to discover what that means for yourself. It is up to you to choose to walk the path. This is a most personal path.

The game of life, the game of human being played properly means an attitude and perspective that transcends the opposites, thus able to see the whole. Must you do it? No. At the end of the day, the choice is completely yours.

I want to end by sharing a favorite anime scene of mine from *Parasyte: The Maxim* where Reiko Tamura relishes in her last moments (translated from Japanese):

On and on, I had been thinking
For what meaning was I born into this world?
At the same time I answer an inquiry
    Another arises
I had sought the beginning
I had sought the end
I've walked alone for so long,
    thinking all the while.
Perhaps nothing will change,
    no matter how far I walk.

And if I stop my journey,
things will remain just as they be.
Even if I am told that everything is about to end,
The thought that will flicker in my mind is...
"I see... is that so..."

ABOUT THE AUTHOR

Kin Lau was born in Hong Kong in 1983. He moved to Michigan in 1995 and finished his bachelor's degree at Michigan State University majoring in Computer Science and Japanese. He later acquired his master's degree in Computer Science at Stanford University.

His interests span from singing and playing the piano to basketball and fitness. His love of reading led him from reading the common finally to the philosophical and the esoteric. He was driven to understand people and the world due to his own experience and questions in life. At the end of the day, he enjoys having a genuine connection with others.

Made in the USA
Las Vegas, NV
07 February 2024

85432223R00163